christian family guide to

Getting Married

Series Editor: James S. Bell Jr.

by Janet Lee and David R. Sanford

ALPHA

A member of Penguin Group (USA) Inc.

International Standard Book Number: 1-59257-174-3
Library of Congress Catalog Card Number: 2003113810

06 05 04   8 7 6 5 4 3 2 1

Interpretation of the printing code: The rightmost number of the first series of numbers is the year of the book's printing; the rightmost number of the second series of numbers is the number of the book's printing. For example, a printing code of 04-1 shows that the first printing occurred in 2004.

Printed in the United States of America

Most Alpha books are available at special quantity discounts for bulk purchases for sales promotions, premiums, fund-raising, or educational use. Special books, or book excerpts, can also be created to fit specific needs.

For details, write: Special Markets, Alpha Books, 375 Hudson Street, New York, NY 10014.

Contents

Introduction

Congratulations! You're getting married. We are excited for you because we know what a thrilling adventure you are about to embark on. We wrote this book to give you the best possible start to a happy and successful marriage. Happy marriages start long before the wedding day and are grounded in the truths of God's Word. Your best chance for success *after* your wedding day is to start with a healthy relationship *now*—one that is based on God's vision of love and marriage, good communication and listening skills, true intimacy, and a solid understanding of each other and your family backgrounds.

Even as you work to make your relationship stronger, you can enjoy the planning and preparations for your special day. From attire to attendants, bands to bouquets, candlelight to cakes, this book outlines the basic ABC's for planning and enjoying your special day. You can write your own vows, add personal touches to your ceremony and reception, and get set for a most enjoyable honeymoon. Use the budget guidelines we've provided and you can have the perfect wedding without going into debt. We hope our guidelines and tips will help you make your wedding dreams come true.

Finally, we've included a few chapters to help you adjust to your new life together during your first year of married life. You both will face many changes in the weeks and months following your wedding day celebration and honeymoon. We want you not only to survive your first year, but thrive! Marriage is a lifetime commitment full of promise and wonder. With God's help it can be the most rewarding challenge you will ever undertake. We wish you Godspeed!

What's in This Book

In this book, you will be encouraged to take a close look at your relationship with your future spouse so that you can build a healthy and happy marriage according to God's Word. You will also discover helpful tips for planning the perfect wedding. This book is organized into the following three parts:

Part 1, "Before You Say 'I Do'," walks you through the early days of engagement up to that all-important walk down the aisle. Each chapter encourages you to take a candid look at your relationship with your future spouse and helps you define what kind of marriage you want. You will find fun and practical exercises and guidelines on family relationships, communication, intimacy, and so much more.

The perfect wedding doesn't just happen! In **Part 2, "Planning the Perfect Wedding,"** you will be given some great tips for putting together the perfect reception, writing your own vows, choosing the perfect invitations, and finding the perfect wedding attire for your entire wedding party.

The plans are in place, your bags are packed, now if you can just relax and enjoy the most important day of your life! In **Part 3, "The Big Day,"** you will find all kinds of practical ways to get beyond the pressures of the day and truly enjoy celebrating with family and friends the wonder of your wedding day before you take off on a romantic honeymoon.

Finally, **Part 4, "Presenting Mr. and Mrs. ____!"** gives you practical information and tips to carry you safely through all those critical "firsts" in the year after your wedding day, including your first doubts, your first fight, and your first anniversary celebration!

Bonus Bits of Information

If you thumb through this book, you'll find interesting sidebars with tidbits of information, inspirational quotes and Scripture, definitions of important terms, and tips for strengthening your family ties.

That's the Spirit

These boxes contain quotes and Scripture verses to inspire you to put marriage into a Christ-centered context, and biblical truths to share together about building a strong, healthy marriage that will last a lifetime.

Bet You Didn't Know

Here you'll find traditions, trivia, and other helpful bits of information about the many elements that go into a wedding. You'll discover wedding traditions from around the world, the symbolism behind wedding traditions, and information to help you in your marriage.

Family Ties

Family Ties boxes hold words of encouragement to help keep you in touch with your family during the pressure-filled months of planning your wedding. That way everyone can join together to celebrate your marriage when the big day arrives.

"I Do" Do's and Don'ts

Here's where you'll look for practical tips—like planning the perfect proposal, how to save money on wedding items, and what it means to fight fair—along with ways to survive the stress of planning a wedding with your relationships intact.

Acknowledgments

I wrote this book for my teenage daughters, Elizabeth and Megan. In it, I have shared what God's Word says and what I feel is important for you to know about marriage. It is a great mystery how two people can become one. Yet with God all things are possible. Remember that while it takes two to start a marriage, it only takes one to end it. Never give up! I pray you will catch the vision and someday find yourselves on the exciting road to a Christian marriage with the man or woman of your dreams.

To my parents, Florence and Virgil Knox, who have remained loving and faithful to each other for over 60 years—you are living proof it is possible. Thanks for always believing in me. To Dave and Karene Sanford, thanks for being my spiritual mentors and friends for all these years. Finally, to Randy Ladenheim-Gil, thanks for giving me the opportunity to write this book.

—Janet L. Lee

My wife, Karene, and I began our journey together without the benefit of the premarital counseling resources available today. Through all these years of discovery she has been my friend and intimate companion in our mutual pursuit of holiness in the laboratory we call marriage. She is the fountain from which flows any relational wisdom I have acquired.

Our son, Tim, has been my mentor in translating counseling principles into practical life applications. His marriage and family are a demonstration of biblical principles in action and the evidence of the generational blessings of God.

The experiences of many couples from around the world that have sought counsel have also helped focus my attention on the critical issues required in building lasting, functional marriages that are shared in this book.

Janet Lee, my long-time friend, is responsible for my participation in this first attempt to put my experiences and insights into words. She has taken the research and thoughts and woven them into an understandable form. I appreciate her encouragement and confidence.

—David R. Sanford

Part 1

Before You Say "I Do"

You're in love. You think you've found the person you want to spend the rest of your life with in a marriage relationship. But what do you really know about love and marriage and your partner? Deciding whom to marry is one of the most important decisions you will make in your lifetime—why not take the time and make the effort to get off to the best possible start!

While premarital counseling may be the best way to ensure that you start your marriage with a healthy relationship, you will find many basic ideas in this book. You will learn what God says about the sanctity of marriage in his Word, the keys to good communication skills, how your family background will influence your marriage, what true intimacy is all about, and many more truths about marriage gleaned from years of counseling engaged and married couples. Make sure to take the time to work through these chapters.

The Choice of a Lifetime

So you think you're in love. You've met Mr. or Ms. Right and you're considering getting engaged. Before you start shopping for a ring, stop and consider the important decision you are about to make. Marriage is intended to be for life. And although in today's culture—and even in many of today's churches—it seems acceptable to view marriage as "'til death do us part or until we no longer love each other," that certainly is not God's view. It takes more than love to have a healthy relationship.

Choosing the Right Mate

The decision of whom to marry is the second most important de-cision of your life (the first being your relationship with Jesus Christ). So you will want to consider carefully your current relationship in light of the following three guidelines:

- Am I ready to get married?
- Are we the right people to marry each other?
- Is this the right time to get married?

Am I Ready to Get Married?

Sometimes in our search to marry the right person, we forget that we also have to *be* the right person for our future mate. Preparing for a lifetime of living happily ever after with your soul mate starts with you. You need to know who you are, what your needs and expectations are, how marriage fits into your life goals, and what you are ready to contribute to a lifetime relationship.

Start with a little personal evaluation. What do you really know and understand about yourself? Make a list of your strengths and weaknesses. Evaluate how you have made important decisions in the past (if getting married is your first important decision, you might consider whether or not you are ready to make it on your own). Think about how you have handled change in your life. Change is always difficult, and marriage is one of the biggest changes you will ever encounter. How important is Jesus Christ to you personally? The first ingredient in a successful Christian marriage is that both partners have a strong and mature faith.

That's the Spirit

Any personal evaluation should start with your spiritual life. Both you and your partner should think about godly character traits and ask yourselves how evident they are in your individual lives and in your relationship.

But when the Holy Spirit controls our lives, he will produce this kind of fruit in us: love, joy, peace, patience, kindness, goodness, and self-control. (Galatians 5:22–23)

What is your level of contentment? More and more singles are choosing to remain single for a longer period of time. If you have used the time wisely—you'll be happier whether you marry or not. It doesn't take a spouse to make a person complete. Whether your present sweetheart ends up being your life partner or not, move forward with the assurance that you can have a happy, full life. If you are able to embrace life with confidence, you will only be that much more attractive to others.

Are you living in a responsible way now? So many singles think that being married will make them or their partner more responsible. Not so! Marriage adds more responsibility to your life—you now have the well-being of another individual to consider in your decision making—but more responsibility alone will not make you more responsible. You will still have to choose how to handle your obligations, your money, and your time. If you are already struggling with managing your personal finances, your time, your health, your commitments, and so on, you might not be ready to handle the added responsibilities of marriage.

Family Ties

Even though we no longer practice the custom of arranged marriages, there are a lot of benefits to including your family in your decision making when it comes to getting married. No one has lived with you longer than your parents, so chances are they know you pretty well. They might not offer their opinion about your future spouse unless you ask. *Ask!*

Beside your own personal evaluation, ask your family and close friends whether or not they think you are ready to get married. Warning! This is risky! You might be giving them permission to say things they have been reluctant to say and things you might not want to hear. It will be a test of your maturity just to be vulnerable enough to allow others to give you this input. But you might also be pleasantly surprised to find that those closest to you and who care about you the most see that you *are* ready to marry and are willing to encourage and support you in your choice.

"I Do" Do's and Don'ts

In their book, *The 10 Commandments of Dating*, Ben Young and Dr. Samuel Adams reinforce the importance of choosing wisely who you marry: "If you date and then marry the wrong person, you will live with significant, negative, and lasting consequences of that decision for the rest of your life. This bears repeating: whether or not you stay married, you will live with significant, negative consequences of that decision."

Are We the Right People to Get Married?

Being the right person is only half of the equation—you have to be the right person *for each other*. There are some wonderful, intelligent, loving Christian people out there, but that doesn't mean they should be married to each other. A good marriage starts with two good individuals who are good together. There are three C's you will see repeated throughout this book—Compatibility, Commitment, and Communication. These three C's are essential ingredients in any healthy marriage. Checking out the three C's in your relationship will help you decide if you are the right people to get married to each other.

Compatibility is more complex than "Do we get along together?" Being compatible means your interactions are harmonious and complimentary. It involves shared interests and goals, values, and beliefs. It is the ability and the desire to bring out the best in each other. It is knowing each other's weaknesses as well as strengths and being willing to accept each other as you are. Do you genuinely enjoy spending time together? How often do you laugh together? When you are alone together, are you content just to be with each other or do you have to be engaged in an activity or involved in physical intimacy? How you answer these questions will help you measure your level of compatibility as a couple.

Commitment is the glue that will hold a relationship together during tough times. When you commit yourself to another person in marriage, it is both a legal and a moral obligation. You are indicating that you are willing to entrust your well-being—now and in the future—into the safekeeping of another individual. Commitment will be tested over and over and over again. No matter how secure you are in your love for each other presently, as the circumstances around you change—and they will!—you will have to go back over and over again to recommit to your relationship or your marriage will falter. Two questions to ask at this point about commitment: Can I trust my partner with my present and future well-being? Am I ready to do whatever it takes to build a strong marriage with this person?

That's the Spirit

There is no fear in love. But perfect love drives out fear, because fear has to do with punishment, The one who fears is not made perfect in love. We love because he first loved us. (1 John 4:18–19)

A loving relationship is founded on trust. Just as we trust God with our future because of his great and perfect love for us, we should not be afraid to entrust ourselves—body, heart, and spirit—to our future spouse.

Communication is essential in relationships. Chances are good that neither you nor your partner can read minds. So how will you learn about each other, make decisions together, work out problems, and even express how much you love each other? Communication! We learn how to talk when we are about a year old. But we start learning to communicate even *before* we are born and we never stop learning.

There's more to communication than talking—much more! In fact, there is so much more that we will be dedicating an entire chapter to helping you and your partner become better communicators with each other (see Chapter 5). Everyone can learn better communication skills. How you communicate now with each other can be a key indicator of your readiness to marry, for example …

- Are you able to listen to your partner for more than five minutes without interrupting?
- What percentage of the time you spend alone together is involved in talking as opposed to physical interaction?
- Do you feel your partner values what you have to say?

Being able to express yourself to your partner and with your partner in a healthy and godly way now will be crucial to the success of any future relationship you have together.

Is This the Right Time to Get Married?

There is a lot of truth to the phrase "Timing is everything!" Even if you are the right person and together you are the right couple that doesn't guarantee that this is the right time for you to get married. There are several aspects to the timing question that we will discuss. But first consider this: You are committing to spending the rest of your life together, so what's the rush? If you feel a need to marry quickly, chances are there is something not quite right about your relationship.

For every couple we know who met and married within a short period of time and have built a happy and healthy marriage, we probably know dozens who were unsuccessful because they rushed into marriage. It's important that you know each other well before you commit to a lifetime together, and there is no substitute for spending time together. You might be deeply in love but if you haven't known each other for longer than three months you probably don't know each other well enough to get married. And there is nothing magical about the three-month mark—what really matters is how much time you have actually spent together, observing each other in a variety of life situations and relationships. Two years in a long distance relationship might not be enough if you have not been together for a sufficient amount of time.

Family Ties

> How well do you know your future spouse's family? There is a lot of truth to the saying that you aren't just marrying an individual but you are also marrying his or her family. Understanding and accepting each other's families is a crucial first step to building a family of your own.

Another aspect of timing is where each of you are in your life goals. Have you finished the college degree that you have worked so hard for? Are you just starting the career of your dreams? Do you have other responsibilities that might affect your ability to give yourself completely to the task of building a strong marriage from the start? Are you just coming out of another relationship? Are you currently burdened with financial responsibilities and debts? All of these timing issues can affect your ability to make wise choices in the beginning of this important relationship. Remember: Not getting married *now* doesn't mean not getting married *ever*. Maybe you just need a little more time to insure that your lifetime relationship gets off to the best start.

Building a Healthy Relationship

Marriage—under the best of circumstances and with the best of people—is hard work! Happy marriages just don't happen, they have to be built by two willing and able partners. No one becomes involved in a bad relationship knowing it is unhealthy. Often when we become emotionally involved with another person we tend to ignore any warning signs that would indicate either that the relationship is unhealthy or that the other person might not be safe.

Signs of a Healthy Relationship

A healthy relationship is a joy to participate in and to observe. It is also an awesome testimony to others of the grace and love of God. Think about a married couple you know whose relationship you admire—what is it about their relationship that draws you? What is it about your relationship with your partner that will draw others? Check out these check points for a healthy relationship:

- Treat each other with respect
- Feel safe when you are together
- Feel free to voice your thoughts, feelings, and opinions without fear
- Needs are equally met

- Feel free to spend time with friends, family, or by yourself
- Make decisions together
- Take responsibility for your own choices

Signs of an Unsafe Person

As much as you love your partner, there might be some nagging doubts in your mind that you need to confront. Don't fall into the trap of thinking that marriage will solve your relationship problems. If you are in love with a person who is unsafe, the only solution is to separate from that person until they have dealt with their issues. Forcing him or her to confront their destructive behavior might be the most loving thing you can do for each other. You might be in a relationship with an unsafe person if you observe any of the following behaviors:

- Controlling behavior
- Unfounded jealousy
- Volatile temper
- Constant criticism
- Blames others
- Abuses alcohol and/or other drugs
- Uses physical force to "solve" problems

Relationship Red Flags

We can't say this enough: Marriage is meant to be a lifetime commitment. Choosing your future mate is the choice of a lifetime so "being in love" is not enough! No one can predict if your marriage will fail or succeed, but there are certain warning signs that you should consider. You might discover areas in which you and your partner need to invest some time and energy before you marry. Or you might decide that this relationship requires a greater risk than you are willing to take at this time. Check out the following relationship red flags:

If you or your partner …

- Has been really drunk or used drugs heavily three times in the past three weeks or about ten times in the past three or four months, there might be a problem that will require professional help. No marriage should begin if one partner is clearly unstable, troubled, and in need of professional help.

- Makes statements like, "My family is everything to me" or "I owe it to my mother (or father) to make her (or him) happy," *and* if such statements are coupled with behavior that shows an unhealthy need for parental approval and an inability to leave the home nest, you should consider how such a close relationship with in-laws will affect your marriage.

- Says things like, "You are my life. If you ever leave me I'll kill myself," and if such statements are accompanied with dependent behavior including unreasonable control or jealousy, this partner might bring nothing to the relationship beyond deep draining needs. Being needed so desperately might flatter the ego for a while, but if that is all there is, the relationship will become dull and draining. You cannot be a wife to a man you have to mother nor can you be a husband to a woman who wants a father.

- Are spending the majority of your time together quarreling, fault-finding, engaging in irritating behavior, or hurting each other, perhaps you are subconsciously trying to tell each other something. Think about it—are you trying to find a way out? This type of behavior doesn't just go away after you say "I do."

- Don't share a vision for what marriage together will look like, including the purpose of marriage, the roles of husbands and wives, and the design for the family, you could be in trouble. How will you meet the complex demands and commitment level necessary for a healthy marriage if you don't share a plan?

- Has been involved in any kind of abuse—sexual, physical, and/or verbal—in the past. Victims of abuse carry deep wounds that might not surface until after marriage. If either of you have abuse in your backgrounds, it is important to ask the questions now and work with a counselor to deal with issues before the wedding.

If the person you are dating often exhibits any of the following behaviors, think carefully before pursuing your relationship with him or her. You should not feel unsafe or worry about the safety of others when you are with someone you love or who loves you. Undesirable behaviors include the following:

- Pushing
- Shoving
- Spitting
- Pinching
- Slapping

- Hitting
- Grabbing
- Kicking
- Throwing things
- Forcing sexual acts

Don't be persuaded or coerced into accepting this type of behavior—it has no place in a loving relationship. If you feel you need help in evaluating your relationship in light of these warning signs, talk to a trusted friend, your pastor or a counselor. You owe it to yourself and your partner.

Is It Love?

What is love and how can someone know if what he or she is feeling is the right kind of love for starting a lifetime relationship? This is the time to honestly evaluate your feelings for and actions toward one another. Love is a very complex emotion. Yet in our culture we have romanticized and trivialized genuine love. The Hollywood formula in many successful movies is boy meets girl, boy and girl fall in love, boy and girl commit to a lifetime together—all within a matter of hours, days, or weeks. Love is rarely that instant in real life. Genuine love needs to grow through time and testing.

What Is Love?

In 1 Corinthians 13, the Apostle Paul gives the Bible's definition of love. As you review these verses, ask yourself if this is how you truly feel about your partner. Then ask your partner to go through the same exercise. Finally, discuss together as a couple each point and evaluate which of these elements of genuine love are present and absent in your relationship with each other.

Infatuation is the counterfeit of love—it masquerades as love in many relationships. Infatuation is defined as lacking sound judgment; completely carried away by foolish or shallow love or affection. It keeps couples from doing the work of getting to know each other and from confronting and working through problem areas in their relationship. It is the worst possible foundation for a successful marriage. Here's a look at what infatuation looks like:

That's the Spirit

Here is the true meaning of love in a healthy marriage.

Love is patient and kind. Love is not jealous or boastful or proud or rude. Love does not demand its own way. Love is not irritable, and it keeps no record of when it has been wronged. It is never glad about injustice but rejoices whenever the truth wins out. Love never gives up, never loses faith, is always hopeful, and endures through every circumstance. Love will last forever .... (1 Corinthians 13:4–8)

Infatuation rushes decision making. Infatuation idealizes marriage and sex, leaving couples disillusioned and wounded. Infatuation wants what it wants when it wants it. It focuses on romantic feelings, viewing the object of affection in an unrealistic way. It goes by emotion rather than reason, values, or principles. It avoids honest evaluation, prayerful consideration, and deliberate planning. Infatuation will never last.

Test Your Love

A lifetime commitment needs to start with genuine love. There are many feelings that can be mistaken for love. Feelings are unpredictable. Because it is sometimes difficult to really determine if what you are feeling is genuine love, here are several tests that can help you determine if what you are experiencing in your relationship is genuine love or a poor substitute:

The Happiness Test: If you had to choose between making yourself happy or making your partner happy, which would you choose?

The Energy Test: Does your love give you a new strength and fill you with creative energy? Or does it take away your strength and energy?

The Respect Test: Do you really admire each other? Are you proud of your partner or do you find yourself making excuses for his or her behavior?

The Habit Test: Has being together become a habit or do you genuinely enjoy being together? Do you like each other well enough to choose to be friends if you were not getting married?

The Quarrel Test: How do you make up after a quarrel? Are you able to forgive each other and give in to each other? The ability to be reconciled after a real quarrel must be tested before marriage.

The Time Test: Never get married until you have summered and wintered with your partner. In other words, spend at least a year together to give your relationship time to evolve. Has your love summered and wintered? Have you known each other long enough to know each other well?

The Separation Test: Do you feel an unusual joy while in the company of each other? Is there pain in separation?

The Giving Test: Love and marriage are about giving, not getting. Are you in love to give? Are you capable of self-giving? Is this quality of self-giving constantly evident?

The Growth Test: Is your love dynamic in its growth? Is it progressively maturing? Are the characteristics of Christian love developing?

The Sex Test: Is there mutual enjoyment of each other without the constant need of physical expression? If you cannot be together without physical intimacy, you do not have the maturity and love essential for marriage.

The Dream Test: Are you loving the person you have now or an imaginary dream? Can you be happy with this person if he or she changes in ways you never dreamed of or if he or she never changes?

Bet You Didn't Know

Although we've come a long way from the picture of the caveman hitting his future mate over the head with a club and dragging her back to the cave by her hair, mating for love is actually a fairly modern custom. For centuries, marriages were arranged to achieve the greatest benefit to the family financially, socially, and politically. Even as recently as the previous century, finding a mate was a pragmatic pursuit more than a romantic engagement. Men looked for women who were good workers and could bear children and women looked for men who were good providers. Love, if it developed, was an added bonus for the couple.

Should You Marry Your Best Friend?

Not all friends should marry, but no couple should marry unless they are friends! Friendship grows from companionship—time spent together, doing and talking and sharing. Friends love each other without physical intimacy and yet, many friendships have lasted as long *and longer than* many marriages. So married couples that begin as friends have an edge. Are you and your partner friends? Can you put his or her name in front of each line in the following description of what makes a person a friend?

A friend is someone who ...

- Takes care of you when you're sick.
- Shares willingly with you his or her personal possessions.
- Helps you up hill when you are sliding down.
- Speaks up to defend you when others speak against you.
- Believes in you when no one else but God does.
- Cares enough to speak the truth to you in love.
- Shows pride in introducing you to family and friends.
- Does all these things without expecting anything in return.

Do Not Compromise

No matter how much you love each other, if only one of you is a believer in and follower of Jesus Christ, you are already in trouble. The nature of the marriage relationship is so deep and profound as to be a living example of how God feels about the church and his people. So much of who we are as individuals—our attitudes, values, and beliefs—come from our faith foundation. Couples who share a common foundation of spiritual beliefs and practices find that it deepens their love, helps them to grow closer together, and enables them to achieve their common goals.

Scripture is clear that we should not seek to be joined to an unbeliever. (2 Corinthians 4:14–15) God does not tell us this just to be difficult and restrictive. He knows how we are wired and wants us to be spared the grief and anguish that so often comes in these unequal unions. While we will discuss this more in the following chapters, we implore you—on this point, do not compromise!

Chapter 2

Congratulations! You're Engaged!

Together you've asked the tough questions and faced the tough issues in your relationship. You are convinced that your love is genuine and that God has brought you together. After much prayer and consultation with those who know you best, you're ready to take the next step in commitment to each other—engagement.

In early history, the ritual of betrothal involved an exchange of property from the man's family to the woman's family. More than a ceremonial gesture, the exchange of property was a necessary part of sealing the contract. Because in marriage the woman left behind her family heritage and became a part of her husband's family, the gifts were meant to compensate her family for their loss.

The custom of a period of engagement or betrothal prior to marriage has been around for thousands of years and comes with many interesting traditions. Although engagement is no longer legally binding, the promise to marry is an important decision and a joyous occasion. You will share over and over again the memories you create together during this time, so give a lot of thought to the days and weeks ahead.

A Moment to Remember: Planning the Perfect Proposal

No matter where, when, or how the question gets "popped," it is a moment to be cherished. It is a story you will tell and retell to family and friends. It is a memory you will hopefully share with your children and your children's children. So take the time to think through what would be meaningful for both of you and carefully plan the details of your perfect proposal.

The first step in planning the perfect proposal is deciding who will do the asking! Although traditionally it is the man who proposes marriage, it may be perfectly appropriate in your relationship for the woman to plan the proposal. Next, consider carefully what would delight your partner in a marriage proposal—take into consideration family, cultural customs, religious beliefs, and personality. Man or woman—you will want to discover what kind of proposal will fulfill the dreams of your partner.

What makes a proposal perfect? Contrary to popular thinking, it's not the amount of money you spend or how elaborate the setting. A proposal should be personal, showing deliberate consideration of the other person. It should demonstrate that a lot of thought and planning went into this special moment. Here are a few samples to get you thinking about what will make *your* proposal perfect.

That's the Spirit

The moment when someone asks you to commit to a lifetime relationship with him or her is a very precious time. Both the question and the answer need to be prayerfully considered and the words you use should be carefully chosen. Thoughtless words spoken at such an important time can wound deeply and might long be remembered.

Everyone enjoys a fitting reply; it is wonderful to say the right thing at the right time! (Proverbs 15:23)

Traditional

Tom and Mary had been dating for about two years. During the past three months, they had begun to seriously discuss getting married. Tom knew Mary's family well and both were sure their families would support their decision to marry. Even though Mary's dad used to tease her about the hard time he was planning to give the man who "dared to ask him for her hand" in marriage, Tom knew that asking her father's permission was important to Mary.

A few weeks before he planned to propose to Mary, Tom took Mary's dad to lunch. He explained how much he loved Mary, answered questions about his plans for the future and then popped the question—to Mary's dad: "Sir, Mary and I would like to get married but we will not do so without your permission. I promise you to love her and take care of her all my life. Do I have your permission to ask your daughter to be my wife?" Mary's father was delighted (and Tom was relieved!) when the answer was "yes."

Three weeks later, after dinner at the restaurant where they had had their first date, Tom took Mary to one of their favorite outdoor spots. There he proclaimed his love and devotion, told about his meeting with her father, and asked "Will you marry me?" Over the next few weeks, they shopped together for the perfect ring to seal the deal.

Creative

Eric wanted to propose in a way his girlfriend Sarah would never expect. One May night, while Sarah thought Eric was playing in a church softball league game, Sarah accepted the invitation of a friend to see the professional baseball team (and 2002 World Series winners), the Arizona Diamondbacks, play a home game. Sarah and her friend were watching the pregame batting practice when she was approached by a camera crew and told she had been "randomly" selected to throw out the opening pitch. Sarah happily agreed.

In the meantime, Eric was also at the stadium—he was suiting up with the catcher's gear in order to receive the opening pitch. When the time came, the stadium announcer called out Sarah's name over the PA and she made her way down to the pitcher's mound as the catcher stepped behind home plate to receive her pitch.

Sarah threw the ball to the catcher, who jogged out to the pitcher's mound. But instead of handing her the souvenir baseball, he whipped off his catcher's mask, dropped to one knee, and asked her to be his wife. Eric and 40,000 fans waited for her answer. Sarah's "yes" appeared on the gigantic scoreboard and the crowd roared its approval!

Romantic

Todd was admittedly inept in the romance department. His girlfriend, Meredith, had learned to accept that about him even though she loved all things romantic—flowers, poetry, candlelight, and so on. Todd wanted his proposal to prove that even though it didn't come naturally to him, he could and would be romantic for her sake. So he enlisted the help of family and friends to plan the most romantic proposal setting Meredith could imagine and he could afford.

The Smiths, close family friends of the couple, had a gazebo in their backyard. It was in a beautiful, wooded setting, secluded from the main house. Friends and family got together to decorate the gazebo with white twinkle lights and flowers. Inside they placed a table for two complete with gorgeous linens, china, silver, and a candlelight centerpiece. The Smiths happily acted as servers during the gourmet dinner Todd had planned himself to include Meredith's favorites.

During dinner, the string quartet from church played quietly just outside the gazebo. When dessert had been served, the couple was left alone. Todd pulled out a poem he had written with much effort for the occasion. It wasn't Shelley or Keats, but they were his words asking the woman he loved to be his wife. When Meredith said yes, Todd produced a small music box with a ring inside. Meredith was delighted with her romantic proposal and thrilled that Todd had put so much thought and effort into the occasion.

> **Family Ties**
>
> The custom of asking the father of the bride for permission to marry his daughter never goes out of style. What a great way to acknowledge that marriage is more than the union of two individuals—it is the union of two families. As you make your proposal plans and celebrate your engagement, include your families as often as possible.

Some Proposal Do's and Don'ts

If you still need some help planning that perfect proposal, there's more help out there than you might imagine. Paul Alden, President of Will You Marry Me®, has helped hundreds of couples achieve their perfect moment. Check out his website www.2propose.com. Here are some tips from Paul's list of Proposal Do's and Don'ts:

Do ...

- Select a location that has some significance to the two of you, such as where you first met, had your first date, first kiss, first "I love you," or special place the two of you go.
- Incorporate details that show you pay attention—favorite flowers, song, food, and so on.
- Take advantage of your moment of greatest impact. Pop the question before they see it coming.
- Remember, it might be your proposal but you have to take into account how the other person will feel being put into this situation.
- Drop to bended knee. It may sound corny, but it adds impact!
- Have a contingency plan in case your proposal doesn't happen exactly the way you planned.
- Bring along a cell phone. They're going to want to tell everyone how romantic and creative their spouse-to-be is.

Don't ...

"I Do" Do's and Don'ts

When planning the perfect proposal, don't become so involved in the details that you forget the purpose and the person you are doing all this for. Even if things don't go completely according to plan, relax! This is about a lifetime of love, not a moment of romance. Your devotion and thoughtfulness to your partner's wishes will win the day!

- Make your proposal too complicated. The more complicated it is, the more likely it is that something can go wrong.
- Propose how you would want to be proposed to, propose the way she would want you to propose to her. The scoreboard at a football game won't mean much to her if she's not a sports fan.
- Get so caught up in the details that you don't get to enjoy the moment.
- Hide the ring in food. Many of these proposals are followed by a trip to either the dentist or the emergency room.
- Be too obvious. If you never take her out in a limo, she's going to immediately be suspicious if you show up at her front door with one.

And the Answer Is ...

There are only three possible answers to the "Will you marry me" question—"Yes," "No," or "I need to think about it." In most cases, the decision to get engaged should be one you've thoroughly discussed and considered together. When that is the case, the question only gets popped when the answer "yes" is pretty well assured. Even so, the person proposing is sure to breathe a sigh of relief when the answer is finally given.

If you are thinking of popping the question and you think it is possible the answer will be no, you might want to reconsider. The reasons for a no answer may represent areas of your relationship that need work. Or it might simply be that you have not had enough time together. Don't propose, however, thinking that you will persuade your partner to marry. You want and need a willing partner in marriage. Forcing the issue prematurely will not make things better and could make things worse.

If the time comes and you are having doubts, be brave enough to ask for more time before committing yourself. Although engagements can be broken (and *should* be if either partner has any hesitation about the permanency of marriage to the other person), engagement should not be entered into lightly. Remember, it is a promise; and promises are meant to be kept.

Bet You Didn't Know

Originally, both the man and the woman received a ring at the time of engagement. The custom of the diamond engagement ring did not become popular until the mid-1800s after huge diamond deposits had been discovered in South Africa. The solitaire setting was introduced in the late nineteenth century. Now nearly half of all rings feature or include side stones of other gemstones.

The Engagement Ring

Engagement rings go back to ancient times when golden rings were used like money. A man would give a gold ring to his bride-to-be as partial payment to her family and as a symbol of his intentions. The woman wore the ring as an indication that she was no longer available. For today's couples, the engagement ring is a visible symbol of their love and intention to marry. It is also often coupled with the wedding ring on the wedding day, becoming a lasting reminder of their pledge to love, honor, and cherish each other for the rest of their lives.

New or Heirloom

Many people like to use rings that have been in their family for years or even generations. The value of family heirlooms can have more to do with sentiment than the actual market value of the settings or gems. A family heirloom can have great significance to one partner but not the other, so be certain that you both agree that this family piece is the perfect ring for you.

If you are thinking of buying an antique ring, it is worth noting that modern laser cutting techniques give a superior cut to a diamond, so older diamonds may not be as valuable as their more modern counterparts. Consider combining the sentiment of an antique setting with a new diamond or gemstone. This may give the greatest appeal and best value in the long run.

If you are going for a new ring, there are many things to consider in going after the perfect ring. Just remember—the engagement ring is a symbol of something beautiful, precious, and rare—your love and commitment to each other.

Check the Bottom Line

The engagement ring might be the first joint financial decision you make as a couple. So realistically, what can you afford? Set a budget for the ring and do not increase it after you have begun looking. It is very easy to find "the perfect ring" and talk yourself into spending considerably more than you can afford. Financial advisors suggest that you keep your spending in the range of one to two months' salary. Another guideline is don't buy a ring you cannot have paid off before the wedding.

A ring can be beautiful and meaningful without being so expensive that it creates a hardship financially. Remember that a fancy, expensive ring will not make your marriage better and if it means going into debt, it might actually be a hurdle to a healthy start.

Speaking of the wedding, remember also that there will be many additional costs—expected and unexpected—for your special day and then, of course, there is the honeymoon! As you talk about the ring, talk also about other expenditures that will be coming up and prioritize together. You will have many anniversaries in the future that can become occasions for presenting a more expensive ring.

What a Girl Wants

Many future grooms still like to spring a ring on their partner at the time of proposal. If the ring is to be a surprise, there are several things to keep in mind when choosing for her:

- Pay attention when she admires someone else's ring.
- Ask friends and family what she prefers.
- Notice other jewelry she wears—Does she wear gold or silver, modern styles or more traditional? Are her tastes simple, elegant, or more ornate and elaborate?
- Take her to the mall and window-shop at several jewelers.

To keep the surprise, you might need to use devious methods to get her ring size. Here are a few suggestions:

- Try to get a hold of one of her rings (maybe one she has left lying around) and make an impression of it to get a fairly reliable measurement. You can use a bar of soap, a small piece of clay, or even a slice of bread.
- Put one of her rings on your finger and mark the spot where it stops on the finger. Show the marking to a jeweler who can measure it.
- Ask a friend or family member to find out her ring size and pass it on to you.

Purchasing the Ring

Make certain that the store or jeweler you are dealing with is reputable. Ask friends and family for referrals. A good jeweler will take the time to answer all your questions and will voluntarily share information with you so that you feel empowered to make the wisest choice. Have him show you several rings, placed side-by-side for comparison.

If you are looking at a number of different rings, don't be afraid to take notes on the ones you like. It is easy to forget what you liked about a ring or where you saw your favorite when you have been to several stores and looked at dozens of rings.

Never buy the ring the same day. Go home, think about it, and go back after a few days to make certain you like it as much the second time. Don't worry that you might miss out on the perfect ring, and don't be pressured into buying on the spot so as not to lose a one-time-only discount.

Get warranties and guarantees in writing. If you buy the ring and your bride-to-be would rather have something else, will the jeweler exchange or refund your money so she may select the ring she wants? Is there an unconditional money-back guarantee if the stone is returned within a certain number of days?

Check out the repair policies. Sizing, cleaning, and tightening of the stone should be done free of charge for the first six months or year.

Be sure your receipt describes the ring and setting in detail, including the weight, shape, and color so that you may use it for insurance purposes. Some insurance companies, however, will require a written document from the jeweler; the receipt alone might not be adequate proof. While chances of your ring being lost or stolen may seem remote, it does happen. Secure insurance on the ring as soon as possible.

Gemstones

Although diamonds remain the favorite choice for most engagement rings, many women today are choosing gemstones as either the primary stone or as accent stones. Gemstones can add a very personal dimension to an engagement ring. And in most cases, they are more affordable than a diamond. Here are some interesting tidbits about gemstones:

- **Garnet**—January birthstone; symbol of eternal friendship; semitransparent and dark red in color.
- **Amethyst**—February birthstone; symbol of faithfulness and sincerity (biblical folklore); clear purple or bluish violet quartz.
- **Aquamarine**—March birthstone; symbol of intelligence and courage; color can be transparent blue, blue-green, or green.
- **Diamond**—April birthstone; symbol of innocence and matrimonial happiness; colorless or hint of blue or yellow.
- **Emerald**—May birthstone; symbol of domestic harmony and success in love; transparent in shades of green.
- **Pearl**—June birthstone; symbol of health and longevity.
- **Ruby**—July birthstone; symbol of love and contentment; dark red. Legend suggests that the stone in a ruby engagement ring will darken in color if the course of true love is not running smoothly.

- **Peridot**—August birthstone; symbol of happiness and friendship; lime green stone.

- **Sapphire**—September birthstone; symbol of truth and faithfulness; same family as the ruby but is rich blue in color.

- **Opal**—October birthstone; symbol of hope; iridescent mixture of colors against a soft, milky white or vivid, fiery background.

- **Topaz**—November birthstone; symbol of fidelity; yellow to yellow-brown in color.

- **Turquoise**—December birthstone; symbol of prosperity; blue, bluish-green or green in color.

Some of the more popular gemstones for engagement rings are emeralds, sapphires, and rubies. These gemstones come in a variety of cuts and make beautiful primary stones with diamonds used as accents.

That's the Spirit

In promising to marry someone, you have made a very important decision. But if God is at the center of your relationship and you are committed to following his will for your life, you can relax and enjoy this next step in your walk with him.

So I pray that God, who gives you hope, will keep you happy and full of peace as you believe in him. May you overflow with hope through the power of the Holy Spirit. (Romans 15:13)

The Four C's of Diamonds

Because diamonds remain the gemstone of choice for most engagement rings, it will be helpful to understand the important terms used in evaluating diamonds. In general, diamonds are described according to the four C's—cut, color, clarity, and carat. Cut and carat are probably the most important factors in determining the value of a diamond. A well-cut diamond, even if the stone is slightly flawed, can be beautiful; and a diamond that weighs .90 carats is virtually indistinguishable from a 1 carat stone, but the savings can be significant. So before you start diamond shopping, get to know your C's:

- **Cut**—The cut is the way that the stone is cut from a rough natural gemstone to a beautiful jewel. The better the cut, the better the diamond sparkles, reflecting the light back in brilliant rainbow colors. Your diamond can be cut in many different shapes, but usually has a full 58 facets. The shape of the diamond—emerald, marquise, oval, princess, pear, heart, or radiant—has little affect on the value.

- **Color**—The best diamonds are perfectly clear. Diamonds are graded from "D" which is exceptionally white, to "Z" which is light yellow, right down to "J" diamonds, which are nearly colorless. The clearer the diamond the rarer and hence the more expensive.

- **Clarity**—Most diamonds have very small flaws or "inclusions." These don't affect the durability of the stone, but they can hinder the light flow through the stone. Obviously the fewer flaws a diamond has the more valuable it is. Diamonds are graded from:

FL	(flawless)
IF	(internally flawless—minor surface blemishes)
VVS	(very, very small flaws)
VS	(very small flaws)
SI	(small flaws)
P	(flaws which are visible to the naked eye)

- **Carat**—Carat is the weight of the diamond—one carat is divided into 100 points and is equal to 200 milligrams. Although diamonds can be found over 3 karats, even 0.05 carat is a big stone in most people's eyes. The average size of an engagement ring today is about .75 carat.

The Setting

The gemstone is only one aspect of the perfect ring. The same gemstone in different settings can look dramatically different. Traditionally, the most popular choice for any setting, regardless of the design, is yellow or white gold, although platinum is growing in popularity, it has the same general appearance as white gold, and is stronger.

Gold is a very soft metal and is usually combined with other metals for strength. Pure gold is 24-karat and is too soft for most jewelry. Twelve karat gold is half gold and half another metal—usually silver, copper, or platinum. The other metal combined with the gold helps determine the color of the gold. Most gold rings have platinum prongs that hold the gemstone, because platinum is the strongest of the metals used in jewelry.

Besides the type and color of the metal, there are other aspects of the setting to consider. Style, whether contemporary or classic, antique or traditional, is a matter of personal taste. Another consideration is whether or not the engagement ring will be paired with the wedding band and if the groom will have a matching ring. Take your time looking at and discussing the wide variety of settings available and the advantages and disadvantages of each.

Engagement Gift for Future Groom

The engagement ring is the future groom's gift to his future bride. Although it is not necessary to give the groom-to-be a gift, it is a nice gesture. This gift should be more extravagant than utilitarian and show thoughtful consideration to your man's likes and dislikes. Some ideas, besides a ring, that you might consider: leather wallet, watch, an engraved pen or pencil, leather briefcase, leather-bound journal, a collectible for his hobby, and so on.

Sharing the News

The joy of good news multiplies when it's shared! But how you decide to share the news of your engagement is an individual decision. Some couples like to keep the news to themselves for a few days. There are some real advantages to that course of action:

- It gives you both time to think about your new level of commitment apart from the romance of the moment and the scrutiny of others.
- It's fun to have a secret that only the two of you share.
- It gives you time to talk about your plans before others begin sharing their opinions.

Of course, both sets of parents should be the first to learn of the upcoming marriage. Even if your parents have been in on some of the proposal plans, try to find a special way to let your families know about your decision. After your immediate family, you may have one or two close friends you want to tell before everyone else hears the news.

Traditionally, the bride's family hosts the first social gathering to share the good news with family members and close friends. If the groom's family lives far away and cannot be included in the same party because of the distance, they may also host an engagement party for the couple in their hometown. Official announcements by mail or in the media follow after the engagement party.

"I Do" Do's and Don'ts

After you make your announcement, be prepared to field questions about the wedding: What's the date? Where will it be? Who's in your wedding party? Although you don't have to have all the answers yet, especially if you are planning for a long engagement, you might want to think about how you can graciously answer each question. Keep in mind that most people ask because they care.

The Engagement Party

A party is a great way to both announce and celebrate your engagement. Sometimes the party is planned under the guise of another celebration like a birthday or holiday. It is only after the guests arrive that the real reason for celebrating—the engagement—is announced. One advantage of this type of announcement is that guests don't feel like they have to bring an engagement gift.

Some ideas for this type of celebration include the following:

- A backyard barbecue in the summer for the Fourth of July or just because
- A springtime brunch to celebrate Easter or Mother's Day
- An open house during the holiday season from Thanksgiving to New Year's Day

Of course, you don't really need an excuse for a party. However you plan it, getting everyone together for the announcement can be exciting and fun. Traditionally, the father of the bride-to-be announces the engagement at some appropriate point in the festivities. It might be nice to have both fathers share in the honors—the father of the bride can make the announcement and the father of the groom can offer a prayer or blessing for the couple.

Even after the news is out, an engagement party is a great way to celebrate this new stage in your life together. Normally, engagement parties are held on or about the same day any official announcement appears and within 6 months to a year of the wedding date. Generally guests are not invited to the engagement party who will not be invited to the wedding.

Can you host your own engagement party? You bet! If the circumstances in either of your families make a family-hosted party difficult or uncomfortable, it doesn't mean you have to forgo an engagement party. Plan your own open house or dinner party for your closest friends and family. In a smaller, more intimate setting, you might enjoy talking even more about how you met and why you want to spend your lives together.

The most important thing to remember about your engagement party is that it is a celebration for both you and your fiancé. So much about the wedding plans will focus around the bride that at times the groom can feel left out. The engagement party is a great place to set the tone for the months ahead. If you are the bride-to-be and your family is hosting the engagement party, make sure that your future groom has some input into the planning. During the party, stick close to his side and introduce him to family members and friends he might not already know. Make it your job to ensure that your partner has a good time.

Setting the Date

When an engagement is announced, the first question nearly everyone asks is "When is the wedding?" Although it is nice to have the date of the wedding set and confirmed before the engagement is announced, it is not essential. But you will need to have some time frame in mind—early next summer or after graduation—in order to answer the inquiries of family and friends.

There are a lot of decisions that go into setting the wedding date—availability of the location for the service and the reception, finances, seasons, availability of wedding party members, life stages (such as finishing college or starting a new job), and so on. You will want to discuss all these decisions together and with your family, as well as get the necessary permissions from the church and reception hall before announcing a firm date.

Engagement Gifts

Guests are not expected to bring gifts to the engagement party, but many do. Save the opening of these gifts for after the party when you and your fiancé can take your time to read the cards and appreciate the thought behind each gift. Within two weeks of the party, each person who gave you a gift should receive from you a personal thank you note.

Formal Announcements

Many couples still choose to announce their engagement in the local newspaper. If this is your choice, there are a few guidelines to follow. Every newspaper has its own policies, but the following Engagement Announcement Worksheet will help you gather all the important information.

Engagement Announcement Worksheet

Bride-to-be's Last Name _____

Fiancé's Last Name _____

Date to appear in paper _____

Bride-to-be's

Full Name _____ Daytime Phone _____

Address _____ City/State _____

Bride-to-be attends/attended/

graduated from _____

Bride-to-be's occupation _____

Employed by _____ City/State _____

Bride's parents' full names _____ Phone _____

Address _____ City/State _____

Fiancé's

Full Name _____ Daytime Phone _____

Address _____ City/State _____

Fiancé attends/attended/

graduated from _____

Fiancé's occupation _____

Employed by _____ City/State _____

Fiancé's parents' full names _____ Phone _____

Address_____ City/State_____

Month of wedding _____ Place of wedding _____

Will photo be submitted? Yes/No

Other information: _____

The announcement is traditionally worded so that it is coming from the bride-to-be's parents. For example, "Mr. and Mrs. John Smith are pleased to announce the engagement of their daughter, Mary Smith to Tom White, the son of Mr. and Mrs. Frank White of Phoenix, Arizona." Even when the announcement is to be printed in the future groom's hometown paper, it should still be worded so that it is from the bride-to-be's family.

Family relationships can be complicated today, even in the Christian community. If your parents are divorced, there are many acceptable ways to word the announcement. They may still make the announcement together and include the names of stepparents. Start checking out the wording in your newspaper and look for the model that feels most comfortable to you.

After the Party's Over

Going public with your engagement is a big step. What was once a private relationship between two now includes a host of family and friends. As easy as it will be to get caught up in all the planning and wedding preparations, now is not the time to neglect your relationship. In fact, you will soon see that in terms of making sure your relationship is ready for the commitment of a lifetime, you've only just begun.

If you care about your future marriage, don't skip the next few chapters! Although these chapters are not meant to take the place of any one-on-one premarital counseling that might be available or required by your church, we will walk you through some of the more important aspects of building a healthy relationship that result in a successful marriage.

What Is Marriage?

Marriage can mean different things to different people. It's important that you and your partner share the same vision for marriage. Your vision for marriage will be your road map for your relationship in the future. Imagine that you and your future mate are going on a road trip. You're looking at a map of California, but your partner is looking at a map of Maine. The problem is obvious! Neither of you will get where you want to go, and the trip is going to be miserable! How can you make sure you are reading from the same map?

Your Vision of Marriage

First, recognize that you both already *have* a vision of what marriage is. Your vision has been formed by the family you grew up in, the faith training you have had, and the values you have accepted from all you have seen and heard about marriage. Even if you and your partner had shared the exact same life experiences (and we know that's not possible), your vision for marriage would be different.

Myths About Marriage

There are many common myths about marriage. Many of these myths are perpetuated in books, movies, and on TV. It is important to separate myth from reality. Otherwise, you will face certain disappointment when your expectations are not met. Here are some common myths about marriage and a reality check for each:

Marriage Myth: Marriage is a cure for loneliness.

Reality Check: Many married people are still lonely. Even in healthy marriages, there will be occasions when you will experience loneliness for a time.

Marriage Myth: Marriage makes you a complete person.

Reality Check: There are thousands of single adults today who are living very complete and fulfilling lives. Although marriage will not make you complete, it will add a new dimension to your life and character.

Marriage Myth: Married couples should do everything together.

Reality Check: It is important that couples spend quality time together. But it is not necessary, nor advisable, that all your time be spent together.

Marriage Myth: Couples who truly love each other won't have problems in their relationship.

Reality Check: *Every* couple will experience difficulties in their relationship, but happy couples learn to work through their difficulties while remaining committed to each other.

Marriage Myth: Happy couples don't argue.

Reality Check: Every couple will experience conflict. It is better to confront conflict than ignore it. Happy couples have learned to disagree in a way that helps them resolve their conflict.

Marriage Myth: He or she will change after we're married.

Reality Check: What you see is what you get. Never marry with the expectation that your partner will be any different after you marry.

Marriage Is ...

Talk about your vision for marriage with each other. By confronting your own conceptions of marriage, communicating with each other about your vision for marriage, and consulting God's Word for his guidelines for marriage, you can map out together what you want your marriage to be. Here are some statements about marriage to get you started:

- Marriage is an opportunity for love to be learned and lived.
- Marriage is fragile.
- Marriage is fun.
- Marriage is affected more by our inner communication than our outer communication.
- Marriage is more often influenced by unresolved issues from our past than we realize.
- Marriage is a call to servanthood.
- Marriage is a refining process—more for our holiness than our happiness!
- Marriage is a way of life, not a one-time event.
- Marriage is a lifetime commitment.

Marriage takes us on an incredible journey. As travelers, we are faced with many choices, and we are responsible for every choice we make. But when two companions travel together on the same road with the same destination in mind, the journey can be fun and rewarding. Enjoy your trip!

God's Vision for Marriage

Have you ever stood in front of a sculpture or painting in an art museum, pondering the work of the creator and wondering "What was he or she *thinking*?" If you could get inside the artist's head and see the work from his or her point of view, you would no doubt have a new appreciation for it. Because God created marriage, it would make sense then to get his perspective on it.

Marriage as God intended it is the union of a man and a woman in a relationship that is mutually satisfying because it provides companionship on the highest level. God's vision for Adam and Eve is the same vision he has for you and your marriage. If you want your marriage to be godly as well as good, then it is important that you understand God's view of marriage.

It All Started with Adam and Eve

In Genesis 1, we learn that when God created mankind in his own image, he created both male and female. (Genesis 1:27) The reason for creating the first couple is made clearer in Genesis 2:18 where we read "And the Lord God said, 'It is not good for the man to be alone. I will make a companion who will help him.'" Only woman was found to be a suitable companion for the man. (Genesis 2:20)

After God presented Adam with his perfect mate, Eve, Scripture tells us "This explains why a man leaves his father and mother and is joined to his wife, and the two are united into one." (Genesis 2:24) In this one verse, God outlines three crucial marriage principles: leaving, cleaving, and becoming one. Before you and your partner can become one in marriage, you both must make the conscious choice to leave your family in order to cleave to your new spouse. Leaving involves much more than packing up the Subaru with all your worldly goods and saying good-bye to the family home. And cleaving is more than joining together in a sticky embrace.

Leaving

Emotional separation from your family of origin is necessary to establish your own family unity. The ties that bind us to our family of origin can also keep us from total commitment to our spouse. As a child, you depended on your family for just about everything—physically, emotionally, spiritually. That's not only natural, that is the way God planned it. But in a healthy family, every child gradually grows less dependent on Mom and Dad and more independent as he or she matures.

Part of the leaving process is recognizing that it is no longer appropriate for you to depend on your parents to meet your needs in the same ways they have in the past. After you marry, your parents no longer have authority over you. God still desires and requires that you honor your parents, but leaving requires a shift from being dependent to being dependable. You must leave behind your financial dependence on your parents. You must be willing to leave behind the control of your parents, honestly evaluating their attitudes and influences on you.

Family Ties

As the two of you begin to discuss wedding arrangements, keep in mind the leaving and cleaving process. The wedding day is the beginning of your life together, so although you will want to be sensitive to the wishes and needs of both your families, make sure you do not cave in to the will of the majority just to keep peace. It is *your* special day.

You can't cleave until you leave! Imagine trying to hug your future spouse with your mom or dad standing between you. It would not be a very satisfying embrace for either you or your partner. In the same way, emotional dependence on your family can stand in the way of a husband and wife being able to fully connect with each other.

Cleaving

The union of a man and woman in marriage is deeper and more complex than most of us can understand. The Hebrew word for "cleave" (dabaq) means "to be permanently glued or joined together." This level of commitment results in a love that is wholehearted, satisfying, and completely interdependent. The concept of cleaving embodies absolute, unswerving loyalty to your spouse—for better or for worse, for rich or for poor, in sickness and in health, 'til death! Only death can break the bond God desires between a husband and his wife. Talk about your super glue!

Unfortunately, cleaving is not a once-and-for-all-time occurrence—you say "I do" on your wedding day and whammo!—you are "cleaved" together for all time. To cleave or not to cleave is a choice you will each have to face many times in the course of your life together. But because of the nature of the covenant relationship that you enter into in marriage, cleaving is the only right choice.

That's the Spirit

As the Scriptures say, "A man leaves his father and mother and is joined to his wife, and the two are united into one." This is a great mystery …. (Ephesians 5:31–32)

Think about it! The only time that $1 + 1 = 1$ is when a man and a woman join together in marriage. How can that be? It is the same mystery that we see in the church—the unity of believers regardless of their race, age, background, and so on. It seems impossible, but with God you can be one with another.

When Two Become One

What God intended when he said that two become one involves so much more than sex! Sexual intercourse is meant to be the final expression of oneness. Physical intimacy is where it should end, not where it should start. And God clearly intended that sexual intimacy be reserved for and confined to your spouse. But there's more—this is about living together as man and wife, celebrating your differences, and learning the joy of oneness. Becoming one takes time and is achieved only when both the husband and the wife make it a priority.

Becoming one starts with your attitude. Take a look at the verses listed below. They all talk about how we as Christians are to act toward one another. Why not study them together with your future spouse and talk together about making the rules of "one another" a priority in your relationship starting now?

Be devoted to one another. (Romans 12:10)

Honor one another. (Romans 12:10)

Live in harmony with one another. (Romans 12:16)

Stop passing judgment on one another. (Romans 14:13)

Accept one another. (Romans 15:7)

Instruct one another. (Romans 15:14)

Agree with one another. (1 Corinthians 1:10)

Serve one another. (Galatians 5:13)

> **"I Do" Do's and Don'ts**
>
> You might want to start carrying around a small notebook just for the wedding so that as ideas come to you for the ceremony, you can jot them down. Many of the Scripture verses regarding marriage you will be studying together in preparation could also make good readings for you wedding service. Or you might want to incorporate some in your wedding vows.

Be patient with one another. (Ephesians 4:2)

Be kind and compassionate to one another, forgiving each other. (Ephesians 4:32)

Submit to one another. (Ephesians 5:21)

Teach and admonish one another. (Colossians 3:16)

Encourage one another and build each other up. (1 Thessalonians 5:11)

Encourage one another daily. (Hebrews 3:13)

Spur one another on toward love and good deeds. (Hebrews 10:24)

Love one another deeply, from the heart. (1 Peter 1:22)

Live in harmony with one another. (1 Peter 3:8)

Clothe yourselves with humility toward one another. (1 Peter 5:5)

Have fellowship with one another. (1 John 1:7)

Love one another. (1 John 3:11)

Love one another. (1 John 3:23)

Love one another. (1 John 4:7)

Love one another. (1 John 4:11)

Love one another. (1 John 4:12)

Love one another. (2 John 5)

Get the picture? The only way two individuals can become one is for each 'one' to focus on the well-being of the other. This is God's model for marriage and his model for all our relationships as Christians.

Marriage Is a Covenant, Not Just a Contract

Sometime before your wedding day, you and your future spouse will apply for a marriage license in the state where you will be wed. That's because today throughout North America in Europe, there are laws regarding the institution of marriage. Marriage is a legally binding contract that, after entered into, can only be undone by a court of law.

But to God, marriage is more than a legal contract—it is a covenant agreement between two people. What's the difference, you ask? Let us outline them for you:

Contract	Covenant
Civil	Sacred
Binding for limited time	Binding forever
Can be broken, for a price	Cannot be broken, but can be violated, resulting in great personal loss
Institutional	Relational
Witnessed by people	Witnessed by people and God
Bound by the State	Bound by God

The fact that marriage is a covenant relationship should be very reassuring. When God guarantees a covenant, he promises to enable and equip each individual in the covenant so that he or she can fulfill the obligations of the covenant relationship. I'm pretty sure you won't find *that* kind of guarantee in the fine print on your state marriage license!

> ### Bet You Didn't Know
>
> There is a difference between a marriage certificate and a marriage license. A marriage certificate is not a legal document but more of a keepsake. A marriage license is required for your marriage to be legal in the United States and is issued in the county were the wedding will take place and it can take three to six days to receive your license after you apply for it. Requirements for a marriage license vary between states and counties and must be obtained before your wedding day.

God Hates Divorce

Too many couples today go into marriage with the idea that if it doesn't work out, divorce is an option. For the Christian couple, divorce should not be left as an escape clause. God is very clear about divorce in his Word:

> "For I hate divorce!" says the Lord, the God of Israel. "It is as cruel as putting on a victim's bloodstained coat," says the Lord Almighty. (Malachi 2:16)

You might be so in love with each other today that you cannot even imagine that either of you would consider a life without the other. But that day will almost surely come. So decide now, before the turmoil of circumstances and emotions that come to every marriage, what your view is on divorce. Look at other Bible verses on divorce. (Matthew 19:3–6; Mark 10:2–9; 1 Corinthians 7:10–11) How does your partner feel about divorce? Is divorce an option for you? Why or why not?

The Roles We Play

It's important to look at the many roles you play because each will be affected by your new role as a husband or wife. Today a wife can be a sister, a daughter, a daughter-in-law, a granddaughter, a mother, an employer or employee, a homemaker, a neighbor, a friend, a citizen, and a church member. A husband can be a brother, a son, a son-in-law, a grandson, a father, an employee or employer, a neighbor, a friend, a citizen, and a church member. Each role carries with it certain responsibilities and opportunities that will likely change as you begin your new marriage roles.

Balancing Your Roles

The Bible has something to say about every role in your life. It can also help you prioritize your time, energy, and finances as they relate to your many roles. Of course, we could make it easy for you and suggest you always think God first, family second, and work third. But that little formula has gotten many in trouble because they have applied it legalistically and forgotten the values and beliefs behind it. It has become an excuse for some to serve the church (God first) to the neglect of their marriages (family second) and often resulting in financial irresponsibility (work third).

You and your marriage will be happier and healthier if you concentrate on the biblical values associated with your roles so that you can keep them in perspective and balance your daily responsibilities and opportunities.

Roles in Marriage

Most of what we believe about our role in the marriage relationship is the product of our family background. As children, we learn what a wife is by watching our mothers and we learn what a husband is by watching our fathers. Hopefully, you have had godly role models in your own homes. We add to that any ethnic or cultural traditions that influence what we think a wife or husband should be. In most cases, these influences are neither good nor bad, but if they are different from the influences that our future mate grew up with, there is the potential for misunderstanding, conflict, and grief.

How can you avoid misunderstanding over your definitions of the marriage roles before you marry? First, define for yourself what makes a man a good husband and what makes a woman a good wife. Next, try to unravel why you believe what you believe. Is it cultural? Is it what you grew up with in your home? Is it what you were raised in the church to believe? Understanding

---

Family Ties

Your parents may be able to offer you valuable insight into how they adjusted to their new roles as husband and wife in the beginning of their own marriage and during the years after. Why not invite them to dinner to share some of their stories and advice? It might be fun and instructive!

where your view originated can be helpful as you work together to accept and affirm each other's beliefs about the roles you will each play in your marriage.

To me, the perfect husband is …

His view: _____

Her view: _____

To me, the perfect wife is …

His view: _____

Her view: _____

Having trouble getting started? The following is a little exercise called "What Do You Think?" Check it out—it might help you come up with your own definitions.

What Do You Think?
Husband-Wife Relationship Expectations

AGREE	DISAGREE	STATEMENT
❑	❑	The personal ambitions of a man should be subordinated to the family as a group.
❑	❑	An ambitious and responsible husband does not like his wife to work.
❑	❑	A man needs the responsibility of marriage to develop fully.
❑	❑	The needs of a family come before a woman's personal ambitions.
❑	❑	It is unfair that men are obliged to compromise their personal goals and ideals for the sake of a good marital relationship.
❑	❑	A woman who works cannot fulfill her children's and husband's needs as well as one who stays home.
❑	❑	A man feels his work to be an extension of his personhood, and his relationships at work are primary to him.
❑	❑	According to Scripture, a wife may not try to change the marriage situation other than through submission.

AGREE	DISAGREE	STATEMENT
❏	❏	A man will have achieved the main goal of his life if he rears normal, well-adjusted children.
❏	❏	Single women need personal success, but all a married woman needs is her husband's success.
❏	❏	There is no conflict for a married man between fulfilling himself as a husband and fulfilling himself as an individual.
❏	❏	A woman feels insecure if her husband is insecure.
❏	❏	Marriage and children should take precedence over everything else in a man's life.
❏	❏	It is unfair that women have to give up more than men in order to have a good marriage.
❏	❏	A father's place is in the home when he is not working.
❏	❏	A husband who insists on being the sole provider will be more ambitious and responsible.
❏	❏	In seeking God's will about decisions that affect both spouses, the husband should take the lead and give final direction.
❏	❏	Women should be the primary educators of their children in the home as related to matters of spiritual knowledge and practice.

Bet You Didn't Know

In the late 1800s and early 1900s, the ritual of courting became more formalized. Men, considered to be too intensely emotional in the affairs of the heart, were restricted to calling on their love interest at her home under the watchful eyes and listening ears of her parents and family. Courting was not conducted in the public eye. In fact, PDA's (public displays of affection)—holding hands, hugging, kissing—were strictly prohibited!

What Do You Expect?

Unacknowledged or unexpressed role expectations have deeply wounded many young marriages. What do you believe about your role in marriage? Use the following key to respond to each statement. Next to each statement, write the number that best reflects what you feel (not what you think you are *expected* to believe):

Response Key:

5—Strongly Disagree
4—Disagree
3—Not sure
2—Agree
1—Strongly Agree

- The husband's primary responsibility is to his job, and the wife's primary responsibility is to the home and the children.
- The husband and wife should plan the budget and manage money matters together.
- The husband should have at least one night a week out with his friends.
- The wife should not be employed outside of the home.
- The husband should help regularly with the laundry and dishes.
- Money that the wife earns is her money.
- The wife should read Bible stories and teach the kids about their faith.
- The wife should always be the one to cook.
- Money can best be handled through a joint account.
- Marriage is a 50-50 proposition.
- Major decisions should be made together, but the husband has the tie-breaking vote.
- The husband should baby-sit one night a week so the wife can get away and do what she wants.
- A couple should spend their leisure time with one another.
- It is all right for the wife to initiate lovemaking with her husband.
- Neither the husband nor the wife should purchase an item costing over $100.00 (or another amount you agree on) without consulting the other.
- The father is the one responsible for disciplining the children.
- It is the wife's responsibility to have the house neat and clean.

- The husband should take his wife out somewhere nice twice a month.
- Disciplining the children is a shared responsibility.
- It is the husband's job to do the yard work.
- The mother should be the teacher of values to the children.
- Women are more emotional than men.
- Children should be allowed to help plan family activities.
- Children need to be strictly disciplined.
- The wife should always obey what her husband asks her to do.
- The husband is the spiritual leader of the home and is the primary decision-maker.

After you have each completed this survey individually, talk it through together. Apart from what God has clearly defined in his Word concerning the roles of husbands and wives, many of our notions about our roles in marriage are unimportant. What is important is that you both understand each other's expectations and can agree together on what your roles will be in your marriage.

Be Realistic!

Not all expectations are realistic, and even if you both agree now on certain expectations, life has a way of changing the best of intentions! So the next question is "what will you do when your expectations are not met?" First, you can ask yourself a series of questions to see if your expectation is realistic: Am I fulfilling the expectations set for me? Can I easily change my expectations? Is the expectation based in reality? Is the expectation essential to attaining any specific spiritual goal? How does the expectation affect my partner's perception of me? Will I be hurt in any way if the expectation is unfulfilled?

Unfulfilled expectations generate frustration and anger—often becoming demands. There are five conditions that escalate the possibility of unmet expectations:

- Unrealistically *high* expectations
- Differing expectations
- Confused expectations

> **That's the Spirit**
>
> If God meant woman to rule over man, he would have taken her out of Adam's head. Had He designed her to be his slave, he would have taken her out of his feet. But God took woman out of man's side, for He made her to be a helpmate and an equal to him. —Augustine

- Unexpressed or assumed expectations
- Unrealistically *low* expectations

Okay, we know this is tough stuff! But take it from us, it is much better to talk through these things now than to face them in the midst of your marriage. For most couples, these exercises help make a strong love stronger. But for some—the fortunate ones—it might point out differences that are so problematic that you either need professional help to sort it all out or you might decide not to marry. No matter how difficult and painful that choice may be, do it! It will only be worse if you marry first.

Submission Is a Good Thing

What does submission mean to you? Most people think that by submitting to another person, you are assuming a subservient position—one of less value, less power, and less worth. The world's idea of submission means you become a doormat or a lapdog. Even some Christians are confused about what God's Word means when it talks about submission, especially within the marriage relationship. The concept of submission has gotten a bad rap.

For husbands and wives to practice submission the way God intended it, they must understand that it is not meant to be restrictive but freeing. Submission is to be mutual. In Ephesians 5, the Apostle Paul clearly outlines that submission is evidence of a life controlled by the Holy Spirit. Every Christian is called to submit to every other Christian. Submission is a reflection of our respect for God's authority and him loving others through us.

In marriage, both the husband and wife have an important role to play for submission to be possible. God says that the husband is the head of the wife. In our human bodies, the head is vitally connected to the body—it cannot live or function without all the systems that connect the two. The head can make decisions but it would be foolish to make any decision that would bring harm to the body. The head is as dependent on the body as the body is to the head.

The Apostle Paul said in Ephesians 5: 28–29: "In the same way, husbands ought to love their wives as they love their own bodies. For a man is actually loving himself when he loves his wife. No one hates his own body but lovingly cares for it ....." To take the analogy one step further, the head will not only refrain from decisions that might harm the body but will *only* make decisions that will *benefit* the body. *The husband's part in the submission equation is tremendously important—he is to be to his wife what Christ is to the church.* In marriage, the husband may have the ultimate responsibility for decision making, but he is expected to make decisions that are going to help the wife become all God intended her to be.

Women, you're not off the hook. Even though it will be easier for you to submit the more your husband fulfills his role as God has defined it, *your husband's conformity to God's ideal for a husband is not a prerequisite to your submission.* It is God who calls you to submit to your husband. Submitting to your husband shows that you understand God's plan for you and can trust God even when you are afraid to trust your husband. (Jeremiah 19:11)

Because God requires submission within the marriage relationship, the character of the person you choose to marry takes on more importance. Again, ask the tough questions now, before you marry:

> 💡 **"I Do" Do's and Don'ts**
>
> Preparing for marriage is serious business—but if all the time you spend together is too intense, that can also hurt your relationship. Make sure you make time to do together the things you enjoy. And, by all means, laugh!
>
> We cannot really love somebody with whom we never laugh.
> —Agnes Repplier

Women:

- Is this man someone you respect enough to submit to?
- Do you trust this man enough to give him control over future decisions in your life?

Men:

- Is this woman someone you love enough to put what is best for her ahead of your own wants and needs?
- Do you love this woman as much as you love yourself?

Both:

- Are you clear on what God expects of you in terms of submitting to each other?
- Do you agree on what submission will look like in your marriage?

If either of you are confused about any aspect of submission in marriage, talk together and with someone else until you are clear. Confusion over the role of submission in marriage has caused serious problems in marriage relationships. Here are some additional Scripture verses to study. (Colossians 3:18–19; 1 Peter 3:1, 5–7; Ephesians 5:1–33)

Why Can't We Just Live Together?

Many couples today consider cohabitation before marriage as a way to test their compatibility before entering into the legal and moral arrangement of marriage. The majority of all marriages in the United States today—60 to 75 percent of first marriages and 80 to 85 percent of remarriages—are now preceded by cohabitation. In the last 30 years, the rate of couples who live together outside of marriage has increased from 500,000 to 5.5 million (U.S. Bureau of Census, 2000). Although this trend is still more prevalent outside the church, many Christian couples have also adopted this cultural trend with the mistaken notion that it is an acceptable alternative as long as marriage is in their future.

Excuses Couples Use for Living Together

Every couple thinks they have good reasons for moving in together—that their situation is unique. But most couples who choose to cohabit give very similar excuses:

"Two can live cheaper than one." The financial gain from sharing living expenses is often applied to a more expensive wedding or an elaborate honeymoon or a down payment on a house. There are other ways to save money.

"You can't really know someone until you live with him or her." Although living together does reveal habits and character traits that courtship might not, that's not necessarily the best barometer of compatibility. Getting to know someone takes a lifetime, and cohabitation falls short of that goal.

"As long as we get married eventually, it's okay for us to be intimate." Nearly half of couples who live together do *not* end up married to each other. Never assume! God is serious about marriage being a prerequisite to sex.

"Living together is better than facing a messy divorce." Although this might be true, it's not a very good basis for a permanent relationship! If you are already questioning whether or not your relationship can survive, there is no evidence that living together will help. In fact, the majority of evidence is to the contrary.

The Problems of Cohabiting

Several studies indicate that cohabitation has negative results, including a higher probability of divorce, lower levels of personal happiness, increased incidence of depression for women, less likelihood of financial support, and more negative attitudes toward marriage.

Couples who live together often have a different view of their relationship and where that relationship will lead in the future. In fact, one reason couples choose to live together instead of marry is because they have differing views on what marriage is all about.

The level of commitment also varies—one person usually interprets cohabiting to mean a deeper level of commitment than the other person intends. Often cohabiting couples have a different view of what is appropriate sexual behavior. Without the commitment of marriage, one partner might feel that sex doesn't have to be exclusive to that relationship.

Family relationships can become very complicated with cohabiting couples. Holidays become times of tremendous stress, and family gatherings can be full of tension as you, your partner, and your family members try to figure out how to act, what to say, and what is appropriate.

Cohabiting is not an alternative for the Christian couple. God's view of marriage is very clear from his Word, and cohabiting is a cheap imitation of what God wants and expects for his children. God's Word calls cohabitation that includes sexual relations by another term, sexual immorality, and clearly indicates it to be a sin. If you are currently living with your future spouse, we strongly urge you to make other living arrangements until the time of your marriage. Living apart will only help you to build a solid foundation for a lifetime commitment.

"But I Already Know *Everything* About Him/Her!"

Love is like a drug that turns your brain off. It can make it hard to see the big picture. In premarital counseling, you have the benefit of a third party, someone more objective than the two of you, looking at the important aspects of your relationship and helping you to see what works and what doesn't.

Most churches, and some states, require some type of premarital counseling. Many pastors who officiate at weddings require that you and your future spouse participate in premarital counseling—either with the clergy, or a counselor, or program they recommend—before they will perform the ceremony. Premarital counseling should be viewed as more than an obligation—it is an opportunity to get to know your future spouse better and to strengthen your commitment to one another.

Why You Need to Knead

If you've ever baked bread from scratch, you know that it is hard work. You can't just mix together all the ingredients, plop it in a pan, shove it in the oven and turn out a perfectly formed and tasty loaf. You need to knead the dough, sometimes working it several times before it goes into the oven. Love is like the yeast in bread—it is a crucial ingredient, acting as a catalyst for all the other ingredients, to "grow" your dough into something good and tasty. But that's not enough! If you don't go to the work of kneading, the dough cannot achieve its full potential. Your bread will be rubbery and dense. You don't want to be dense!

Premarital counseling is like kneading. It will help you do the work of preparing your relationship for the "heat" you will face later in the course of your life together. It can be hard work, but it will be worth it.

Face the Facts

Premarital counseling works! Multiple studies over the past several years indicate that couples who participate in premarital counseling and other courses that help to enhance a couple's understanding of and further equip them for the marriage relationship have a better chance for a happy and satisfying marriage than couples who don't. In fact, the evidence compiled by The Heritage Foundation (October 25, 2002) is overwhelming:

- An analysis of 85 studies of more than 20 different marriage enrichment programs found that *couples who participated were better off than two thirds of couples who did not.*

 **"I Do" Do's and Don'ts**

We come to love not by finding a perfect person, but by learning to see an imperfect person perfectly.
—Anonymous

That is the purpose of premarital counseling—to help you understand yourself and your future mate, warts and all, so that you begin your marriage on a solid foundation. Get started as soon as possible.

- Among 71 studies that compared counseling to no counseling, *couples who took counseling were better off than 70 percent of couples that did not take counseling.*

- An analysis of 16 studies of another program, Couple Communication, showed that *the average couple who took the course out-performed 83 percent of couples who had not participated* in the critical area of marital communication.

- A 2002 study of the effectiveness of premarital inventory questionnaires and counseling in preventing marital distress demonstrated a *52 percent increase in the number of participating couples who were "most satisfied"* with their relationship and among high-risk couples, more than 80 percent moved up into a more positive category.

Still not convinced? There are dozens of other articles and studies that show beyond a doubt that you and your partner will be better prepared for marriage, be more effective communicators, find more satisfaction in your marriage relationship, and experience less conflict in your marriage if you participate in premarital counseling. So why *wouldn't* you do it?

Back to the Three C's

Successful marriages are built on compatibility, communication, and commitment. In premarital counseling you will be addressing all three of these key components for marriage. As you discover more about each other—your family history, personality traits, values, and goals—you will get a clearer picture of your compatibility. As you discuss key issues like finances, husband and wife roles, expectations, and sex you will learn about your communication styles and uncover better ways to share your needs and resolve conflict.

Commitment is about choice. You will have to choose to be vulnerable, to reveal more of yourself than you have ever revealed before, and to be accepting of each other's differences. But your love for your partner can give you strength, and knowing your partner loves you can give you the courage to make the tough choices.

What You Should Cover in Premarital Counseling

Many couples are surprised to learn just how many factors and issues will influence the success of your marriage relationship. It will take a specific commitment for both of you to seriously and objectively consider the experiences, preferences, and expectations that will impact your marriage relationship. And it is usually wise to have an objective third party help you focus and keep you on track. The closer you get to your wedding day, the more difficult it will be to find the time, or take the time. But with so much at stake, it will be worth every effort.

Factor in the Factors

When a writer sets out to write a biography of someone, he or she has to do his or her homework if he wants to be successful and accurate. He or she will spend a tremendous amount of time talking with the subject of the biography—finding out as many details as possible about his or her past, present, and future goals. If you were to write a biography about your future husband or wife, what would you have to say about him or her? Could you answer questions about your partner in all of the following areas?

- Age
- Education
- Employment/Occupation
- Income
- Religious affiliation
- Ethnic heritage
- Marital status
- Parents' marital status
- Birth position/number of children in family
- Previous relationships
- Alcohol/drug use (personal, partners, parents)
- Abuse—verbal, physical, psychological, sexual by parent(s) or partner

Each of these factors will have an influence on your relationship as a married couple. Don't assume that the influence will always be negative. On the contrary, many of these factors can have a positive impact on your relationship. For example, previous relationships—good and bad—are often God's laboratory for teaching us important lessons that equip us to be better marriage partners.

A good biographer will not depend on the subject's recollections and interpretations alone but will seek out and interview friends, relatives, old school chums, even enemies, in order to get the most complete picture of the person he or she wants to know. That's good advice for couples, too. If you want to really get to know your future mate, talk with the people who know him or her best. Observing your partner in a variety of situations—family gatherings, church functions, work-related situations, and at leisure—will give you the most informed view of this person with whom you plan on spending the rest of your life.

Your values determine your priorities—how you spend your time, your money, and your energy. Your values grow from your family backgrounds, your ethnic heritage, and your religious beliefs. What's important to you? What's important to your future spouse? The more you know and understand about these areas, the better equipped you will be to prevent or resolve conflicts within your relationship.

Family Ties

Comparing your birth position within your families—first, middle, youngest, and only—and the number of siblings you lived with will help you better understand each other, how you relate to one another, and your attitudes toward family matters. The size of your family matters, too. A person who has grown up in the middle of a large family has had experience with children and sharing, but an only child might naturally be lacking in some of those skills.

Bet You Didn't Know

It matters how old you are! According to the National Marriage Project report *The State of Our Unions* (2002), "age at marriage is one of the strongest and most consistent predictors of marital stability ever found by social science research." People who marry as teens are much more likely to divorce; couples who wait until their mid-20s to wed have a higher probability of success.

It is especially important to be honest about the use of alcohol and/or drugs—both your personal use, past and present, and any use in your immediate family. The same is true about abuse. If either or both of you have experienced abuse—verbal, physical, psychological, sexual—in your family, by your partner, or by any one else, you need to be sure the issues have been resolved so you do not bring harmful emotional baggage into your marriage relationship.

It's also important to review your relational histories. What do you know about your partner's past relationships? Has he or she been engaged before? What makes this relationship different? Are there similarities, positive or negative, with this relationship and other relationships you have had in the past? Review your history together. How long have you known each other? Have you broken up or separated from each other? If you have had difficulties in the past, have those issues been resolved?

Goals and motivation are also important to a healthy and growing relationship. Compare your educational backgrounds and goals. Are you on the same intellectual level and able to stimulate each other's thinking? Are you satisfied with your vocation and your ability to earn a respectable income? Are your careers complimentary or competitive? Chat about your social values and political philosophies.

There are also many other preferences that you will discover as your relationship progresses. You will need to seek agreement on how do decorate your home, the furniture style and colors, the geographical area where you would like to live, and the size and style of your home. You will need to agree on where you will attend church and how you will serve. Talk about the holiday traditions that you want to bring from home and new ones you will begin together in your family. Discuss your vacation preferences, activities, and locations. The more you are aware of each other's preferences, the better you will understand, compliment, and encourage each other.

That's the Spirit

Without wavering, let us hold tightly to the hope we say we have, for God can be trusted to keep his promise. Think of ways to encourage one another to outbursts of love and good deeds. (Hebrews 10:23–24)

I love you not only for what you are, but for what I am when I am with you. I love you not only for what you have made of yourself, but for what you are making of me. I love you for the part of me that you bring out … I love you because you are helping me to make of the lumber of my life not a tavern but a Temple, and of the words of my every day not a reproach but a song.
—Anonymous

Get Personal

Have you ever noticed how different people bring out different aspects of your own personality? Marriage is about two personalities coming together for the mutual benefit of both. Making a marriage work smoothly depends on being aware of who you are, who your partner is, identifying and accepting your strengths and weaknesses, and being confident in your ability to express thoughts and needs.

Are you an extrovert or an introvert? Are you assertive, self-confident? Are you independent? Do you prefer to spend your free time alone or are you a party animal? Can you easily show emotion and affection or are you more reserved? Can you answer all these questions about your partner? How do your various personalities compliment each other and in what ways have your individual personalities created conflict in your relationship?

We hope you genuinely like the person you are going to marry, but you also need to be realistic. You both come to the relationship with all your beauty and warts. If you are secure in who you are, secure in your relationship with God, you will be an encouraging partner in a fulfilling marriage.

Get in Touch with Your Roots

It is often said that you don't just marry the person but you marry the person's family! Get to know each other in the family context if possible. Watch how mother and father relate to each other and the children. You will want to observe how they talk with each other, how they make decisions, and the level of respect they show each other. Is there a balance between their togetherness and their separateness? Is it acceptable for the siblings to be different, to express their thoughts and feelings? Is there a positive emotional climate in the home? Do they really enjoy being together? Your partner has spent many years in the family environment and will have many of the same traits as expressed in the family.

Observe the leadership roles. A healthy family will have clear rules and boundaries, flexible leadership from the parents, and strong but reasonable discipline. Everyone knows the rules and the consequence for breaking them, but they also know the rules are fair and sensible, and that exceptions can be made when the situation warrants. A rigid, inflexible home, or by contrast one that is chaotic with no rules nor boundaries, will have a strong influence on the way you will behave in your marriage relationship. Talk about your families and how they have influenced your attitudes and expectations about how to manage your own home.

Stop Playing Games

Just as you have inherited certain characteristics, expectations, and patterns from your parents that affect your relationship, we have also inherited certain traits from the first couple—Adam and Eve—that influence our behavior toward one another. Take a look at some early interactions between the first man and woman and their offspring and see if you and your future mate are playing some of the same games.

The Blame Game (Genesis 3:8–13)

Here's what happened: There was only one tree in the Garden that was forbidden to Adam and Eve by God. Satan, in the form of a snake, took God's instructions, twisted the meaning and convinced Eve to disobey and eat fruit from the tree. Adam was there, too! Eve gave him some fruit and he ate it. After disobeying God's direct command, they experienced shame and guilt for the first time. God confronted Adam and asked him point blank "Did you do it?" and round one of the blame game began.

Adam blamed Eve. " … it was the woman you gave me who brought me the fruit, and I ate it." (Genesis 3:12)

Eve blamed the snake. "The serpent tricked me … that's why I ate it." (Genesis 3:13)

And husbands and wives have been blaming each other or someone else for their problems ever since!

Why we play the blame game:

- It's easy to play. Blaming someone else is so much easier than taking responsibility for your own behavior. In fact, this is one of those games that is easier to play than *not* to play.
- Everyone plays it. Home is not the only playing field for the blame game. You can catch it being played at work, school, and church. Anywhere where individuals face accountability, the blame game is bound to spring up.
- It's better than the alternative. It's hard to own up to your own shortcomings. The main reason people play the blame game is because they are afraid to face the facts about their own behavior.

Playing the blame game keeps us from taking a realistic look at our selves and our relationships. Whether you play this game or not, you will still face the consequences of your actions. God still held Adam and Eve accountable for their individual disobedience. But think of the grief their finger pointing caused. How do you think Eve felt about Adam blaming her? What opportunity for growth and healing did Eve miss by blaming the snake?

No one wins in the blame game. If you and your future spouse have been playing the blame game, it's time to quit. Each of you must have the spiritual, emotional, and relational maturity to take responsibility for your own actions—especially when those actions are harmful to your relationship as a couple.

The Control Game (Genesis 12:10–20)

Abram (Abraham) gives us the rules for this game. Shortly after God tells Abram that God is going to make him famous and bless the socks off him and his many descendents, Abram arrives in Egypt in the middle of a famine. His wife Sarai (Sarah) is so drop-dead gorgeous that Abram is afraid—*not for her* but for himself! So he tells Sarai to "… say you are my sister, then the Egyptians will treat me well because of their interest in you, and they will spare my life." (Genesis 12:13)

Sarai does what her husband tells her to do (I wonder, though, how she *felt* about it). As a result, Sarai is taken away and becomes a prisoner in the harem of the Pharaoh. And get this—Abram is rewarded by the Pharaoh with great riches. Round one of the control game. We all play this game from time to time in our relationships. In fact, Sarai gets into the game as a major player later in their marriage.

Why we play the control game:

- It makes us feel powerful. Most people who try to control their relationships act out of weakness rather than strength. Their self-doubt needs to be bolstered by the feeling they get by controlling someone else.

- It helps us get what we want when we want it. The best players in this game are completely self-absorbed, putting their needs above the needs of others.

- We think it's the best game in town. The main reason we play the control game is fear. We don't believe we can trust God or anyone else to provide for us. It's easier to control that to trust.

This game is also known as the "You're Not the Boss of Me" or "I'm the One Who Matters Most" game. We play the control game because we are afraid that our needs will not be met. We don't trust our partner to care enough about us to pursue our best interests, so we must control not only our own behavior but our partner's as well.

"I Do" Do's and Don'ts

Warning! Everyone plays the control game from time to time. But it can become addictive! People who play this game often become dictators—sometimes benevolent, mostly tyrannical. The meeting of their own needs takes priority and they act without considering what their actions will do to the other person. This is a difficult pattern to break, so it's best not to start it.

In a healthy relationship, neither partner feels controlled by the other. If your love is genuine, it cannot be selfish or self-serving. Who controls your relationship? Do you trust each other enough to let go and stop playing the control game? Here's the really good news! There's a happy ending to our story about Abram and Sarai. Even though Abram betrayed Sarai's trust, God didn't! He went to extraordinary measures to protect Sarai and return her unharmed to her family. When you stop trying to control your partner, God will be your safety net.

Show Me the Money

Money matters! Financial management is one of the top issues that couples need to discuss prior to marriage. Even happy couples disagree more about money than any other issue. Now that you are engaged, discussing finances will become increasingly important. As you plan for your wedding, honeymoon, and first home together, finances will play a key role. Use these opportunities to develop together a financial strategy to carry you into your first year of marriage.

You can start by listing all income, expenses, and debts. Be as accurate and detailed as possible so you have a good picture of where you currently stand financially. Next, talk about your financial goals. Do you want to be debt free by your wedding day? Do you want to buy a home within three years of marriage? Choose some short term (one to three years) financial goals that you can agree to. Be realistic based on what you know, not what you hope will happen.

Keep in mind the stage of life you are in or entering and how that affects your finances. Are you in school with tuition to pay and limited employment opportunities? Will you graduate with major debts to repay? Are you already depending too heavily on credit cards? Can you afford the wedding you both desire on your current timetable and with your current finances? We'll talk more about costs and budgets for your big day in Chapter 8.

Prayerfully set some financial priorities. Ask yourselves often "Is this something we *want* or something we *need*?" Meeting both your needs must come first. Then discuss your list of wants and agree together what you can afford to pursue now and what will need to be postponed. Using the Married Budget Worksheet that follows, create a written budget. Having your budget in writing is important for accountability—you can both refer to it when faced with financial decisions.

According to marriage counseling experts, money is a hot issue in marriage. Yet few engaged couples thoroughly discuss their financial expectations in order to clear these stumbling blocks to a more satisfying relationship.

Here is a list of the top five financial stumbling blocks for couples:

1. **Spending Habits**—Are we happy with each other's spending habits?
2. **Saving**—Do we agree on how much we should be saving?
3. **Priorities**—How should we spend our money?
4. **Debt**—Are we in major debt? How much of our debt is in credit cards?
5. **Control**—Do we agree on who should control our money?

Annual Budget Worksheet

Income:

Male   _____

Female   _____

Other   _____

Total Annual Income: _____

(Divide by 12 for average monthly income):   _____

Expenses:

Housing

Rent   _____

Utilities   _____

Phone   _____

Internet   _____

Other   _____

Transportation

     Gasoline/Oil   _____

     Repairs/Tires   _____

     Public Transportation   _____

     Auto License   _____

     Other   _____

Food

     Groceries—At Home   _____

     Restaurant—Eat Out   _____

Insurance

     Health Care   _____

     Automobile   _____

     House   _____

Medical

     Doctor   _____

     Medicines   _____

     Hospital   _____

Clothing

    Personal Hygiene   _____

        (toothpaste/deodorant/shaving cream/etc.)   _____

Household Expenses

    Supplies (Detergent/etc.)   _____

    Equipment (TV/computer/furniture/etc.)   _____

Additional Services (Dry cleaning/laundry/etc.)   _____

Recreation (Vacations/hobbies/etc.)   _____

Gifts (Birthday/wedding/Christmas/etc.)   _____

Tithe _____

Other Expenses   _____

Total Annual Expenses _____

    (Divide by 12 for average monthly expenses)   _____

Annual Surplus or Deficit _____

    (Divide by 12 for average monthly surplus/deficit)   _____

Your discussions on money are bound to raise some issues between you and your partner. But it might not always be clear what the root of the problem really is. You can use the following discussion points to uncover patterns and attitudes toward money that might be the cause of conflict in your relationship now and in the future. Answer the questions individually first, then compare your answers with your future spouse.

- The primary person responsible for providing an adequate income:
  You / Your Partner / Both / Neither
- Balancing the checkbook and paying the bills should be done by:
  You / Your Partner / Both / Neither
- Is the most concerned about spending money wisely:
  You / Your Partner / Both / Neither
- Is the most capable manager of finances:
  You / Your Partner / Both / Neither
- Never seems to have enough money:
  You / Your Partner / Both / Neither
- Is most bothered about current and/or future debt:
  You / Your Partner / Both / Neither
- Has well-defined financial goals:
  You / Your Partner / Both / Neither
- Is least concerned about saving for the future:
  You / Your Partner / Both / Neither
- Most often feels anxious or angry about our financial situation:
  You / Your Partner / Both / Neither
- Has the best grasp of our current financial situation:
  You / Your Partner / Both / Neither

Remember when you marry, any debt or financial obligations you have accumulated as individuals become equally yours as a couple. Take the time to confront and deal with any spending habits or behaviors regarding money that will create conflict in the future. This is an important part of your premarital counseling.

What You Can Expect

Many couples resist premarital counseling simply because they have preconceived ideas of "counseling" and are fearful of the process. These sessions or classes can actually be very enjoyable. Sometimes the going gets tough, we won't deny that, but when you consider that you are embarking on the journey of a lifetime, it should be worth any investment of time and energy to make that journey more fulfilling.

Tools in the Toolbox

Your premarital preparation program might be done one-on-one with a clergyman or counselor or in a small group with other soon-to-be-married couples. In either setting, the person leading the program might use several tools to help you and your future spouse work through the important issues.

There are a variety of surveys and worksheets that might be used (we have included several in this book). Surveys and worksheets are great tools for getting you to think about and express things you might not otherwise be able to articulate. They can help direct conversation between you and your partner so that you get to the heart of what you think and believe. Worksheets are also practical tools to help you put into writing your plans (like a budget) and goals (like the communication covenant). It is good to keep these surveys and worksheets, along with any other notes or handouts from your sessions, in a notebook so that you can refer to them from time to time and see if your relationship is still on track.

Some counselors and clergy also use some specific tests to help couples understand each other and the dynamics of their relationship. The Taylor-Johnson Temperament Analysis (TJTA) looks at nine traits that represent attitudes and feelings that play a significant role in personal adjustment and interpersonal relationships.

Nervous vs. Composed

Depressive vs. Lighthearted

Active-Social vs. Quiet

Expressive-Responsive vs. Inhibited

Sympathetic vs. Indifferent

Subjective vs. Objective

Dominant vs. Submissive

Hostile vs. Tolerant

Self-disciplined vs. Impulsive

Another test, the Myers-Briggs Type Indicator, is used in many corporations as well as in marriage counseling to help people understand their personality type and how different personality types relate to one another. A series of questions show your dominant character traits such as:

Extrovert or Introvert

Sensing or Intuitive

Thinking or Feeling

Judging or Perceiving

Although many of these tests have made their way onto the Internet, it is best to have a counseling professional help you interpret the results of these tests and others.

Even if your marriage preparation course is conducted with a group, it is essential that you and your partner make time for just the two of you to discuss what is being covered in the sessions.

Finding Premarital Counseling

First check with the church where you plan to marry. As we mentioned earlier, many churches now require premarital counseling if you are planning on using any of their facilities for your wedding. Often these churches have someone on staff who does their counseling or they will recommend you to a counselor who can help you.

Some couples are planning to be married by a clergyman but not in a church. If that is your situation, check with the clergyman to see if he or she can still offer you premarital counseling. Another option is to check with churches in your area to see if they offer premarital counseling or a marriage preparation course for couples in their community.

One of the best marriage preparation programs we know of is the PREPARE/ENRICH Program. This program is offered by over 45,000 counselors and clergy around the United States. There are also international offices in over 10 other countries. The six goals of the program are achieved by having a couple complete six exercises designed to achieve the following:

- To identify a couple's relationship strengths and areas needing growth.
- To teach communication skills, including assertiveness and active listening.
- To teach conflict resolution skills using a 10 Step Method.
- To focus on family of origin and how it can impact a couple.

- To deal with financial goals and develop a budget.
- To develop personal, couple, and family goals.

To learn more about the PREPARE/ENRICH Program, take a Couple Quiz, or locate a professional that offers the program, visit their website at www. lifeinnovations.com.

If you are still unable to find a counselor or pastor to do premarital counseling, ask a trusted married couple—a couples whose godly marriage is an inspiration to you—and ask them to hold you accountable to the work we have outlined for you in this book. Ask them to pray with you and for you, to listen as an objective third party when you and your partner have issues you cannot resolve, and to recommend additional reading or exercises to strengthen your relationship.

That's the Spirit

Get all the advice and instruction you can, and be wise the rest of your life. (Proverbs 19:20)

Of all the decisions you will make in your lifetime, the choice of your life mate is one of the most crucial. Do not neglect the opportunity that premarital counseling offers to get advice and instruction on how to build a solid biblical foundation for your future relationship.

Married Before?

If you or your partner have been married before, you might be tempted to take a "been there, done that" attitude about premarital counseling, and decide you can afford to skip it. Nothing could be further from the truth for two reasons: (1) You've never been married to *this* person before; (2) previously married people bring additional baggage to any relationship.

As we've said before, when you marry someone, you also marry his or her family. When you marry someone who has been married before, you are also engaging in a relationship with his or her former spouse, former in-laws, and children. Even if your partner no longer has any connection to the former spouse, you will still be dealing with any past relationship on a variety of levels:

- **Sexual**—Every previous sexual encounter you or your partner have had go with you into your marital bed. This is true physically and emotionally. It will be very important for you and your future spouse to discuss openly the material in Chapter 6.

- **Emotional**—Regardless of why the marriage ended, no one comes out of a divorce without emotional scars. Has he or she acknowledged the pain of the past? Has your partner had time to heal?

- **Financial**—Your partner might still have financial obligations to either his or her former spouse or their children. Do you understand these obligations, and can you be supportive of your partner's responsibility to meet these obligations even if it means achieving your own financial goals might take longer?

- **Spiritual**—*Every* failed marriage happens because one or both partners are deficient in some spiritual discipline. Whether or not your partner wanted a divorce, has he or she acknowledged the part he or she played in the failure of the marriage? Has he or she grown enough spiritually so that the problems won't be repeated in your marriage?

Although 50 percent of all first marriages end in divorce, the statistic is 60 percent when one or both of the partners have been married before. One of the primary reasons these relationships fail is that these couples did not take the time nor make the effort to get to know each other sufficiently and to work out any difficulties in their relationship before they married.

If your partner has children, your relationship is even more complicated. Are you prepared to take on instant parenthood? It is important that you address many of the issues regarding parenting even though the children might not be living with you. More second marriages break up over parenting issues than for any other reason. Blending families successfully is difficult but not impossible. Just be sure you take the time to understand the issues and work out a plan together.

Yes, there are risks and challenges in marrying someone who has been married before. You need to go into such a union with your eyes wide open. You need to take extra time and care to work through any issues. And you need to be fully convinced that God has brought you together. Only then can you have a wonderful, successful, and satisfying marriage relationship. We believe that God can and will bless these marriages when both partners are fully committed to him and each other.

"I'll Never Understand Him/Her!"

Do you ever feel like the couple who sits facing each other across a table, each one saying to the other "I know you believe you understand what you think I said, but I'm not sure you realize that what you heard is not what I meant." Communication is a complex process—more than just talking and listening.

We all long to be understood, and there is nothing more frustrating or hurtful than to feel you have been misunderstood. Yet it happens—even between two people who love each other and are committed to each other. Misunderstandings are often the result of our differences—differences in our gender, our family backgrounds, our cultures, our education, and our training. Couples who learn and practice good communication skills are much more likely to have a happy marriage.

He Said, She Said

One of the most exasperating hurdles to good communication in marriages is the simple fact that men and women are different. We are wired in totally different ways and the more you are able to understand and accept your differences because of your genders, the better off you will be. Your differences aren't the problem! In fact, they are what make the miracle of oneness so awesome! But it will take a conscious effort on both of your parts to embrace your differences and make them work for you instead of against you.

Viva La Difference!

Besides the obvious anatomical differences (for which we are all thankful!), men and women differ in many ways—physically, emotionally, and relationally. In some cases the differences are obvious and measurable, but in many cases we can only give certain generalizations from observing many men and women over a period of time. Because you love each other, you will want to learn as much about your partner as possible, including how the sexes differ.

There are many physical differences in a man and a woman of which you might not be aware. Of course, every man and woman is unique, but modern medicine can tell us these things:

- A man usually will have a higher metabolism than a woman.
- A woman's thyroid is larger and more active than a man's.
- A man's brain weighs 11–12 percent more than a woman's brain.
- A woman might have larger kidneys, liver, stomach, and appendix than a man, but a man has larger lungs.
- A woman's blood cells contain more water and less oxygen than a man's.
- A man's body weight is 40 percent muscle while a woman's body weight is 23 percent muscle.
- A man's heart beats an average of 72 beats per minute and a woman's heart beats an average of 80 beats per minute.

When it comes to the emotional and social make-up of men and women, more inferences can be made. Many of these differences are shaped by our culture as well as by the way God made us:

- Men are more interested in *problem-solving;* women are more interested in *empathy.*
- Women tend to be more *in touch* with their emotions than men.

- Men tend to gain their identity through *achievement;* women tend to find their identity in close *relationships.*

- Men tend to focus on their *independence;* women tend to focus on *intimacy.*

- Men tend to be more *physically violent;* women tend to express their hostility *verbally.*

- Men are more *logical and abstract;* women tend to be more *intuitive.*

- Men are more *competitive;* women tend to be more *cooperative.*

In studying the communication patterns of men and women, researchers have discovered that not only do men and women talk about different things, there is also a difference in *how* they talk:

- Men use fewer disclaimers like "This probably isn't important, but ..." or "Don't get angry, but ...".
  Women use more qualifiers like "I guess," "I think," and "I suppose."

- Men tell more jokes.
  Women laugh more.

- Men use more aggressive language.
  Women are more likely to use polite words like "please" and "thank you."

- Men interrupt more.
  Women ask more questions.

- Men delay responses in order to shorten interactions.
  Women answer with quick responses to keep interaction going.

The Difference Our Differences Make

Do you know the number one complaint women have about men? "He never listens to me." What is the most frequent complaint that men have about women? "She's always trying to change me." Our differences are important because of the way they affect our interactions with each other.

Many conflicts in marriage arise because of basic differences between the sexes. A woman feels rejected when her man is preoccupied with his work or money. A man might interpret an offer of help not as the sign of support and encouragement the woman intended but as an indication that she sees him as weak or ineffective.

When a woman shares her problems, what she wants and needs is for her man to listen. But if he doesn't know that, guess what? He's going to offer solutions in an attempt to solve her problem, because that's what men do!

Women are motivated when they feel cherished and special. Men are motivated when they feel needed. Men need to receive trust, approval, and respect. Women need romance and place more emphasis on "atmosphere" because they are more sensitive to sounds and smells than men are. Men fear failure; women fear loss of intimacy.

Remember, differences are just different—not better or worse. God created both male and female *before* he said that all he had created was very good. It is essential in marriage that both the husband and the wife learn to remember, accept, and respect these differences when trying to communicate with each other.

That's the Spirit

Like water from a well, your communication with your partner springs from a place deep within you—your heart. A bitter heart will bring forth bitter words; a loving heart will bring forth loving words.

… all of you should be of one mind, full of sympathy toward each other, loving one another with tender hearts and humble minds. Don't repay evil for evil. Don't retaliate when people say unkind things about you. Instead, pay them back with a blessing. That is what God wants you to do, and he will bless you for it. (1 Peter 3:8–9)

What Is Good Communication?

The quality of the communication between you and your future spouse will make or break your relationship. We learn how to communicate primarily from our parents. But communication skills can be learned and unlearned as long as we are willing to make the effort to improve what we say, how we say it, and how well we listen because, in the end, the goal of communication is understanding.

There are several levels of communication. Some levels—clichés, meaningless phrases, reporting of facts not involving yourself—require little personal risk but also yield the lowest personal return. When you begin to express personal ideas, beliefs, and judgments or share emotions or feelings, you are risking more. In marriage, it is important that you move toward complete emotional truth and personal revelation. The risk is great but the reward is well worth it!

What's Your Couple C.Q.?

Marriage is an intimate relationship built on mutual understanding, but in order to truly understand another person you must be able to communicate with him. A husband and wife can know a great deal about each other without really knowing one another. Communication is the process that allows people to know each other, to relate to one another, to understand the true meaning of the other person's life.

Use the following responses to test your Communication Quotient (C.Q.):

1 = Usually
2 = Sometimes
3 = Seldom
4 = Never

[ ] Is your partner's voice irritating?

[ ] Does your partner have a tendency to say things that would be better left unsaid?

[ ] Do you find it necessary to keep after your partner about his or her faults?

[ ] Does your partner seem to understand your feelings?

[ ] Does your partner listen to what you have to say?

[ ] Does your partner pay you compliments and say nice things to you?

[ ] Is your partner affectionate toward you?

[ ] Does your partner let you finish talking before responding to what you say?

[ ] Do you and your partner remain silent for long when you are angry with one another?

[ ] Does your partner try to lift your spirits when you are depressed or discouraged?

[ ] Do you fail to express disagreement with your partner because you are afraid he or she will get angry?

[ ] Does your partner ever complain that you don't understand them?

[ ] Do you feel your partner says one thing but really means another?

[ ] Do you and your partner find it hard to disagree with one another without losing your temper?

[ ] Do you find it hard to express your true feelings to your partner?

[ ] Do you and your partner talk about things that are of interest to the both of you?

[ ] Do you discuss intimate matters?

[ ] Do you discuss spiritual things?

[ ] Is it easier to confide in a friend rather than your partner?

[ ] Does your partner let you know how important you are to him or her?

Compare your score with your partner's score and discuss any areas where you seem to disagree.

Smart couples pay attention to their C.Q. They avoid sentences laced with the deadly phrases "You always …" and "You never …" and don't assume but make sure they understand what their partners are saying. Smart couples don't take good communication for granted but are committed to improving their C.Q. even if they are currently satisfied with their level of communication. Because smart couples know that the only way to survive the changes that will happen in the course of their life together is to keep the channels of communication open and healthy.

What You Say and How You Say It

Words are very powerful! They can be constructive or destructive. They can produce positive or negative emotions. They can engender peace or anger. Control of the tongue is key to effective communication in marriage. How you speak to each other is an evidence of the intentions of your heart. But there is also a right way and a wrong way to talk to one another:

- **Be assertive**—It is important that you feel confident enough in yourself and your relationship to be able to express your feelings and ask for what you need or want from your future spouse.

   Right Way: "I've had a long, hard day at work. I really don't feel like cooking. Let's order out!"

   Wrong Way: "We don't have anything to eat around here. I'm not hungry anyway!"

- **Use "I" statements**—"I" statements are responsible and communicate specific information and your feeling without focusing blame. "You" statements elicit defensive reactions because they communicate blame or accusation.

Right Way: "I feel embarrassed when you make jokes at my expense."

Wrong Way: "You don't care about me; everything about me is a joke to you!"

- **Practice active listening**—Listen attentively and accurately say back to the speaker what he or she said to you, including the feeling component.

  Right Way: "What I heard you say is that you felt left out when I did not introduce you to my friends. Is that correct?"

  Wrong Way: "I'm sorry. I didn't do it intentionally."

Ignoring communication issues between you and your future spouse is dangerous. Communication does not "naturally" get better after you are married. In fact, just the opposite is true. You cannot have a successful and fulfilling relationship until you learn to communication with each other and effectively resolve conflict. And the time to do that is *before* you marry.

Effective (Not Selective) Listening

Listening intently with one's mouth shut is a basic communication skill needed in marriage. Listening effectively means that when someone is talking, you are not thinking about what you are going to say when the other person stops. You must be totally tuned in to what the other person is saying. We often practice selective listening—we choose to hear only what we want to hear. Effective listening is receiving and accepting the message as it is sent. Listening is seeking to understand what the other person really means.

Think you're a good listener? Use the following evaluation of your listening skills to find out. First, complete the survey for yourself. Think about how often you do the following and write in the number that you think matches that frequency. Then, ask your partner to evaluate how well he or she feels you listen.

On a scale from 1 to 5, give yourself a score as follows:

1 = Never
2 = Rarely
3 = Sometimes
4 = Often
5 = Very often

Scores	Behavior
___ ___	I listen to my partner without interrupting.
___ ___	I show my partner that I empathize with him or her.
___ ___	I maintain good eye contact during our conversations.
___ ___	I get angry when my partner doesn't agree with me.
___ ___	I ask questions to ensure I understand what my partner needs.
___ ___	I resist forming my response while my partner is talking.
___ ___	I wish my partner would get to the point more quickly.
___ ___	I respond to my partner with phrases like, "You're wrong."
___ ___	I give my partner my full attention when he or she is talking.
___ ___	I respect my partner's ideas as much as my own.

Add up and compare your scores.

Listening is a skill that requires self-control. To be a good listener you have to set aside your own agenda and focus on the wants and needs of your partner. Most marital misunderstandings can be cleared up if both partners practice active listening. If you really love each other and care about your relationship, you will learn to listen effectively.

Body Talk

Communication happens even when no one is saying anything! In fact, some communication researchers estimate that more than 60 percent of all communication happens in nonverbal ways. Your words might be saying one thing while your body talk is shouting a different message. The study of nonverbal communication includes …

- Touch, physical contact (kinesics)
- Space, conversational distance (proximics)
- Time, punctuality (chronemics)
- Tone, pitch, rhythm, inflection (vocalics)
- Clothing, jewelry, cosmetics, symbols
- Significance of colors (chromatics)
- Eye behavior, staring, winking (oculemics)

- Smell, odors (olfactics)
- Taste, food preferences
- Sounds, noise, music (acoustics)
- Silence

What is your body saying to your partner? When you lean forward, make a lot of eye contact and smile, you are saying "I'm interested and listening." However, when you lean forward while staring and tapping your foot, you are saying "Shut up! It's my turn to talk." Start paying attention to your nonverbal communication. Notice also what your partner is saying without words. Unexplained tension in your relationship might be the result of your words and your nonverbal messages not matching up.

Bet You Didn't Know

Changing the distance between two people can convey a desire for intimacy, declare a lack of interest, or an increase or decrease in domination. Studies in proximics (spatial territory in communication) have identified four space categories: the intimate distance for embracing or whispering (6–18 inches), the personal distance for conversation among good friends (1.5–4 feet), social distance for conversations among acquaintances (4–12 feet), and public distance used for public speaking (12 feet or more).

Resolving Conflicts

Many couples think that a happy marriage is one without conflict. Wrong! Because marriage is a union of two imperfect individuals who have unique viewpoints, backgrounds, and values, conflict will occur from time to time. The happily married couple learns how to deal with conflict in creative, constructive ways.

How important is it to deal with conflict appropriately? Take a clue from what happens to your body when there is unresolved conflict in your life. Every major system in your body responds negatively to conflict. Your adrenal gland pumps adrenaline and noradrenaline into your bloodstream. Your heart rate and blood pressure increases. Muscles tense and shake throughout your body.

Your body undergoes respiratory changes—deeper breathing, holding your breath, more rapid respiration and bronchial dilation. Perspiration appears on your skin and the tissue actually generates a slight voltage, electrical resistance. The pupils of your eyes can contract or dilate and your eyelids flutter in a distinctive pattern. Your liver releases sugar, your spleen produces blood cells, your digestive movements cease, and your stomach produces more acid.

Although all these changes are happening in your body, unresolved conflict can have equally devastating affects on your relationship. You cannot avoid conflict. Every couple has differences and disagreements. Healthy couples find ways to resolve marital disputes without turning them in to major marital wars. Satisfying and successful resolutions can be reached if you can accept and appreciate the fact that your mate has independent opinions. Resolving issues will require a commitment to develop positive communication skills.

Your Personal Style

How do you handle conflict? The way you have learned to communicate and confront differences will influence how you approach and resolve conflict. Your family of origin has a definite impact on your personal communication style. Over the course of life, you and your partner have each developed your own way of handling differences, difficult issues, and conflicts.

Check out the five basic responses to conflict and discuss what responses are typical in your family and your own personal conflict resolution style:

- **Avoidance**—I will physically and/or emotionally withdrawal to avoid conflict.
- **Win**—I must win no matter what the cost.
- **Yield**—I will give in rather than risk confrontation.
- **Compromise**—I will give up what I want in a trade off for your demands.
- **Resolve**—I will engage in open, direct communication until our differences are reconciled.

When conflict comes, it should be faced with the understanding that disagreements do not mean that the entire relationship is on the verge of breaking down. Husbands and wives need to know how to "disagree agreeably" and to "fight fair" so that disagreements don't turn into heated arguments, quarrels, or violent fights.

If you or your partner are using any of the following unfair fighting tactics, you need to learn how to fight fair, for example:

- Thou shalt not pretend your partner has made an unreasonable demand.
- Thou shalt not assume you know what your partner is thinking or feeling.
- Thou shalt not switch the subject in the middle of a disagreement.
- Thou shalt not dredge up the past as a defense of your position.
- Thou shalt not interrupt.
- Thou shalt not deny your partner's feelings.
- Thou shalt not use sarcasm and ridicule to gain an advantage.
- Thou shalt not be overly sensitive.
- Thou shalt not blame your partner for something beyond his or her control.
- Thou shalt not avoid or refuse to deal with the issue.

Fighting fair is not only about the "shalt nots" but also the "I wills," for example …

- I will be aware of how words and actions affect my partner.
- I will take responsibility for my actions.
- I will do my part in make the conflict constructive.
- I will affirm my partner, myself, and the importance of the issue at stake.
- I will make a contribution to the discussion.
- I will be realistic and accept my partner and the issue for what they are, not for what I think they should be.
- I will focus only on the issue at hand.
- I will express compassion for my partner and his or her feelings.
- I will be discreet and respectful in sharing our conflict with others.
- I will be ready to forgive and to renew closeness.

There is a best way to resolve conflict. First, learn to express your needs in a non-threatening way and really listen to each other. Then define the real issue and set up a specific time and place to talk about that issue. Be ready to own up to the part you each play in the problem. Brainstorm together possible ways to resolve your problem and agree on one solution to try. Finally, set a time to check in with each other to see how things are going.

Family Ties

In the beginning, you and your future spouse will probably disagree often over family matters. When you do, keep your families out of it! This might be difficult at times, especially if you are close to your parents, but it is important that you and your partner discuss family issues in private, come to an mutually satisfying agreement, and present a united front to your families.

Choose to Forgive

We all need to experience the act of love called "forgiveness". Whether you need to forgive another who has offended or hurt you or to receive forgiveness from others, forgiveness is essential to your health and happiness. In marriage you will be called upon to participate in both aspects of forgiveness, with no exceptions. The willingness to ask for forgiveness as well as choose to forgive another is critical for a marriage relationship to heal, grow, and thrive. It is basic to conflict resolution, so let's be clear on what forgiveness is and is not.

- Forgiveness is not forgetting. People who try to forget find they cannot. Forgetting might be the result of forgiveness, but it is never the means of forgiveness. When we bring up the past against others, we are saying we have not forgiven them.

- Forgiveness is a choice, a crisis of the will. Forgiveness is difficult for us because it goes against our concept of justice. We want revenge for offenses suffered. Because God requires us to forgive, it is something we can do!

- Forgiveness is agreeing to live with the consequences of another person's sin. Forgiveness is costly. You are going to live with those consequences whether you want to or not; your only choice is whether you will do so in the bitterness of unforgiveness or the freedom of forgiveness.

- Forgiveness is the decision that you will bear the burden of their offenses by not using that information against them. This does not mean you tolerate sin but you decide not to seek revenge from a bitter heart.

- Forgiveness from your heart is acknowledging the hurt and the hate. Forgiveness must come from the emotional core of your life. Let God help you deal with the pain.

- Forgiveness can't wait until you feel like forgiving; you will never get there. Feelings take time to heal after the choice to forgive is made and Satan has lost his place. You will gain freedom, not a feeling.

Here is a prayer of forgiveness to try:

Lord, I forgive (<u>name of person</u>) for (name every hurt and pain the Lord brings to your mind and how it made you feel).

Lord, I release (<u>name of person</u>) to you, and I release my right to seek revenge. I choose not to hold on to my bitterness and anger, and I ask you to heal my damaged emotions. In Jesus' name, I pray. Amen.

What About Anger?

Everyone gets angry. Sometimes we get angry for true and noble reasons—injustice, poverty, hunger, and evil. Even God gets angry over such things. But more often we get angry because we are frustrated—things aren't going the way *we* want them to go. Anger is hard to contain, so don't try living with it! Anger must be dealt with quickly and appropriately or it will lead to bitterness, resentment, and abuse.

That's the Spirit

My dear brothers and sisters, be quick to listen, slow to speak, and slow to get angry. Your anger can never make things right in God's sight. (James 1:19–20)

Don't sin by letting anger gain control over you. Think about it over night and remain silent. (Psalm 4:4)

Anger is not a sin, but it can lead to sin. Jesus himself was angry but never sinned in his anger. That is why God advises us to slow down and be quiet when we feel anger overcoming us. In anger you can crush the heart of your husband or wife by saying something you would not otherwise say.

Christian marriage counselor and author H. Norman Wright tells us that people tend to handle their anger in one of four ways:

1. **Suppress it!** Suppressed anger is like a low fire under a pressure cooker. It is okay to keep your anger under control for a short period of time while you think about what you are going to say or do to express your anger appropriately. But it is essential that you not suppress your anger for too long. If you do, the pressure can build until you blow!

2. **Express it!** It is okay to express anger if it is done appropriately. That usually means waiting until the passion of the moment has passed. Give yourself a

time out—go for a jog, take a shower, or scrub the kitchen floor. Physical activity can help release any pent-up pressure. Then, after you have had some time to carefully consider what you will say, tell your partner about it.

3. **Repress it!** There's a difference between suppressing and repressing. Suppression says "I'm angry but I'm going to control it rather than let it control me." Repression says "I'm not angry. I refuse to be angry. Whatever I am feeling will go away on it's own." Unacknowledged anger rarely goes away on its own, but it might find an alternative way to make itself known—like in your stomach or head or in a critical spirit.

4. **Confess it!** This is the best way to deal with anger in your marriage relationship. Confession says, "I feel I'm getting angry. Give me a few minutes to think things over and then we'll talk more." The important part of confession is taking responsibility for your own emotions. It is not blaming your partner for making you angry but acknowledging that you are angry.

How do you and your future spouse deal with anger? Do a quick check on each other.

When I get angry, I tend to …

When you are angry, you tend to …

If either of you express anger in destructive ways—silence, blaming, yelling, pouting, sarcasm, avoidance, appeasement, crying, threatening, or physical violence—get together with your pastor or a counselor to work on a better way to communicate. Remember, you *will* experience anger in your marriage. The key to a happy marriage is learning how to handle it.

"I Do" Do's and Don'ts

Remember these guidelines when conflict comes (and it will!) to your relationship: Do stick to the issue and avoid personal attacks. Don't dredge up past hurts or problems. Do listen to your partner. Don't use the "silent treatment." Do admit when you're wrong. Don't embarrass each other by arguing in public. Do make up and mean it. Don't be bitter or carry a grudge.

Say What You Mean and Mean What You Say

By now we hope you realize that communication is complicated. Just think about it! In any one exchange, there are six possible messages that can come through:

1. What you mean to say.
2. What you actually say.
3. What the other person hears.
4. What the other person thinks he or she hears.
5. What the other person says about what you said.
6. What you think the other person said about what you said.

Yet communication is the key to you and your future spouse finding fulfillment in your marriage relationship.

Communication is the 'glue' that keeps two people together while a relationship grows and strengthens into a channel of mutual support, counsel, productivity, excitation, and satisfaction. With that goal in mind, can you embrace the commitment that good communication requires? Why not read together the Communication Covenant that follows. Honestly discuss each of the statements. Prayerfully consider this covenant. If you can make this commitment to each other with the full intent of fulfilling it, sign it and ask another couple to witness it. Be prepared to review it often as you move forward in your life together.

Communication Covenant

We agree that communication is essential to our relationship as husband and wife. We agree to intentionally work at understanding each other and to demonstrate our love daily by practicing these communication skills:

- We promise to express our irritations and annoyances with one another in a loving, specific, and timely way.

- We promise not to exaggerate or attack each other in the course of a disagreement.

- We promise to attempt to control the emotional intensity of our arguments, taking time-outs when necessary in order to gain perspective and control.
- We promise to not avoid conflict or run away from each other during a disagreement.
- We promise to practice the good listening skills of:
  - Focusing on what the other is saying instead of what we want to say next.
  - Asking questions when we need more information.
  - Repeating back what we heard the other say.
- We promise to not attack each other by dredging up past failure.
- We promise to admit when we are wrong and ask forgiveness when necessary.
- We promise to resist jumping to conclusions prematurely, giving each other the benefit of the doubt.
- We promise to honor each other's right to be heard by eliminating distractions during our discussions.
- We agree to regularly review this covenant and hold each other accountable for fulfilling the promises we have made to each other in signing it.
- We promise to pray through all our disagreements in a spirit of humility and forgiveness, asking God for the grace of reconciliation.

_____   _____

Husband   Wife

Chapter 6

There's More to Intimacy Than Sex

The term "intimate" has become synonymous with having sex. But the truth is far different. Intimacy is more about character than climax. God created us with a hunger for significance and a desire to belong. Intimacy is choosing to know and be known on the most personal level. It involves strength and vulnerability, risk and security. It is also essential to a marriage.

In this chapter, we will look at several aspects of intimacy—spiritual, relational, and sexual. All three are part of our design as human beings made in God's image and reflect God's vision for the marriage relationship. This is an area of your relationship that needs to be fully discussed before you wed, because you and your partner will have differing needs and expectations when it comes to intimacy.

What Is Intimacy?

We have within us the capacity for an intimate relationship with God and with each other. Developing spiritual, emotional, and physical intimacy is essential for a healthy, satisfying, and meaningful marriage relationship. But don't expect to achieve intimacy with your future spouse in the days, weeks, or even months ahead because intimacy is a process. It's part of the journey of life—one we take first as individuals with our God before we can find it in our relationships.

Intimacy takes a certain self-knowledge and self-acceptance so that you can reveal your inner self to another, including your hopes and dreams as well as your fears and needs. Don't expect your partner to meet all your needs—no one person can ever do that! But you also can't expect your future spouse to read your mind or just "know" what you need.

That's the Spirit

Don't be selfish; don't live to make a good impression on others. Be humble, thinking of others as better than yourself. Don't think only about your own affairs, but be interested in others, too, and what they are doing. (Philippians 2:3–4)

This is good advice for achieving true intimacy with your future spouse. It's not about what others think, but it *is* about thinking of others.

Meeting Each Other's Needs

We all enter marriage with certain basic needs. We might bring the false assumption that our spouse will automatically know what our needs are and be prepared and willing to meet those needs. An important part of communication in marriage is being able to tell each other what you need in a way that your partner can understand. There are some things that all human beings need. We all need physical provisions—shelter, food, water, and so on, assurance and hope for the future, a sense of significance and purpose, and love and acceptance.

But men and women can interpret differently what needs are most important or how those needs should be fulfilled. In the context of the marriage relationship, it is important to reach a level of self-acceptance and self-disclosure that allows you to honestly discuss together what you need.

A woman needs ...

- Affection from her spouse.
- Understanding conversation.
- Respect.
- Devotion.

- Honesty and openness.
- Financial support.
- Family commitment.
- Reassurance.

A man needs …

- Sexual fulfillment from his wife.
- Acceptance and trust.
- Appreciation.
- Recreational companionship.

- Approval.
- Encouragement.
- An attractive spouse.
- Domestic support.

Make your own list of what you feel are your deepest needs—you may or may not use the lists we have given. Then rank your needs in order of their importance to you. Talk about your needs with your partner. Discovering your own needs and the needs of your partner is a process that takes time, commitment, communication, and hard work. Meeting the relational needs of your spouse for feeling accepted, wanted, needed, respected, valued, and understood are often most difficult. Achieving both are an important step in your journey toward intimacy.

Spiritual Intimacy

Christian couples have an incredible advantage over couples who are not believers. In a marriage where both individuals are believers, their relationship has an added spiritual dimension. You can be not only one flesh, but also one spirit and one mind as believers. For married couples, spiritual growth and intimacy should be a shared pursuit. Although each person must have a personal relationship with God, couples must also discover the spiritual dimension of their marriage together. Although you cannot neglect your personal walk with God, you must also nourish the soul of your marriage.

Surveys of couples in America show that the happiest couples are those that pray together. In fact, couples that pray together regularly are more likely to describe their relationship as being highly romantic! As marriage counselors and best-selling authors Drs. Les and Leslie Parrott put it "As strange as it might sound, there is a strong link in marriage between prayer and sex. For one thing, frequency of prayer is a more powerful predictor

"I Do" Do's and Don'ts

Do you know how your partner became a Christian? What would your partner say has been the most significant spiritual experience in his or her life? Sharing with each other your conversion story and the continuing work of God's grace in your life can be a very moving and intimate experience.

of marital satisfaction than frequency of sexual intimacy." Prayer is better than sex! Check it out.

As a couple, make sure you spend time together in Bible reading, worship, and praise. Share your spiritual journey with each other. Encourage each other to grow in an intimate relationship with the Lord. Your relationship will be enriched; your marriage will be transformed. Join together with other believers in regular worship and praise. Be faithful in your commitment to a local church. Worshiping together has a stabilizing effect on the marriage.

If you have both been active in ministry in your church, one of the challenges you might face is finding a way that you can minister as a couple. This is especially important early in your marriage when individual ministries could take away from what little precious time you have together. It is still important to serve in an area that respects your individual gifts, but try to resist taking on ministries that would separate you rather than bring you together.

Having given that caution, serving together in the church or community can build an incredible connection between the two of you. Reaching out to others as a team promotes humility, sharing, compassion, and intimacy in your relationship. It is your joint expression of the love of Christ to others. In serving together your lives are bonded together.

Relational Intimacy

Most people approach marriage with the deep desire to have a mate that is a best friend for life. Is your future spouse someone to whom you can express your thoughts without out fear, someone who listens and supports you, and someone who is a trustworthy life companion? Protecting and enhancing an intimate friendship is a choice that can only be made by someone who is personally mature.

Personal maturity and an understanding of your own needs and expectations are basic to becoming a loving student of another person. Immaturity, the focus on one's self with little or no concern for others, will seriously limit the possibility of a healthy relationship and reduce any possibility for lasting intimacy.

The following principles can help you build the right kind of intimate friendship with your partner and prevent that friendship from weakening:

1. Schedule time to be together as friends. Put a priority on this aspect of your relationship. This will allow you to continue to grow in your knowledge and appreciation of each other.

2. Use your time together as friends to connect instead of resolve conflict. It is important for your intimacy that you do problem-solve, but you also need dedicated time to get to know each other and to just enjoy being together.

3. Treat each other as friends: Listen without being defensive, sharing your thoughts and feelings without fear of judgment, and guard your tongue so that you express your thoughts with wholesome, encouraging, gracious words. (Ephesians 4:29)

Remember that if you enter marriage under the false assumption that you need this person to be complete or that as long as this person needs you, you will be complete, you are destined for disappointment and disaster.

Physical Intimacy

Sexual intimacy within marriage is part of God's plan. He initiated the sexual relationship before sin entered into the human experience. But like so many other good gifts he has given to us, sex has been distorted by sin. The physical union of husband and wife and the climax of the sexual union were intended by God to be the delightful expression of their oneness in every other way.

The foundations of emotional, intellectual, and spiritual closeness, along with nonsexual sensuality, provide the basis for great experiences of love in sexual union. God created us as sensual beings. As a couple you can share in many pleasant sensual experiences that involve touching, seeing, smelling, hearing, and tasting. These sensual experiences do not necessarily have to be associated with sexuality.

Let's Talk About Sex

The pleasure that comes from satisfying sexual relations within marriage is not sinful but holy and good. At least that is God's perspective, but our perspective on sex is more often influenced by what our parents did or didn't teach us, what we observed growing up, our early exposure to sexual relationships, even what we have been taught in school or church. If we received healthy and godly instruction then our view of sex will be healthy and godly. Unfortunately, that is not always the case.

Mutual sexual satisfaction is an important aspect of a strong marriage. It is, therefore, important that you and your future mate have safe and comfortable discussions about your views on sex and your expectations about sexual relations in marriage.

Sexual pleasure is intended not to be self-oriented but other-oriented. Sexual relations are to be regular and continuous to provide adequate sexual satisfaction to both husband and wife. Each party is to provide sexual enjoyment as frequently as the other party requires, controlled by the principle of moderation and consideration for one's mate, rather than uncontrolled lust. Sexual relations are equal and reciprocal. This is not just our opinion. Read what the Apostle Paul has to say about it in 1 Corinthians 7:3–5.

We will talk more about sex when we talk about honeymoon expectations (see Chapter 15) but as part of your preparation for marriage, you and your future spouse need to examine your beliefs about sex so that any differing views you have can be resolved before your wedding night. In some cases, these discussions might indicate the need for additional help or advice from a counselor or medical professional.

Birth Control

Every engaged couple needs to thoroughly discuss and decide on the issue of birth control before the wedding. Views on birth control vary widely even within the Christian community, and the Bible does not address contraception directly. There are some that feel that any form of birth control is interfering with God's will. There are others who believe it is morally irresponsible not to practice some form of family planning.

Our intention is not to present the right or wrong of any particular form of birth control. On the moral and biblical issues, we recommend you discuss them with your family and/or your clergy because the morality of birth control is not directly addressed in the Bible. Because today's couples have so many choices in contraception, we will outline the most common types of birth control so that you and your future spouse can have an informed discussion. However, before you make your final choice, consult your doctor to discuss any possible side effects and which form of contraception is best for you.

Oral contraceptives—The most common form of contraception, "the pill," has been widely used for several decades, and many of the earlier and more serious side effects have been eliminated as lower doses have proven to be equally successful in preventing pregnancy. Oral contraceptives involve the woman taking small daily doses of hormones which prevent pregnancy in several ways—preventing ovulation (release of an egg from the ovaries), shortening the menstrual cycle which thins the uterine wall making implantation of a fertilized egg less likely, and thickening the cervical mucous which prevents sperm from getting to the egg.

> ### Bet You Didn't Know
>
> One form of contraception that has been widely rejected by Christians in the past might be under reconsideration if current research holds up. In the past, the IUD was believed to effectively prevent implantation but *not* fertilization. If you believe that life begins at conception, then this method could be viewed as a form of early abortion. However, new research indicates that the IUD might actually have a strong spermicidal affect. If this research holds up, the IUD might become another contraceptive choice for Christian couples.

With any form of hormonal contraception, there is still the possibility that fertilization can take place but that implantation is prevented. Even though the odds of this happening are very low, for some couples this poses a moral dilemma. Most doctors recommend being on the pill for 3–6 months prior to your wedding date for maximum effectiveness.

Implants and injectibles—Depro-provera is an injectible hormonal contraceptive that prevents fertility and menstruation. Each injection lasts for three months. Another hormonal method, Norplant, consists of six small rods, each about the size of a matchstick, that are inserted under the skin of the inner arm. Implants release a steady stream of hormones preventing fertility for about five years.

Barrier methods—Condoms are still the most common barrier method. They are also the most affective for preventing STD. There are instructions that need to be followed to preserve the effectiveness of condom use, and many men and some women feel condom use decreases sensation and pleasure during intercourse. However, condoms do remain one of the safest and most effective forms of contraception, are readily available (in nearly any grocery store or pharmacy) and do not require a waiting period to become effective.

Diaphragms and cervical caps are two forms of barrier contraceptive used by the woman. They are placed over the cervix along with a spermicide to prevent sperm from reaching any waiting egg. Both need to be fitted by a physician and must be inserted a short time prior to intercourse. But once they are in place, neither the man nor the woman can feel them, and many couples have used them successfully for years.

Spermicides—Some spermicides, with or without a sponge, can be used by themselves as a form of contraception and are most commonly available as suppositories, creams, and foams. With spermicides, timing is everything—some need to be inside the body for 15 minutes prior to intercourse and only last for an hour. Some women and men have experienced irritation from the active ingredient in certain spermicides—some mild, some severe. In many cases, any irritation is caused by a nonactive ingredient and can be cleared up by changing brands.

Fertility Awareness and *Abstinence*—Natural Family Planning (NFP) and Fertility Awareness Method (FAM) are both contraception methods that depend on knowing when the woman is fertile by charting one or more factors such as cycle length, morning body temperature, and condition of cervical mucous.

With NFP, no method of birth control is used except total sexual abstinence during the woman's fertile time. Couples using NFP correctly have a lower contraception failure rate than couples using the pill. While NFP is the only form of contraception approved by the Roman Catholic Church, some Christians feel it violates the biblical command that couple agree to abstain from sex only for the purpose of prayer and fasting. (1 Corinthians 7:5)

FAM and NFP use the same methods of determining the woman's fertility but FAM allows intercourse using a barrier method of contraception or sex that does not include intercourse. While methods for charting a woman's cycle are getting easier to use and more effective, both FAM and NFP require self-control and conscientious tracking and record keeping.

Bet You Didn't Know

Several states in America still require a blood test in order for a couple to obtain a marriage license. You can check with your county clerk to see what your state's requirements are, but even if a blood test is not required, a checkup with a physician before marriage is not a bad idea. It gives you a chance to ask a professional any questions you might have, and a consultation is necessary to obtain many types of birth control.

As your wedding day approaches, keep in mind that some contraceptives require a waiting period before they become effective. And, except for abstinence, no form of contraception is completely effective, although in the majority of cases where contraception fails, the failure is due to misuse or nonuse.

False Intimacy

Beware of behavior that masquerades as intimacy. In many relationships, couples who are sexually active assume that they are intimate. But as we have indicated, sexual intimacy is a poor substitute for true intimacy. More than half of young adults in America today admit to having sex with someone they have no intention of pursuing a relationship with.

Just as sex is not synonymous with intimacy—neither is living together. Intimacy is not achieved just by sharing time or the same space with someone. Intimacy requires deliberate revelation of your inner self to another. Many couples who live together—married or otherwise—often discover after years together that they really don't even know each other.

Some people are masters at talking without telling you anything. The sad part is, they often don't even realize that they are doing it. True intimacy requires a deep level of self-knowledge and self-acceptance. A partner who resists talking about his or her past, puts himself or herself down all the time, and doesn't articulate his or her hopes and dreams might not be mature or self-aware enough to establish a truly intimate relationship.

Control can sometimes be misinterpreted as intimacy. A partner that wants you and only you to the point of controlling your relationships with other people is not a safe person. Resist any pressure to become isolated from others. Strong couples get stronger when they have healthy connections with others outside of their own relationship.

Passion and Purity

Sexual purity before marriage is one of the most important gifts you can give to your future spouse. It demonstrates that you understand the sanctity of sex within the marriage relationship and the importance that God places on sexual purity. It also helps to establish trust in your relationship. Will you be tempted? You bet! But rather than see abstinence as an inconvenience you just have to endure, you can choose to see sexual purity as proof of your mutual love and respect for each other.

Sexual purity is more than abstaining from sexual intercourse. Many engaged couples are tempted to allow petting and other forms of sexual stimulation to become a part of their relationship. The reasoning is that (1) we're going to get married anyway; and (2) as long as we don't have intercourse, it's okay. While this kind of reasoning is all too common today, it is contrary to the intent of God's Word and creates guilt and embarrassment should the engagement end.

You *can* remain sexually pure. But it will require a thoughtful and prayerful choice on your part and on the part of your partner. The time to make that choice is now because as your passion and desire for one another grow and the closer you get to your wedding date, the more difficult it will be to resist. Here are a few guidelines to help you follow the path of purity.

Keep God at the Center of Your Relationship

Purity starts with a heart attitude. It's recognizing and actively seeking God's best. Make spiritual intimacy your first goal. It will be difficult to yield to temptation when your heart and mind are focused on spiritual things. When temptation strikes, believe that you can resist because God has promised to help. (1 Corinthians 10:13)

- Pray regularly—together and individually. Your prayer times should include confession, thanksgiving, and petition for God's guidance and protection.
- Study God's Word together. Start with the many Scripture verses we have given throughout this book or get involved in a study with a small group from your church.
- Serve together. Serving others will keep you stay active as well as give you the opportunity to see another aspect of how your partner relates to different people and different situations.

Set Ground Rules and Stick to Them

The best way to resist temptation is to have a plan. You and your partner should have a plan that is unique to your relationship and your needs. Part of your plan should involve talking together about when, where, and how temptation strikes and then setting up rules to help you control those situations. You might want to start with the following rules that address common situations where your resolve to remain pure will be tested:

- Restrict where and when you can be alone together. If purity is your objective, it just doesn't make sense to spend long periods of time alone together in a house, a car, a hotel room, or a circus tent! Don't place yourselves in compromising situations.

- Make certain areas of your bodies "off limits" to touch. Any area of your body that you would be embarrassed to have your partner touch in front of your parents should probably be off-limits in private as well.

- Avoid entertainment that stimulates your desires. Now that you're in love, it's more fun to watch romantic movies. But some movies and other sources of entertainment can be overly stimulating. This is especially true for guys because men are stimulated visually.

- Stop immediately when either person indicates that he or she is uncomfortable. The responsibility for purity does not rest on one partner more than the other. Both of you have the responsibility to maintain discipline and practice self-control.

- Stay in control of your senses. Obviously alcohol and drugs impair your ability to make wise choices. But lack of sleep and even some prescription medications can have the same effect.

Don't Put Each Other to the Test

Accept responsibility for your purity. You can say no. But because you will soon be one, you should also earnestly seek to protect the purity of your partner. If you or your partner indicates that it is time to stop what you are doing, respond immediately, even if you don't feel especially tempted at the moment. Move apart physically, but don't retreat from each other. It is important at these times to use good communication skills to discuss what you are feeling and why what you are doing makes you uncomfortable.

It is natural to want to be desired by your partner and it is important that you both can express that desire for each other in a healthy way. However, love does not provoke each other to sin but to godliness. Don't act, talk, or dress in a way that will tempt your partner and never take advantage of your partner's weakness. You can decide to stop any behavior that is leading toward compromise.

That's the Spirit

For where two or three gather together because they are mine, I am there among them. (Matthew 18:20)

As believers, any time you and your partner are together, God is there with you. This can be convicting if your behavior has been inappropriate. But it can also be very inspiring and encouraging because where God is, there is love!

Take the Purity Pledge

Read the verses that follow and prayerfully consider whether or not these are promises you can make to each other. If so, sign the pledge and review it together when faced with decisions about the guidelines and rules you have established for purity in your relationship. You might want to have another couple—friends, parents, or mentors—witness your pledge. If you do, give them permission to question you and hold you accountable to the promises it contains.

"God wants you to be holy, so you should keep clear of all sexual sin. Then each of you will control your body and live in holiness and honor—not in lustful passion as the pagans do, in their ignorance of God and his ways." (1 Thessalonians 4:3–5)

I promise to protect your sexual purity now and until we become husband and wife before God and man.

Run away from sexual sin! No other sin so clearly affects the body as this one does. For sexual immorality is a sin against your own body. (1 Corinthians 6:18)

I promise to respect and honor you by guarding my thoughts and behavior so that I might present myself to you in all purity.

Or don't you know that your body is the temple of the Holy Spirit, who lives in you and was given to you by God? You do not belong to yourself, for God bought you with a high price. So you must honor God with your body. (1 Corinthians 6:19–20)

I promise to focus on building up the inner person of your heart, putting your spiritual good above my own desires.

Be humble and gentle. Be patient with each other, making allowance for each other's faults because of your love. Always keep yourselves united in the Holy Spirit, and bind yourselves together with peace. (Ephesians 4:2–3)

I promise to express my love for you in ways that allow both of us to maintain a clear conscience before God and each other.

You are to live clean, innocent lives as children of God in a dark world full of crooked and perverse people. Let your lives shine brightly before them. (Philippians 2:15)

I promise to preserve my purity and yours as a testimony to others of God's love and grace.

This is my promise of purity.

_____   _____

Man   Woman

I have witnessed this pledge of purity between this man and woman and promise to hold them accountable to it according to the Scriptures.

_____   _____

Witness   Witness

Date _____

It's Not Too Late

Perhaps you feel that you have already violated God's call to purity, either with your current partner or with someone from a previous relationship. Although you cannot undo what has been done, you can find complete forgiveness and restoration in Christ. How do we know? Let's take a look at Psalm 51: 6–10, written by King David *after* he had committed adultery with Bathsheba.

> Honestly confess your sin to God and admit that what you did was against his laws and contrary to his will for you. "But you desire honesty from the heart, so you can teach me to be wise in my inmost being."
>
> Accept God's forgiveness and His power to make you pure again. "Purify me from my sins, and I will be clean; wash me, and I will be whiter than snow.
>
> Rejoice in your renewed purity. "Oh, give me back my joy again; you have broken me—now let me rejoice."

Commit to remaining pure and ask God to give you the heart and will to do it. "Don't keep looking at my sins. Remove the stain of my guilt. Create in me a clean heart, O God. Renew a right spirit within me."

After you confess to God, do you need to confess to your future spouse? That depends. If you have been involved in sexual behavior and feel burdened to tell your partner even after asking God's forgiveness, we recommend you take the following steps:

1. Write down specifically what it is you feel you need to tell your partner and why.

2. Ask yourself who will benefit if you tell. If telling is for your benefit only, then you probably need to talk with God and/or a counselor before you talk to your future spouse. But if you feel that your partner has a need and a right to know, then it might be right for you to confess.

3. Ask yourself, will my confession hurt others?

4. How will telling change my relationship with my partner? If you decide to share past sexual sins, you need to be prepared for your relationship with your future spouse to change. It could get better after he or she has had time to process and forgive. It could get worse, creating tensions and conflicts that need to be worked out before you marry. Or it could end the relationship completely.

5. There is wisdom in righteous counsel. Before you confess, talk it over first with a trusted spiritual advisor.

If after careful consideration of all the steps above, you still feel God is leading you to confess, then choose a time and location that is appropriate. Be willing to give your partner time to process this new revelation. Don't demand forgiveness and acceptance on the spot. Be prepared to postpone or cancel the wedding if your partner asks you to do so. It would be unwise to go ahead with the marriage if either of you feel the issue is unresolved.

Chapter 7

Family Matters

Getting married is probably the most important event in a person's life. It is also a very significant family event involving the future of three family units—the bride's family, the groom's family, and the new family the couple is beginning together.

When you announce your engagement, you will begin to sense a shift in your family relationships. As you become less dependent on your family of origin, your connection to your future spouse and his or her family grows. And if you or your partner is a child of divorce or have been married before, you are dealing with extended family ties. Although weddings can bring families together, they can also put a strain on even the best of family relationships. You'll want to get off to a good start, so pay attention to family matters because families matter!

We Are Family

There's nothing like a wedding to test the strength of family connections. Even in the healthiest of families, planning a wedding can cause financial, emotional, and relational tension. The more you are able to understand your family of origin—how you interact with one another, your communication styles, and any family expectations—the better prepared you will be to handle the merging of your family values and plan a wedding that honors both families.

Family Ties

As you evaluate your family ties, resist the urge to confront your parents over perceived failures in your upbringing. The value of reviewing the relationship styles within your family of origin is not in trying to fix the past, but in avoiding the same mistakes in the future as you and your spouse create your own family.

Understanding Your Family

As well as you and your partner think you understand each other, understanding and accepting your family dynamics can still be a challenge. Your responses to the following statements will help you discuss with your future spouse the kind of family you grew up in. Respond to each statement based on your own recollection and perception of your family experience. Someone else in your family might have a completely different set of responses and that's all right. What is important is how *you* experienced your family.

1 = Almost Never

2 = Sometimes

3 = Almost Always

In my family …

[ ] We stick together when any family member has a problem.

[ ] We can speak our minds without risking rejection.

[ ] We don't let our differences divide us.

[ ] We enjoy doing things together.

[ ] We share beliefs and values.

Total 1: _____

Growing up …

[ ] Our parents included us in decisions regarding discipline.

[ ] Our family enjoyed discussing problems and solutions together.

[ ] Our friends were welcome in our home.

[ ] Our family shared chores and responsibilities.

[ ] Our family clearly understood the house rules.

Total 2: _____

When you marry, you are also marrying your partner's family of origin. Especially in the early years of your marriage, marked differences in attachment (the closeness between family members) and adaptability (the amount of flexibility in the family) styles of your families can present problems for you as a couple.

Total 1 reflects attachment. In a well-adjusted family, there is a balance between separateness of individuals (autonomy) and relational connectedness (attachment). A low total might indicate a family that is disconnected or unable to connect with each other. If you or your partner scored 1–6 for attachment, you might have difficulty establishing or maintaining emotional closeness in your relationship. On the other hand, a total over 12 might indicate family members are overly connected to each other. If that is true of you or your partner, you might have difficulty establishing a separate family identity.

Total 2 reflects flexibility, or the ability to adapt to change. Too much flexibility leads to insecurity—you never know what the rules are or what to expect. As human beings, we naturally resist change because it makes us uncomfortable. But change is a very real and natural part of life. A very low score on flexibility might indicate that you or your partner will have a difficult time adjusting to the changes that come naturally with getting married. On the other hand, a high score (12 or more) might leave one or both of you constantly wondering where you stand in the relationship. And, if it is the man who scores high on flexibility, the woman might feel a lack of leadership in the marriage relationship.

The key, obviously, is balance! Families that are balanced on the attachment scale encourage family members to be independent while still remaining connected to the family. Families that are balanced on the adaptability scale are better able to cope with crisis situations because they have established a firm foundation but are able to be flexible when necessary.

Just as with a healthy marriage, healthy families recognize the individuals within the "we" of the family. They do not ask individuals to surrender their own identities because they recognize the richness each adds to the whole. They enjoy being together but don't always *have* to be together to be fulfilled. A healthy family recognizes that it takes commitment, communication, and compatibility (our three C's) to establish and maintain a balanced family.

Can We Talk?

Communication is essential in keeping your relationship with your family, your in-laws, and your future spouse healthy and happy. We've written a whole chapter (see Chapter 5) to help you and your partner learn good communication skills. However, because you and your partner learned your communication skills from your family of origin, you might want to talk about how your family communicated and discuss how that style of communication might impact your ability to relate not just to each other but to your future in-laws.

When our family talks …

- We play close attention to details and want all the facts.
- We all talk at the same time.
- We just want the bottom line.
- We talk mostly about impersonal things—events, the weather, and other people.
- We avoid arguments.
- We are comfortable talking about our feelings and personal situations.
- We can often finish each other's sentences.
- We think it's rude to all talk at once.
- We have certain "forbidden" subjects in my family.
- We don't mind loud discussions in my family.

Unpacking Your Baggage

As you examine the function (or dysfunction) in your family of origin, you might find some serious family issues that you and your partner need to work through with a counselor. But in most cases, remembering that your parents loved you and did the best job they could will help you extend grace and forgiveness so that you can wholeheartedly include your families in your wedding celebration.

Christian marriage counselor Dr. David Stoop, in his book *Forgiving Our Parents, Forgiving Ourselves: Healing Adult Children with Dysfunctional Families*, gives seven excellent descriptions of the most common types of dysfunctional families.

Take a look at the following list and see if any apply to your family:

1. **Isolated Islands.** The members share a common name but are isolated from each other. In terms of internal dynamics of family life, they are almost totally detached from one another. Relationships are typically devoid of emotional content, existing for utilitarian purposes only. This is probably the most severely disturbed pattern of family dysfunction.

2. **Generational Splits.** This family lacks significant interaction between parents and children—not just the two generations currently living in the same household, but also between the parents and their parents. Significant interaction takes place only within generations. A frequent pattern for this type of family is for emotional and relational connections to skip generations.

3. **Gender Splits.** This is similar to the generational split except it happens along gender lines within families. Very little emotionally significant interaction takes place across gender lines. The men and boys stick together, as do the women and girls. There is often a very strong notion of sex-based roles for men and women.

4. **The Fused Pair.** Two members of this family cut themselves off from the others. The pair becomes the nucleus around which the rest of the family revolves. The other members experience the family as extremely disengaged and detached. The two who are fused are strongly enmeshed.

5. **Queen of the Hill.** This family is completely dominated by one person. In the vast majority of cases it is the mother. She becomes the reigning matriarch. In some extended families it is the grandmother. Everyone knows where the power lies. No one questions her decisions.

6. **The Quiet Dictator.** This is similar to the "Queen of the Hill," but the dominant member's control over the family is far more subtle and manipulative in nature. They work behind the scenes, skillfully manipulating others' emotions. There are clear, unbreakable rules and expectations, enforced by a firm set of roles that the members are to fulfill without wavering.

7. **The Family Scapegoat.** This family will make one member bear the blame for the family's problems. "Blame" is a theme in a chemically dependent family. After a member is labeled, it might be very difficult to break out of the expected behavior pattern.

No family is perfect! Not even the first family of Adam and Eve with the advantages of being created perfect, living in a perfect environment, and walking and talking with God every day. Don't be afraid or embarrassed to discuss honestly and openly with your future spouse and your clergy or counselor areas of dysfunction in your family of origin that will impact your marriage.

> ### That's the Spirit
>
> So each generation can set its hope anew on God, remembering his glorious miracles and obeying his commands. Then they will not be like their ancestors—stubborn, rebellious, and unfaithful, refusing to give their hearts to God. (Psalm 78:7–8)
>
> If you can trace your spiritual heritage back several generations, you are especially blessed. But even if your family ties are tangled, twisted, or broken, there's hope! You do not have to follow the unhealthy patterns of the past. Give your heart to God and live your life in obedience to God's commands and you and your children and your children's children will see God's glorious miracles.

Family Treasures

In every family there is a treasury of experiences, values, memories, and beliefs. For some, the treasure is buried, hidden in failures and hurts. But for many, the treasure is lying there, just waiting to be discovered and claimed. Christian families can have the most valuable treasure of all because their treasure is of eternal worth. What family treasures have you uncovered in your family or in your partner's family?

My family treasure: _____

_____

My partner's family treasure: _____

_____

Paternal Relationships

Of all your family relationships, none has more of an impact on your marriage relationship than your relationship with your father. As a woman, you can tell a great deal about the kind of man, husband, and father your future spouse will be by learning more about his dad. And men, if you want to know what your future wife expects from you, find out how she views her father. Even your view of and your ability to relate to him have been shaped—positively or negatively—by your relationship with your dad.

That's the Spirit

There is treasure in the house of the godly .... (Proverbs 15:6)

For you bless the godly, O Lord, surrounding them with your shield of love. (Psalm 5:12)

Take a look at the treasure you are inheriting from your family and from the family of your future spouse. As you thank God for a rich spiritual heritage, determine to be intentional in leaving your children with just as rich of a spiritual inheritance.

Identifying how your father interacted with you during your childhood and through your teen years might help you understand how you respond to your partner and to God. Read carefully each of the following characteristics and determine the number that indicates how you remember your father as you were growing up:

1 = Always
2 = Seldom
3 = Occasionally
4 = Often
5 = Never

[ ] **Demonstrable Love**—My father expressed his love in words and actions to me. He confirmed the fact that his love did not depend on my performance but upon his choice and commitment to me.

[ ] **Encouraging Words**—My father verbally confirmed my personal worth, acceptable behavior, and positive attitudes and expressed interest in and approval of my accomplishments.

[ ] **Consistent Demands**—My father set firm but flexible guidelines and standards of behavior for me and was consistent in their application. He was reasonable and fair which was a course of security for me.

[ ] **Understanding Discipline**—My father reacted to my unacceptable behavior and attitudes rationally, not in anger, and applied discipline that was appropriate, instructive, and understandable.

[ ] **Admit Error**—My father was open to recognize his mistakes and would apologize when wrong or inappropriate words, behavior, or attitudes were evident. He was able to ask for forgiveness as well as give it.

[ ] **Always Accessible**—My father was available to talk, play, laugh, cry, counsel, console, touch, and encourage me when I needed him. He also respected my privacy.

[ ] **Share Life**—My father was open to share his successes, problems, hurts, future prospects, answered prayer, and other experiences that affected the family and me.

Perhaps after reviewing this section, you realize that your experience with your father was woefully lacking. Don't despair. Yes, your relationship to your father is important to your future relationships. But God has promised to be a father to the fatherless. If you ask, he will make up anything lacking from your earthly father.

Healthy Relations with In-Laws

You've spent a lifetime getting to know and understand your own family members, so one of the first guidelines for a good relationship with your in-laws is to get to know them. The more you understand not only your spouse's childhood but the family life of your partner's parents, the better equipped you will be to build a healthy connection with them. Remember that family ties are for life—and that includes in-laws. Here are a few tips for getting off to a good start:

- Accept your in-laws as they are.
- Focus on the good points.
- Treat your in-laws with kindness and respect.
- Allow them time to adjust to their changing relationship with their child.
- Think positive thoughts—they did raise the partner you love.
- Refrain from telling your in-laws what's wrong with your future spouse.

> **"I Do" Do's and Don'ts**
>
> Get off to a good start in your relationship with your in-laws. Be sincere in wanting to get to know them better. Give them credit for raising a partner you love and adore. Invite them to participate in the wedding plans and incorporate their traditions and beliefs whenever you can without compromising your own wedding day wishes.

Interference from either family cannot ruin a healthy marriage. Couples who give their relationship priority over other family relationships will have a sound marriage. The process of leaving (see Chapter 3) doesn't always go smoothly. If conflicts arise between you and your partner's family, remember that your first loyalty is *always* to your spouse. The husband should be his wife's advocate to his parents and the wife should run interference for her husband with her family.

Becoming An In-Law Exercise

We've listed here one of the best premarital exercises we know of for establishing healthy connections with in-laws. Make a copy of this exercise and give it to both sets of parents. Include an envelope for them to use when returning it. After they have completed the exercise and returned it to you, *resist the urge to read it!* until you and your partner can set aside some quality time to read them together. You will also want to add these to your notebook or file to review throughout your first years of marriage.

Dear Parent(s):

As part of our preparation for marriage, we want to ask your help in building positive family relationships. Please read and consider the questions in this letter and complete the form without discussing the questions with your son or daughter. When both families have completed the form, we will discuss the results with our pastor, counselor, or mentoring couple.

How would you describe your relationship with your parents during the early years of your marriage?

What was your relationship with your in-laws like during the early years of your marriage?

Would you like your married children to approach you in the same way you approached your parents and in-laws? Why or why not?

What would you list as some major needs of your soon-to-be-married son or daughter?

What will be your greatest adjustment as your son/daughter leaves home?

If you could ask your son/daughter to pray during this transition, what would be your request?

Will you expect your children to visit you often? How do you define "often?" How will you go about suggesting that the newly married couple visit you?

When your children choose something that is not your choice, will you graciously accept it as their decision or feel personal rejection? (Can you think of an example?)

Can you accept your child and his/her spouse with love and not criticism? Do you think and speak of your soon to be son-in-law/daughter-in-law as a positive addition to your family?

In what way are you taking into consideration the feelings of the other family in making wedding plans, giving gifts, scheduling holiday visits, and seeing the grandchildren.

Please describe six expectations that you have for the couple after they are married:

1. _____
2. _____
3. _____
4. _____
5. _____
6. _____

On another piece of paper, please compose a letter describing in detail why you are looking forward to your son/daughter's partner becoming part of your family. Address it to your soon-to-be son-in-law/daughter-in law. Include your letter with this form when you return it.

Blending Families

Today's families can be a little complicated! A young couple marrying today might need to deal with issues that arise from remarriage, multicultural marriages, and mixed faith marriages. Have you every made a fruit smoothie? Think about the work of a blender! It doesn't change the various ingredients into something they are not—strawberries don't become bananas. And it's not a process without difficulty—in fact, the success of the blending is in direct proportion to the amount of turbulence! But the result is worth it! Keep your eye on the prize—the goal of your wedding is to create a new family founded on scriptural principles.

Marry Me, Marry My Kids

We've mentioned in previous chapters that you will face special challenges if you or your partner have been married before. If either of you have children, the challenges are multiplied! The sensible couple will recognize and accept these challenges. We sincerely believe that you can enjoy a marriage that involves ex-spouses, stepchildren, ex-relatives, and often-complicated finances and tangled schedules. Here are a few quick tips to consider:

1. Attend to your attitudes. You are entering a long-term commitment to a number of individuals, not just your future spouse. You will need patience, forgiveness, and tolerance. You will not be successful if you harbor vengeful thoughts or selfish desires.

2. Train for a marathon. Blending families is not a sprint. You have to be in it for the long haul. Stay focused and committed and in time you will win the prize.

3. Face the challenges. Some partners enter into a relationship with the idea they will just "wait it out" until the kids are grown. Trust us, that won't work! You need to face the challenges together.

4. Enjoy the realities. Life doesn't have to be easy to be enjoyable. As difficult as blended family life can be, it also has rich rewards. Be realistic, but also take time to enjoy your unique family blend.

Bet You Didn't Know

According to a recent survey in *Reader's Digest* (March 2003), 43 percent of all weddings involve at least one partner who has been married before. But the odds are against these marriages. Census 2000 and other family-oriented surveys have given us some fascinating information on the state of American families:

60 percent of second marriages end in divorce.

66–70 percent of marriages and/or live-in relationships end in break-ups when there are children involved.

50 percent of all Americans are currently living in some form of step relationship.

With a divorce rate equal to or higher than that outside the church, every church has members in step relationships.

Beating the Odds

If you or your partner has been married before, you should know up-front that the odds are against you. Although 50 percent of all marriages end in divorce, 60 percent of all *second* marriages end in divorce. We say this not to discourage you but to encourage you and your partner to spend the time necessary to get to know each other, do your premarital counseling, and lay a healthy foundation for a successful marriage.

Mixed-Faith Marriages

When God created us in his image, he imparted to us a spiritual component. That spiritual part of our being is essential to our being healthy, well-grounded individuals. And the marriage relationship involves a union of two individuals emotionally, physically, and spiritually. Although we strongly counsel against marrying someone who is a nonbeliever, it is possible that you and your future spouse might be coming from different religious traditions within the Christian faith.

An interfaith marriage involves individuals from different religions. Most Christian denominations and churches discourage interfaith marriages because they fall under the admonition in 2 Corinthians to not be unequally yoked together with unbelievers. Believers in other religions are sometimes more open to marriages between faiths. An example of this would be a Lutheran marrying a Muslim.

An interdenominational or intrafaith marriage involves individuals who follow different traditions within the same religion. An example of this would be two individuals from differing denominations within the protestant religions, such as a Lutheran and a Baptist. Even if both individuals are born-again believers, the practices of their churches might be significantly different and require discussion and counseling. Even if your differences are not causing problems now, that doesn't mean they won't in the future. Many couples in intrafaith relationships face real difficulties when they are faced with a crisis or when they decide to have children.

Bet You Didn't Know

Although the Jewish faith discourages interfaith marriages, it is estimated that 50 percent of all American Jews marry non-Jewish partners. Roman Catholicism allows interfaith marriage, but the ceremony must be performed in the church by a Catholic priest and both husband and wife must agree to raise the children of their marriage according to the beliefs and practices of the Catholic Church.

Do you know what your church's stand is on interfaith or intrafaith marriages? Many clergy will not marry interfaith couples, and others will only marry intrafaith couples who agree with certain core beliefs that most Christians find essential to salvation:

- Jesus Christ is the Son of God
- Belief in the death and resurrection of Christ
- Salvation is through faith in Jesus

A shared faith is key to a happy and successful marriage. You will want to investigate both the beliefs of your church and your future spouse's church if you are planning to be married in either. And if you or your partner do not agree on the three principles listed here, you should seriously reconsider marrying and seek additional counseling.

Multicultural Marriages

Experts in the field of multicultural marriages have identified four possible responses to the union of couples from different cultures:

- **Submission**—One partner submits to the culture of the other, abandoning his or her (most often the woman's) own culture completely.
- **Compromise**—Each partner gives up certain aspects of his or her own culture to make room for the habits and beliefs of their partner. Both lose something, but both win something too.
- **Obliteration**—Both individuals agree to deny both of their cultures and form a new cultural identity. This leaves them with no history, collective memory, or traditions. It also often leaves them with no support system as well.
- **Consensus**—Neither sacrifices things that are essential, but agree to keep what is important from both cultures. This is a win-win situation.

Many couples involved in multicultural relationships do not feel the full impact of their decision until after the ceremony. It is after the wedding that they encounter the pitfalls of blending two cultures successfully. The most common pitfalls occur in the areas of defining the male and female roles, choosing a place of residence, in-law relationships, raising children, and dealing with stress.

But there is hope! Intercultural marriage expert, Dugan Romano, gives the following 10 factors for success:

1. Good motives for the marriage
2. Common goals
3. Sensitivity to each other's needs
4. A liking for the other's culture
5. Flexibility
6. Solid, positive self-image
7. Spirit of adventure
8. Ability to communicate
9. Commitment to the relationship
10. Sense of humor

Your Families vs. Your Wedding

In most cases, you will want to include your families in the planning process for your wedding, especially because in most cases they are paying for the majority of the expenses. It might take some effort and good communication to find the best way to include your family in any decision-making. You want to ensure that your wedding remains your wedding without causing family friction or hurt feelings.

Set Boundaries

Do this for everyone involved in the planning—even your parents! Using the suggestions and guidelines in the next chapter, sit down with your partner and create a list of elements about which you don't want to compromise. For example, if you absolutely want a midmorning ceremony with a sit-down luncheon at the reception, agree that you won't ask anyone for input on that decision. Be aware, however, that to get the nonnegotiable elements, you might have to compromise on other elements, such as the date or the cost of your dress.

Be Specific

When asking for opinions or advice, give family members specific choices. For example, you want help deciding on the flavor of the wedding cake. Avoid using broad questions like "What kind of wedding cake do you think we should have?"

That question solicits an opinion on size, style, color, and so on. Instead start first with your future groom, narrowing down your choices to two or three. Then ask your mother for her opinion between white with lemon filling or chocolate with raspberry filling. (Of course, with a multiple tier cake, you could end up with both!)

Be Tactful

Planning a wedding that involves both families can require United Nations level diplomacy! Be sensitive to how important this event is to every member of both families. To keep from hurting anyone's feelings, try to equally include everyone in the process. If you ask your mother about the cake, ask your future mother-in-law about the flowers. And keep everyone up-to-date on how the plans are progressing.

Know When to Let Go

Careful planning, good organization, and thoughtful negotiation will take you a long way toward reducing the stress of your big day. But you must also recognize when it is time to let go. Don't try to do everything yourself! Invite your two families over to discuss how each can contribute. Be prepared with a list of tasks and responsibilities you are ready to release. This doesn't mean you are giving up control! But you will discover that as your wedding day draws closer, the demands are your time and energy will increase! And this all happens at a time when you need to be spending more time with your partner.

It just makes good sense to delegate some responsibilities to others. Use the guidelines in the following chapters to make up "to do" lists for volunteers. Provide specific dates and times, as well as instructions for their individual duties.

Handling Conflicts

Even with the best planning, conflicts can flare up unexpectedly. One hot zone is the decision among parents and future in-laws regarding whom should pay for what. Wedding etiquette (covered in Chapter 10) hasn't changed much over the years and will give some clear guidelines on some of these issues. But it will still take a spirit of cooperation to bring it all together.

Deciding to include your family in your wedding plans and preparations will be challenging. However, as long as you can maintain control over your wedding, there are a lot of benefits to sharing your special day with those closest to you.

Part 2

Planning the Perfect Wedding

The perfect wedding doesn't just happen—it takes good planning and organization. Get a notebook (with pockets) before you read through the following chapters. Start with a realistic budget that includes all the important elements of your special day. Work with your future spouse to choose those elements of your wedding that will mean the most to the two of you.

Communication between you and your partner and your families will be crucial as you work out the details: When will you marry; how formal of a ceremony do you want; where will you get married and by whom; what will you wear; who will be in your wedding party; what kind of reception fits your dreams? The following pages will help you organize your dreams and find practical ways to get what you want most without blowing your wedding budget.

Chapter 8

Organizing Your Dream Wedding

Dream weddings don't just happen. They take thoughtful planning and good organization. If you want your special day to reflect your love for each other and the values you share, you will want to decide the important elements of your wedding together—the date, the budget, the wedding party, and the style of ceremony—before you move into the particulars. Talking about your wedding dreams now will reduce the chances of conflict and controversy as the planning and preparations continue.

As you talk through your wants and wishes for your wedding, practice good communication skills. Be honest—don't say it doesn't matter if it does! But remain flexible—you may have little control over some elements of your wedding. Talking through what's most important to both of you will help you prioritize and present a united front when discussing wedding arrangements with others—family, friends, wedding planners, clergy, and so on.

Elements of Your Wedding

Most brides have a pretty clear idea about what they want in a wedding, but many grooms have given it little thought. Don't take "I don't know" for "I don't care." Start your marriage off right with a ceremony that acknowledges both of you and celebrates your coming together as one. In the course of your discussion of the who, what, where, when, and how, make sure you cover the following questions:

- Which elements are most important to us?
- Which elements are least important to us?
- How much money can we afford to spend?
- What should the atmosphere be at our wedding?
- How large should the wedding be?

That's the Spirit

As you and your future spouse plan the perfect expression of your love and commitment, don't forget to include prayer as a part of your planning process. Praying together about the elements of your wedding will help you to prioritize and find peaceful solutions when you do face disagreements.

May he [God] grant your heart's desire and fulfill all your plans. (Psalm 20:4)

When

Elements of your wedding—such as indoors or outdoors, colors, availability of reception location—may decide the date you choose. If a certain date is your primary concern, other wedding elements may be dictated by it. Either way, it's best to give yourself at least a year for planning. There are some buying advantages to planning for a season a year or more away, too. Whatever season you choose, consider any major holidays that might interfere with your wedding arrangements or with the travel of guests or wedding party attendants.

If you are planning to marry in your home church, check the master calendar before you make any other plans. Some churches only allow weddings on Saturdays and have a cap on how many are allowed each month.

Where

The location of your wedding is also a key element that might influence many other elements in your wedding plans. How formal your wedding will be and how many people you will invite are key elements that might affect your choice of location.

Specific and meaningful sites can sometimes be difficult to book. For example, our town is home to the Air Force Academy. Couples wanting to marry in the Air Force Academy Chapel have to meet certain criteria and then must take whatever dates are available. Spots fill up quickly and certain months are booked years in advance.

If you have your heart set on an outdoor wedding, you will also have to plan your date around the weather (which is always unpredictable!) and the season. We'll talk more about location in the next chapter. But be aware that if a specific location—be it church, park, or castle—is a nonnegotiable element for you or your partner, then you need to say so and work other elements around it.

"I Do" Do's and Don'ts

One of the first things a new bride-to-be will do is buy a bridal magazine hoping for advice and answers to her wedding questions. While thumbing through these admittedly gorgeous glossy cover-to-cover advertisements is entertaining, it is important to remember that the advice contained in these magazines is rarely realistic or applicable to your individual situation. Enjoy the pictures, but don't take any of it too seriously.

How

This gets at how formal or informal an affair you want your wedding to be. The how is really a reflection of your individual personalities, your values, and your beliefs. What is it you want to say with your ceremony? What is it you want your wedding to *do* for you, for each other, and for the guests you invite.

For most Christian couples, the ceremony is held in a church or chapel in acknowledgement of the sanctity and holy nature of the marriage covenant. But that doesn't mean it has to be a strictly formal affair. A small outdoor service can still convey an attitude of worship but allow for a warmer, friendlier atmosphere. It might also be a more child-friendly celebration.

Again, all the elements are inter-related. So your how is bound to affect your where and even your when!

Who

This element has two parts: (1) who will participate, and (2) who will attend. If you absolute must have your college roommate as best man or maid of honor, then by all means do it! Just realize that you might need to make other adjustments to make it happen. If he can't afford the airfare, are you willing to cut back on something else to pay for it? What if she is in grad school and can only come in the summer months? Can you live with a summer wedding? An outdoor, summer wedding? An outdoor, summer wedding in Arizona?

Bet You Didn't Know

In Mexico, it is traditional for an engaged couple to be sponsored by their godparents or *padrinos*. The godparents assist financially with the wedding arrangements and also act as mentors to the bride and groom throughout their engagement and into the early years of their married life. At the wedding, the bride and groom honor the godparents with a special place during the wedding ceremony where the padrinos present the couple with a rosary and a Bible.

One of the most difficult elements to manage is the number of people you invite. This will be an important area to discuss with your family and future in-laws. They might have good reason for including people you might not even consider important. It's all about compromise. If having a sit-down formal dinner at the reception is a nonnegotiable, can you afford that and 200 guests? Maybe you can keep the formal dinner if you cut the guest list to 100. Or you can keep the 200 guests and cut the dinner back to a buffet.

Most couples realize during this process that they can't have it all. Yet the great thing about working together on the essential elements for your special day is that you soon realize you don't *have* to have it all. You only need to have what's important. What's important to you?

Who Pays for What?

By now you're probably starting to think that planning a wedding is all about money. It certainly doesn't have to be! But the financial considerations do play a big part in the planning and the preparations. Your wedding can be as expensive or inexpensive as you plan it. And while traditionally the bride's parents pay the lion's share of expenses, more and more couples are marrying later in life and are able to contribute a substantial amount to their own wedding expenses.

The key to who pays for what is being sensible and considerate and sticking to your budget. As long as your requests are reasonable given the resources of the families involved, and as long as everyone works diligently at communicating throughout the process, there need not be friction over wedding expenses. On the following pages, we have listed for you the way expenses are traditionally broken down between the families. These lists are meant to be guidelines for discussions. You can set your own goals and guidelines with participation from your partner and your families.

> **"I Do" Do's and Don'ts**
>
> Many brides save hundreds of dollars on their dream wedding by enlisting the help of talented friends. My artistically gifted good friend Sheri made all my floral arrangements from silk, including my bouquet, the bridesmaids' brass lantern arrangements, and the top for my wedding cake. We had a great time shopping together for just the right flowers to match my color scheme and everyone in the wedding party had a floral keepsake to take home.

Traditional Family Expenses: Bride

The following are traditionally expenses paid by the bride and her family:

> **Bet You Didn't Know**
>
> The average cost of a formal wedding in the United States is around $15,000. That includes all the extras—rings, flowers, photos, clothing, invitations, and dinner for 200. More than 50 percent of that cost goes to paying for the reception. Of course, you can spend half as much and still have a dream wedding.

- Services of a wedding consultant
- Invitations, announcements, enclosures, and postage
- Bride's wedding dress and accessories
- Bride's bouquet and bridesmaid's flowers
- Rental of site for ceremony and/or reception
- Decorations for ceremony and reception
- Formal wedding photographs
- Videotape recording of the ceremony
- Music for the ceremony and reception
- Transportation of the bridal party to the ceremony
- Transportation for the wedding party to the reception

- All expenses for the reception
- Bride's presents to her attendants
- Bride's gift to groom
- The groom's wedding ring
- Bride's physical and/or blood test
- Accommodations for bride's attendants, if from out-of-town
- Bridesmaids' luncheon
- Thank you notes

The following are traditionally expenses paid by the bride's attendants:

- Dress and all accessories for wedding
- Transportation to and from the town where wedding takes place
- An individual gift for the couple
- A shower and/or luncheon for the bride

Traditional Family Expenses: Groom

The following are traditionally expenses paid by the groom and his family:

- Bride's engagement and wedding rings
- Groom's present to his bride
- Groom's attire (rental of formal wear)
- The minister's fee
- The marriage license fee
- Groom's physical and/or blood test
- Gifts for groom's attendants
- Accommodations for groom's attendants, if from out-of-town
- Boutonnieres for the groom's attendants
- Going away corsage for the bride
- Corsages for immediate family members of both families (unless the bride has included them in her florist's order)

- Transportation for the groom and best man to the ceremony
- All costs of the rehearsal dinner
- Bachelor dinner
- Transportation and lodging for groom's parents
- All honeymoon expenses

The following are traditionally expenses paid by the groom's attendants:

- Rental of wedding attire
- Transportation to and from the wedding location
- An individual gift for the couple
- A bachelor dinner or party

Make a Budget and Stick to It!

As you and your future spouse discuss and decide on the important elements of your dream wedding, you need to talk seriously about a wedding budget. Budgets can feel as friendly as a trip to the dentist for a root canal. But few of us have the resources to spend without limit. Start looking at your budget as a tool that will help you:

- Negotiate with parents and vendors.
- Decide what is most important to you and your partner.
- Manage a very stressful part of planning your major event.
- Act as a reality check when wedding fantasies get out of hand.

So start saying to yourselves "Our budget is our friend!" Be realistic when setting it—the goal should be keeping everyone involved out of debt—and write it down. Writing it down is important so everyone is clear on what was decided and how you are doing with the overall expenses as the planning progresses. For example, if you have budgeted $800.00 for the wedding dress but find your "dream" dress for $1200.00, a written budget will show you what other wedding elements you will need to compromise on to buy that dress. With that information on hand, the "Is it worth it?" question practically answers itself.

Your wedding is a once-in-a-lifetime celebration. You want everything to be perfect—just as you have envisioned it! Or you might find yourself comparing your wedding preparations to those of others. As the financial realities hit, you might feel cheated by having to stick to a budget. A marriage that starts out with financial debt faces additional stress and frustration and long-term sacrifice. It just doesn't make sense to allow your wedding celebration to add to this burden.

> **That's the Spirit**
>
> Many couples give in to the temptation to "have it all" by going into serious debt for their dream wedding. Try to keep your wedding preparations in perspective. Your marriage is for a lifetime; your wedding is just one day.
>
> Just as the rich rule the poor, so the borrower is servant to the lender. (Proverbs 22:7)

With careful planning and creative willpower you can have a beautiful wedding without blowing your budget. Don't forget to use the Wedding Budget Worksheet (Appendix B) we have prepared for you in the back of the book. Make a copy of it and put it in your wedding planner, notebook, or file. Refer to it often as you make the many decisions necessary for putting together your dream wedding, and stick to it!

Selecting Your Attendants

Most people are very honored when asked to be part of a couple's very special day. You and your future spouse want to surround yourselves with people you love and enjoy and who will encourage and support you. Two key members of the wedding party—the maid or matron of honor and the best man—should be a part of your early discussions with your partner. Other attendants can be chosen from close family members and friends. It is not essential to have the same number of bride's attendants and groom's attendants unless you are planning to pair them up for the processional or recessional. And there are a lot of other opportunities to include family and friends who want to be a part of your special day.

The Maid or Matron of Honor

Usually the maid or matron of honor is the bride's sister or best friend. The term maid of honor is used for an unmarried woman and matron of honor is for a married woman. Her primary responsibility is to attend to the bride before, during, and after the ceremony. She might be asked to help with the planning of the wedding, attend to the bride before and during the ceremony, and the assist in any other way needed. It is also acceptable to have both a maid and matron of honor. These are the duties of the maid or matron of honor:

- Helps the bride address the invitations
- Makes decorations or favors for the reception
- Runs errands
- Plans and/or hosts a shower for the bride
- Attends the wedding rehearsal and rehearsal dinner or party
- Arrives at least an hour before the ceremony (or earlier) at the bride's request
- Walks down the aisle just before the bride (unless there is a flower girl)
- Signs the marriage license as a legal witness
- Helps the bride dress on her wedding day
- Holds the bride's bouquet during the ceremony
- Keeps the groom's ring
- Assists the bride with her veil and train at the altar

Your maid or matron of honor should be someone who is responsible and willing to take on some additional tasks to make your wedding day perfect for you. She should be someone you trust and who will put your wishes first. She might also be asked to participate in the ceremony by reading Scripture, a poem, or other text. Above all, she should be someone you feel comfortable around—someone who can put you at ease and help calm your nervousness.

Bridesmaids

You might choose as many sisters or relatives (from both families) and close friends as seems appropriate for the size of wedding you have chosen.

Bridesmaids should …

- Assist with prewedding errands and preparations when asked.
- Help the maid or matron of honor with the bridal shower.

- Attend the wedding rehearsal and rehearsal dinner or party.
- Arrive at the church at least one hour before the ceremony or earlier at the bride's request.

Most relatives and friends consider it an honor to be chosen as an attendant for a wedding. But for some, it might present a financial hardship or it might conflict with other plans or commitments. And sometimes the reasons just don't make sense. Don't be thin-skinned. If someone turns down your invitation to participate in your wedding for reasons that cannot be overcome, try not to let it interfere with either your friendship or your perfect day.

One bride had a close friend who refused to be a bridesmaid because she didn't think the style of the bridesmaids' dress was flattering to her and she didn't want to invest money in a dress she would not wear again. All the other bridesmaids were pleased with the dress, and the bride did not have time to start her search over. Not wanting to exclude her friend from the wedding party entirely, the bride decided to ask her friend to attend to the guest book and chose another friend as a bridesmaid. Her friend agreed, bought her own dress in a complimentary color, and the friendship survived this wedding drama.

Best Man

Traditionally, the best man is the groom's brother and/or best friend. He is the groom's counterpart to the maid of honor and should be a trusted and responsible assistant to the groom. Some of the best man's duties include the following:

- Assists the groom with wedding transportation
- Organizes the bachelor party or dinner
- Participates in rehearsal and rehearsal dinner
- Makes sure all groomsmen attend their fittings
- Organizes and contributes to gift for groom from groomsmen
- Helps groom dress and prepare
- Encourages and reassures the groom
- Accompanies groom to wedding, arriving early for photos
- Holds marriage license and officiant's fee
- Keeps the bride's wedding ring until the wedding ceremony

- Makes sure the ushers know the schedule of wedding day events
- Makes sure that the ushers know of special seating arrangements
- Decorates the bride and groom's departing car
- Holds the bride's ring during ceremony
- Participates in ceremony as requested by the groom
- Offers first toast or blessing at the reception

The best man should be someone who can put the groom at ease and is willing to jump in and help keep the groom organized by running errands, making telephone calls, and so on. In Hollywood, he is usually the former boyfriend of the bride, but that doesn't work well in real life!

Ushers or Groomsmen

Additional friends, brothers of the bride and groom, and other close relatives can be asked to be groomsmen or ushers. The responsibilities of the ushers or groomsmen include the following:

- Attends fittings for formal wear
- Attends bachelor party and/or dinner
- Participates in rehearsal and rehearsal dinner
- Contributes to gift for groom from groomsmen
- Arrives on time at ceremony for photos and instructions
- Checks with wedding coordinator or best man for special seating assignments at ceremony
- Knows of any special events for the ceremony or reception
- Helps best man decorate departing car for wedding couple
- Helps seat guests in appropriate areas at the ceremony
- Attends the reception

There is some art in good ushering. If some places have been reserved, the ushers should have a list of guests to be seated in the reserved section. Guests should be treated courteously. The usher should always extend his arm to a lady. If seating is being arranged with the bride's family and friends on one side of the aisle and the groom's family and friends on the other, the usher needs to ask each guest "Are you a friend of the bride or groom?" Otherwise, the ushers should balance the seating between both sides.

Children in the Wedding Party

There is nothing more adorable than a little girl or boy all dressed up and making their way down the aisle. Children in a wedding add a very special touch and are especially endearing if they are a close part of your family circle. But remember—kids say and do the most kidlike things! They are not very predictable and have short memories for instructions. They tire easily and get restless and cranky. Still, many couples wouldn't have a wedding without them. Here are some parts children can play in your wedding party:

- **Flower girl**—The flower girl is usually three to six years of age. Traditionally, she carries a basket and scatters flower petals down the aisle just before the bride's entrance. Or she might simply carry flowers arranged in a basket. Her dress is paid for by her parents, and she should be included in the wedding rehearsal. Whatever wedding activities she is invited to should also include one or both of her parents.

- **Ring bearer**—The ring bearer is usually a boy and also three to six years of age. He is responsible for carrying down the aisle a decorated cushion (usually white velvet or satin) with a ring or rings fastened with white thread. Often the rings on the cushion are fake—the real wedding rings are carried by the maid of honor and best man. The ring bearer also attends the rehearsal attended by his parents. His outfit is paid for by his parents.

- **Junior bridesmaids and groomsmen**—These young people are traditionally 10 to 13 years of age. They are part of the processional and dress to match the adult attendants. They attend the rehearsal and the rehearsal dinner. Their parents pay for their outfits. Their jobs might include lighting candles, unrolling the aisle runner, distributing programs, or any other duty suitable to their age.

Other wedding positions for children include the following: train bearer (age: 4 to 8); gift attendant (age: 13 and up); Scripture reader (age: 14 and up); greeter (age: 13 and up); guest book attendant (age: 12 and up); candle lighter (age: 10 and up); program attendant (age: 10 and up).

Schedule

Part of getting organized is listing all the tasks that need to be completed and when they should be done. The more you can do early, the less stressful your final month before the wedding will be. But some tasks have to be done within a certain time frame. Listed here are some general guidelines for scheduling the many tasks that go into planning and preparing for your dream wedding.

What to do 6 to 12 months before the wedding:

- Announce engagement
- Arrange for families to meet
- Have a formal portrait taken of you and your partner
- Decide on wedding elements and priorities
- Create a budget. Use the Wedding Budget Worksheet (Appendix B)
- Select a wedding date
- Hire a wedding consultant, if desired
- Select and invite friends and relatives to be part of your wedding party (attendants): maid or matron of honor, bridesmaids, flower girl, ring bearer, best man, groomsmen, and ushers.
- Compile a list of guests for the bride's side and for the groom's side
- Reserve ceremony site
- Investigate and reserve reception site
- Schedule premarital counseling
- Select invitations, enclosures, and other wedding stationery
- Order bridal gown, headpiece, and veil
- Select color scheme
- Choose attire for bridal party
- Investigate and interview: photographers, videographers, caterers, florists, bands/DJs, baker (wedding cake and desserts)

What to do three to six months before the wedding:

- Contract the following: photographer, videographer, caterer, music for reception

- Finalize floral selections and contract with florist
- Finalize wedding cake selection and contract with baker
- Interview and investigate transportation companies, if desired
- Schedule fittings for wedding dress
- Reserve location for the rehearsal dinner
- Request dimensions and set-up diagram of hall or garden for reception site so you can plan a seating chart
- Finalize honeymoon plans
- Finalize music selection for ceremony and arrange for musicians

Family Ties

There are lots of ways besides the wedding party to include family members in your wedding celebration. The *guest book attendant* greets guests as they arrive and encourages them to sign the guest book. *Readers* during the ceremony can bless the couple with a scriptural, inspirational or poetic reading. And someone needs to ensure that guests receive birdseed, flower petals, or bubbles to "shower" on the newlyweds as they depart the festivities.

What to do two to three months before the wedding:

- Finalize your guest list
- Order invitations
- Address and mail out invitations
- Make accommodation arrangements for out-of-town guests
- Get physical and/or blood tests
- Schedule a wedding day appointment for hair, nails, and make-up
- Confirm wedding day itinerary with a transportation company
- Buy gifts for attendants: (best man, ushers, maid of honor, bridesmaid's and others)
- Purchase party favors for reception

What to do three to eight weeks before the wedding:

- All RSVPs should be in so you can finalize your seating arrangement
- Purchase a guest book and special pen for wedding day
- Attend final fittings for the bride and her attendants
- Finalize church plans with clergy
- Check with all vendors to make sure everything is on track
- Confirm rehearsal events
- Pick up wedding rings
- Get marriage license and complete necessary forms for name change

Bride's Final Checklist

In the final weeks, there are many remaining tasks that can tax your energy reserve at a time when you are already feeling stressed and vulnerable. This is the time to let go of certain tasks that others can confidently do for you. It is especially important not to neglect your future spouse during these final days before your big day. Let others work with the final arrangements (consulting you as necessary) so that you can spend time as a couple.

What to do two weeks before the wedding:

- Finalize ceremony seating and make a list for the ushers of special guests and where they should be seated
- Give caterer a final count for reception
- Reconfirm with all vendors
- Pack for honeymoon
- Check your checklist to make sure you haven't forgotten anything

What to do the day before the wedding:

- Pick up rented attire.
- Attend the rehearsal and dinner. Rest easy, everything is going to be beautiful.
- Get a good night's sleep.

For a complete guide to what to do on your wedding day, see Chapter 13.

What to do after the wedding day:

- Keep a list of wedding gifts received
- Mail out personal thank you notes

Groom's Final Checklist

Your main duty in the final days before your wedding is to attend to your bride! Try to keep her as relaxed and stress-free as possible. Remind her often of how much you love her. Then attend to the other responsibilities listed for you here.

What to do one to two weeks before the wedding:

- Give the best man the rings
- Give the best man a sealed envelope with the officiant's fee
- Pick up the honeymoon tickets

What to do the day before the wedding:

- Pick up rented attire
- Attend the rehearsal and dinner
- Pack for honeymoon
- Get a good night's sleep

What to do the day of the wedding:

- Pack a bag with essential toiletries, a hairbrush, and a change of clothes for after the reception
- Arrive early for photos
- Relax and enjoy!

Chapter 9

Finding the Perfect Spot

Where you get married should have special significance to you and your partner. Because of the sacred nature of Christian marriage, most couples choose to have their ceremony in a place of worship—the home church of the bride or her family, the home church of the groom or his family, or in a church or chapel chosen for its location or ambiance. However, God will be present wherever you choose to marry, and vows exchanged in a garden, at the seashore, on a ranch, or in your own backyard will be just as sacred and just as blessed as those exchanged in a church.

Your choice of location for your wedding ceremony and reception is a decision that should be made early in the planning process because it might influence many of the other elements for your big day. It is a key element in establishing the kind of wedding you and your groom are dreaming of: Do you want formal or informal? Will it be indoors or outdoors? By talking through your wedding desires and with careful planning, you can find the perfect spot for your wedding day.

> **Bet You Didn't Know**
>
> More than 75 percent of all wedding ceremonies are held in a house of worship, but that percentage can vary by state (from 97 percent in West Virginia to less than 40 percent in New York). Although a church, chapel, or temple remains the site of choice for most couples, there are many other wedding site options available. Here are just a few: city or state parks, historic sites, private homes, museums, ranches/farms, private clubs, and gardens.

A Significant Site

Your home church might be the only location you've ever considered appropriate for your special day. Weddings are one of the best things about being part of a community of faith. It's a great blessing to get married among people who have watched you grow from childhood to the young adult you are today. But it's also likely that you, your parents, or your future spouse attend a different place of worship. No matter which church you choose, you'll need to check out the following to ensure your special day goes smoothly.

What Do You Need to Do First?

Requirements for marrying in a church can vary greatly—from one denomination to another and between churches within the same denomination. Some churches require that you have completed a membership course and have been accepted as a member of their congregation before you can get married in their sanctuary. In some cases, you can get married in a church if your parents are members there even if you are not.

Most churches now require that you complete a series of premarital classes or that you complete premarital counseling with a pastoral staff member. If this is not a requirement, we still highly recommend it (see Chapter 4). You and your future partner will want to get started with your premarital counseling right away.

Who Will Officiate?

Another common requirement in churches is that the person performing the ceremony be the pastor of the church or an ordained minister who is part of the church staff. If you have a family member or close friend who you would prefer perform the ceremony or if you and your partner are from different churches and you want

to involve both of your ministers, you can often arrange to have more than one officiant share in the ceremony responsibilities.

That's the Spirit

I was glad when they said to me, "Let us go to the house of the Lord." (Psalm 122:1)
A wedding ceremony is first and foremost an act of worship because marriage is a sacred
covenant. It is also a celebration that embraces your family and friends. It seems then that a
place of worship would be the right location for such a significant event.

If you wouldn't dream of getting married by anyone other than your own pastor,
make sure he will be available for the date you have planned. Ask him about premarital counseling—what does he require and will he conduct it? How involved will
he be in the planning of the ceremony? Can you have input? Can you write your
own vows (see Chapter 12)?

Ask if he will file the paperwork after the ceremony. Finally, let him know you
would like to pay him and ask how much is customary.

Is the Date Set?

You, your partner, and your family can discuss the perfect date for your wedding,
but until you book the site of the ceremony, you might have to stay flexible. One of
the first questions you'll want to ask the church staff is whether or not the date you
have chosen for your wedding is available. Many churches give church program-
ming priority over weddings and might only open their facilities for weddings on
Friday evenings and Saturdays. So if you have your heart set on a June wedding,
you only have four Saturday dates to choose from, so call early. And while holiday
weddings can be lovely, Christmas is one of the busiest seasons for a church.

When asking about the availability of the church for a specific date, don't forget to
ask what other events are scheduled the day before, the day of, and the day after the
date you've chosen. You will want to be sure you can use the sanctuary the day
before your wedding for your wedding rehearsal. The day of your wedding, it will
be important to know what other groups might be using the facilities or if there is
another wedding before or after yours that might create conflict. Other activities at
the church can affect your access to parking, the availability of church staff (including musicians and clergy), and the ambiance of your special day (imagine Youth

Group Blowout vs. Your Wedding). And if your church is planning a major musical/ theatrical production for the day after your wedding, you might find the sanctuary under construction or full of props (think of a holiday we all know that might include stable, straw, and live animals).

Who's in Charge?

Many churches have either a paid or volunteer wedding coordinator you must use. The responsibilities (and power) of the church wedding coordinator varies greatly from church to church. In most cases, she will be your main point of contact with the church and will tell you all about church policy and what you can and can't do. If she's been in her position for a while, she might prove to be a great source of recommendations for photographers, caterers, florists, and other wedding contacts. The right person in this position can be a tremendous blessing—giving advice, negotiating difficult situations between family members, and ensuring that your wedding day goes off on time and without a hitch. But remember, as a church staff member her primary job is to represent the interests of the church.

Is What You See What You Get?

Don't assume that because you are a member of a congregation that you will be able to use the facilities for free. Keep in mind that the church incurs certain expenses whenever the facilities are in use, so any fee you might be charged will go toward reimbursing staff, covering utilities, and paying for clean-up and maintenance. Fees for use of the site vary widely from church to church and even state to state. Ask up front about all costs for using the facilities and make sure to write them into your wedding budget.

There are many details you will want to make clear before you book your church. Here is a list of things to think about and guide you in your conversations with the church staff:

- Is there a wedding coordinator?
- Can you bring your own, and how will the coordinators work together during the event(s)?
- Can you bring your own officiant or do you have to use the church's? Can you use both?
- Do they require approval of your vows or music?

- What is the cost for using the facilities?
- Does that include the ceremony, rehearsal, clean up, musicians, and sound system person?
- How many people does the sanctuary seat comfortably? How many additional people could be accommodated, if necessary?
- How is parking handled and are there additional fees?
- Are there any restrictions on decorations—candles, flowers, and so on?
- Do they require you to use their candelabras, arches, arbors, kneelers, and other equipment or can you bring in rental equipment?
- Do they have a sound system? Can they provide someone to run it?
- Are there restrictions on what kind of music you are allowed to have and who can play it?
- Can you use their instruments? Who can play those?
- Can you photograph inside the building? During the ceremony?
- Is there a place for the bride to dress before the wedding? What about the groom and other bridal party members?
- What can be thrown after the wedding (petals, rice, birdseed)?

With so many details going into your special day, you can see how important it will be to start out and remain on good terms with those at the church who will help make your day perfect. Be polite and respectful, patient and forgiving as you deal with these hard-working servants of the Lord.

The Party's Here

Right after you book the ceremony site and wedding date, you need to turn your attention to the reception site! The best reception sites are often booked 9 to 12 months in advance. If you are having the ceremony at a church, you might want to see if they also have a facility for receptions. If they do, check it out. Keep in mind, however, that if you hold your reception at the same place as the ceremony, all guests should be invited to both. More and more couples are choosing an alternate location for their after-wedding celebration. So don't hesitate to check out other spots for your after-the-wedding celebration.

Family Ties

If your parents are footing the bill for your wedding, then by all means include them in the decisions you are making regarding your location. Take Mom along to check out reception sites and include Dad for the taste tests. Sometimes it's good for them to see what their money is buying. Be sensitive to their budget limitations and don't take them places where the price list will give them cardiac arrest.

What You Need to Know

Before you pick up the telephone and schedule any appointments to view sites, you will need to know how many guests you plan to invite to your reception. The number of guests at the reception can vary significantly from the number of guests at the ceremony. You might want to have a very, small private ceremony followed by a larger reception, or you might want to have a large number of people witness the exchange of wedding vow but have a smaller number attend the celebration after. These decisions will need to be decided before you can choose a reception site.

There are a lot of options besides your church when it comes to reception sites, some you might be familiar with and others you might not. Hotels, catering halls, private clubs, and restaurants are popular options. But you might also look into museums, historic sites, theaters, ranches, private estates, and bed and breakfast inns. If the location and ambiance for your reception is high on your priority list, you'll want to start looking early because the best places tend to book up quickly.

Be Sure to Visit the Site

Recommendations from friends and family, bridal shows, advertisements in bride magazines, and the Internet are all good places to start your search. But don't make any decision until you actually visit the site. Use the telephone to narrow down your choices by calling and confirming whether or not your wedding date is available before you schedule an appointment for a visit. Visit several of your top choices to check out the following:

- Will this location accommodate your number of guests comfortably?
- Is the space adequate for the type of reception you want (buffet, sit-down dinner, dancing)?
- Can we afford it?

- How is the lighting?
- Does it have the right atmosphere?
- Is it well managed?

When you meet with the catering manager, be honest about your budget. Ask for examples of how the site can be set up and see if you can stop back by before an actual reception to see the real thing. Find out what the rental fee includes: food, beverage, china, linens, centerpieces, service, and so on and get any verbal promises in writing. Ask about your particular date: Is there anything else happening at the site on your day? It's best to get exclusive use of the facilities if possible. What hours—from when to when—does the rental agreement cover? Does that include any necessary set-up or tear-down time?

After you make your decision, put down the smallest deposit possible and use a credit card. Deposits made by cash or check leave you little legal recourse should things go terribly wrong.

Make sure the contract states all the specific details including the date, hours, rental fee, any other charges, and number of guests. Also, confirm that whoever signs the contract will be available or on-call at the time of your reception to take care of any problems. Make a note to check back at least a month prior to your wedding date to go over the details one last time so they are fresh in everyone's mind and to answer any last-minute questions.

"I Do" Do's and Don'ts

Watch out for the surprise costs of home weddings. If your backyard is your ceremony/reception site, you will probably want to work on the landscape a bit to make it just perfect. If you're thinking of renting a tent, you might be looking at a $500 to $1,000 bill. Need more tables, chairs, plates, silverware, linens, and glassware? All can be rented, for a price. Before you know it, any savings from hosting the event yourself can be quickly eaten up with unexpected costs.

Home Sweet Home

For small, informal weddings, you might choose to use your home or the home of a close family member or friend. A backyard wedding can be very intimate and can be less expensive. But it does take a great deal of planning to pull it off perfectly (think about the movie *Father of the Bride*). Home weddings often include both the wedding ceremony and the reception and at least one or both are held outdoors, so you will need to keep in mind the season and have a "foul-weather" plan in place just in case. Having your wedding in your home can provide a delightful location and serve as a lasting family memory.

Things to Consider First

Keep in mind the number of guests you plan to invite and evaluate whether or not the location can handle it. If you are planning to have the ceremony and reception outdoors, sketch out a plan that shows realistically how you can place enough tables and chairs to accommodate your guests. Consider also any access to the house that will be needed: kitchen, bathrooms, and so on. Talk with your neighbors to ensure cooperation with the increase of traffic and noise. If the weather turns foul, what will you do? Is the location for the ceremony in a place where guests can see and hear what is going on? If not, what's the point?

Family Ties

A wedding at home is a great way to involve your entire family in your wedding preparations. Even younger brothers and sisters can pitch in and feel like they've made a big contribution to your special day. Home weddings can also put a lot of pressure on your family. You want your wedding to be an enjoyable occasion for your parents as well. Try to keep things simple, help out as much as you can, and if you see that mom is stressing out, try to arrange for her to have a break.

Let's Get Organized

It takes someone very organized to successfully pull off a home wedding. If that's not you or your mother, get some help! Set up a timeline and a list of who is responsible for doing what. Be realistic in your expectations of what any one person can do in an allotted amount of time. Try to delegate as many duties as possible to those outside of the wedding party: prepping the lawn and flowerbeds, picking up rental equipment, setting up tables and chairs, decorating, food service, and clean-up are all responsibilities that can be handed off to other capable hands.

Do as much preparation ahead of time as possible. Don't try to cram everything into the last day or two before the wedding. If you are preparing your own food, choose dishes that can be made up ahead of time. Rearrange furniture and clean indoors as far ahead of time as possible. Try not to schedule the ceremony too early on the wedding day so that you have plenty of time for last-minute preparations.

Mind the Details

It's important to take in every detail when planning a backyard wedding. For example, latticework over the ceremony site sounds quaint but the shadows it might cast on the bridal party can make for checkered photographs. Here are a few other details to watch for:

- Your invitations should clearly indicate the location is a private home. Be sure to give an exact address and consider including a map and/or parking instructions.

- The ground should be level and not too soft. Set up a few test rows of chairs and actually sit in them to see if your weight sinks the legs into the ground or if you find yourself listing to one side.

- Cakes are fragile and should not be left outdoors for very long. Do you have a place indoors designated for the cake until just before it's needed?

- Nice linens and covered chairs add a classic touch to a wedding and reception. Covered chairs are also more comfortable than metal chairs that have been sitting out in the summer sun. Ouch!

- If your yard is smaller than your reception guest list, consider having a smaller number of guests for the ceremony and schedule the reception as an open house where guest can come and go.

- If using cut flowers, choose varieties that hold up well in the heat of the day.

- Set up your serving tables under shade and have plenty of ice on hand to keep things fresh.

- Post a list of emergency numbers next to the telephone and have a first aid kit and a fire extinguisher where they can be easily accessed.

- Provide a special area in the house for changing diapers—far away from the festivities and out of the view of other guests.

- Designate one room just for wraps and handbags and ask someone to keep an eye on it.

That's the Spirit

For the Lord is a great God, the great King above all gods. He owns the depths of the earth, and even the mightiest mountains are his. (Psalm 95:3–4)

You can choose to have your wedding in the quiet calm of a church sanctuary or against the majestic backdrop of God's magnificent creation. Wherever you are, you will find yourself in his presence.

Whether the site you choose is a church or a ranch, your backyard or the beach, there is a lot you can do to transform your ceremony and reception locations into the perfect setting for your wedding. Flowers, plants, candelabras, and canopies can all be used to change the ordinary to the extraordinary. Just a note of caution: Costs for creating the perfect atmosphere can add up quickly. Always keep in mind the bottom line, stick to your budget, and remember what's really important is that you and your life mate are happy with the effect that is created.

Perfectly Pretty Posies

Flowers play an important part in any wedding. In fact, some brides spend more money on flowers than they do for their dress and wedding ensemble. Although it's important to "dress up" your ceremony and reception site, it's also possible to have a beautiful selection of floral arrangements without blowing your budget.

One of the first choices you will make regarding flowers is whether to use real or silk. There are pros and cons for both, so the decision can be a tough one. Let's take a look at what each option has to offer you:

- **Real flowers**—Traditionally, brides have chosen real flowers for their scent and texture. Many people have an emotional attachment to real flowers and feel that a wedding is one occasion that "deserves" the extravagance of something so lovely yet so temporary. But don't let emotion or tradition make your decision for you. There are some drawbacks to real flowers. Real flowers fade and wilt after a few days and can become torn or bruised during transportation. Using real flowers might also significantly limit your selection depending on your location and the season of your wedding. Cost is another factor to consider. If you have your heart set on a particular out-of-season or exotic posy for your bouquet, you can expect to pay a pretty penny for it.

- **Silk Flowers**—As the quality of silk flowers has increased, they have become a more popular choice for wedding arrangements. Today, there are many realistic looking silks out there in rich colors and textures. One advantage to silk flowers is that they are generally less expensive. And there's no need to worry about not being able to get your favorite flower even if it is out-of-season. Another advantage is that silk arrangements can be made up several weeks in advance instead of the day before required by fresh flowers. Perhaps the biggest advantage to silk flowers is that after the wedding you and your bridal party can have a lasting keepsake of your special day. The biggest disadvantage is that silk flowers don't smell like real flowers so you'll have to find another way to have the romantic scents of traditional bridal flowers like roses, orange blossoms, and lily of the valley if you choose silk.

One last factor in your choice might be a major one—allergies. If you or anyone in your bridal party will be made miserable by the presence of real flowers, silk might be the better option. You want only tears of joy on your special day.

Bet You Didn't Know

The average florist's bill for a medium-sized wedding can run between $600 to $1000. Why so expensive? Unless you've chosen exotic or out-of-season flowers, the posies themselves are relatively inexpensive, making up about a third of the total cost. In most cases, you're paying for the arrangements, service and delivery, and the florist's overhead. You can save big bucks by buying your own flowers wholesale or in silk and getting a talented friend or relative to arrange them for you.

Whether you choose silk or stick with real flowers, you'll want to work with a florist you can trust. Start by asking for recommendations from family or friends, your wedding consultant, or bridal shows and publications. Before you make up your mind, meet with two or three different florists to get estimates. Use the Floral Worksheet that follows to help you think through your floral needs.

Worksheet for Floral Needs

Wedding colors: _____

Floral preferences:_____

Bridal bouquet: _____

Bridesmaids' bouquets: _____

Boutonnieres: _____

Mothers' corsages: _____

Flower girl basket:_____

Others: _____

Ceremony site: _____

Altar flowers: _____

Aisle runner: _____

Arrangements for pews: _____

Arch or canopy: _____

Candelabras: _____

Reception: _____

 Cake table flowers: _____

 Flowers for cake top/decoration: _____

 Centerpieces: _____

 Other: _____

Here are a few other things you might like to know before you go:

- It helps to take along any photos that show the type of flowers or the style of arrangement you like. You can collect pictures from magazine or photos from friends' weddings.

- A swatch of cloth from the bridesmaids' dresses indicating the color and style and a picture of your wedding gown will help your florist choose colors and arrangements that match.

- Be clear on your budget and don't compromise. Make sure that any estimates you're given include "hidden costs" such as delivery and set-up fees. Don't use a florist that charges a consultation fee.

- Ask if the florist has pictures from weddings he or she has done that you can look at and how many weddings they do in a day.

- If you are considering renting other items from the florist, such as an arch, candelabras, or aisle runner, call a rental store that specializes in occasions first so you have an accurate cost comparison.

Even on a budget, you can have beautiful flowers for your special day. Instead of a big and expensive bouquet, consider carrying a single elegant long-stemmed flower such as a calla lily or a few roses. Assign the bridesmaids' bouquets double-duty by using them after the ceremony at the reception to decorate the cake table. If you know someone else who is having a wedding the same day and at the same location as you, consider sharing floral arrangements and/or rentals for the sanctuary. This can add up to a considerable cost savings for both of you. Finally, think about alternative ways to dress up your location that might save you time and money—fabric and ribbons; potted trees and plants; greenery and baby's breath for the pew decorations; and seasonal decorations such as ivy or evergreen swags and branches from flowering bushes and trees.

"I Do" Do's and Don'ts

Do have your florist or whoever is handling your flowers label the personal flowers—corsages for mothers and servers, boutonnieres for fathers and groomsmen, and bouquets for bridesmaids—with names according to the list you provide. It will help to sort out and distribute the flowers quickly before the ceremony and you won't have to worry about Aunt Candice walking off with the special corsage you ordered for your groom's great-grandmother.

Delightful Lighting

Light is symbolic of the sacred, both passionate and pure. The right kind of lighting can help create the perfect setting for your wedding ceremony. Sometimes the right lighting might be just a matter of timing. Just picture a late morning wedding in a sanctuary where sunlight is streaming through stained glass windows.

For evening weddings, candlelight provides the perfect blend of the sacred and the romantic. Candelabras can be placed at the front of the sanctuary and decorated with ferns, flowers, ribbons, or tulle. You can also rent lanterns that can grace the aisle. Imagine walking through the glow of candlelight. One bride had each of her attendants carry candles in small brass hurricane lamp decorated with small flowers and ribbons instead of the traditional bouquet.

Lighting can play a big part at your evening reception as well. Floating candles in shallow glass dishes make inexpensive centerpieces and they're also not too tall to talk over. A single pillar candle surrounded by a floral ring is another centerpiece option that combines flowers and candlelight for a nice romantic effect.

Start paying attention to how lighting is used to enhance weddings and other ceremonies in your church. Check for any regulations your ceremony and reception sites have regarding candles before you make any final decisions.

What's the Deal with Destination Weddings?

This is such a fast-growing trend that we just had to mention it. More than 10 percent of all weddings today are destination weddings. So what is it? A destination wedding is when you and your future spouse travel to a special place for your wedding. The location is usually exotic or offers activities you can't really get just anywhere. The difference between a destination wedding and eloping is that with a destination wedding you take your family and friends with you!

What's the Attraction?

More and more couples getting married today are ready to pass up the hassle of planning a big traditional wedding in favor of a smaller, more meaningful ceremony and celebration. They would rather have a wedding that allows them to spend quality time with their closest family and friends instead of several hours with hundreds of people they might barely get to speak to in the course of the day.

Keep in mind that a destination wedding is a combination of wedding, reception, honeymoon, and family vacation! Although some destination weddings geared more for fun and entertainment (like Disney World and Las Vegas) are not in keeping with the worshipful nature most Christian couples desire, there are other spots that can provide the sacred experience you want and still deliver the benefits of a destination wedding. For instance, a wedding with mountains or ocean in the background helps you both to contemplate the wonders of God's creation. You can keep all the elements of your wedding that are important to you—writing your own vows, your dress, the cake, and so on.

How Does It Work?

The two main elements to consider are where to go and who to invite. Unless you or your family is picking up the tab for everyone, guests are responsible for paying for their own transportation and lodging. Think also about the season and weather patterns for the location you want and make sure you are planning to go at a good time. The cost of a destination wedding can be the same as or less than a traditional wedding.

The first thing to do is *choose a location*. Any resort location can probably accommodate a wedding so check out your favorite resort destination first. Or check out one of the websites (we've listed a couple in the resources) that offer wedding destination packages. Some airlines even offer discounts for wedding event travel. Here are just a few popular choices you can check out on the Internet or at their state Visitor's Bureau of Tourism:

- **Hawaii**—A real tropical delight. Imagine taking your vows on a black sand beach or at the foot of a misty waterfall.
- **Yosemite**—Mountains, pristine lakes, and fields of wildflowers.
- **Vermont**—A riot of color in the fall and oh, so romantic in the wintertime.
- **Rocky Mountains of Colorado**—Snow-capped mountains and shockingly blue skies with many affordable locations.
- **Florida and Key West**—Mickey's place isn't the only wedding destination spot in this versatile state. Beautiful beaches and warm sunny weather are available even in the winter months.

Overseas destinations require a little more planning but are well worth the effort. If you plan on getting married overseas, be sure to check out thoroughly any legal requirements. Take a look at England, Wales, Ireland, Scotland, France, and Italy. You can even have a safari wedding in Kenya, Africa, and there's always a cruise to the Caribbean.

Next, you need to decide on the *guests to invite*. One of the benefits to a destination wedding is the quality time it allows you to spend with close family and friends, so keep your guest list short. Destination weddings can be for a week or a weekend. The atmosphere is relaxed instead of rushed, allowing your families to get to know each other better—a good way to introduce the relatives. Only invite those people you are fairly certain will be able to come. Because this number will be small, you can send handwritten invitations, make telephone calls, or invite your guests personally.

Because arrangements for some destinations need to be pretty far in advance, and invitations traditionally go out just four to six weeks before the wedding, couples who choose destination weddings sometimes send a "Save the Date" letter to their guests several months prior to the event. After the wedding, it is perfectly appropriate to send out invitations to a reception in your hometown or announcements to share the good news of your nuptials.

Although destination weddings are not for everyone, only you and your partner can decide if it's the right choice for you. Be ready to encounter some resistance from traditional family members and friends, especially if they are paying for the wedding. It does take the cooperation of everyone invited to make it work. On the flip side, destination weddings allow couples to be surrounded by a loving community of people for more than just a few hours or a day. For some couples, it might be the perfect way to start their married life together.

Chapter 10

Perfect Wedding Etiquette

For an occasion as important as your wedding, it's only natural to want to be sure you are doing everything properly. But with so many things to think about, you might find your thoughts in a whirl over whether to go formal, semiformal, or casual, who to place on the guest list, and wording the invitation correctly. The good news is that there are books and websites galore that can walk you through every possible etiquette question.

Rules of wedding etiquette have changed significantly with the changes in our culture over the years, and they continue to change. So before bowing to a rule that doesn't seem to fit your situation or what you desire for your wedding, consider if it isn't one of those areas where you can apply some flexibility. Keep the main thing—your marriage—the main thing, not the rules.

What's Your Wedding Style

The style of your wedding sets the tone for many aspects of your wedding and depends on the choices you make regarding the location of your ceremony and reception, the size of the wedding party, and the number of guests you will invite. The simple question is "Just how fancy do you want your wedding to be?" The level of formality might also determine the amount of money in your wedding budget. Other aspects that will be reflected in your decision of style include your attire, your invitation, time of day for ceremony and reception, and so on.

Here are some guidelines to help you decide what style of wedding you want:

Formal—Typically church weddings are either formal or informal. A formal wedding includes more than three but less than ten attendants to the bride. Generally, the guest list is between 150–350 people but even a very small wedding can be formal in its other elements. The invitations are engraved or printed on a heavier white or cream stock paper with wording in the traditional style.

Formal wedding ceremonies are usually conducted in the late afternoon or early evening followed by a buffet or sit-down dinner reception. Decorations include candles and flowers and are usually more traditional and more extensive. The bride will wear a floor-length gown with either a full- or chapel-length veil and the attendants' dresses are also full length and in a style that compliments the complexity of the bride's dress. All the men in the wedding party should wear a tux.

Semiformal—Semiformal weddings are less elaborate and usually less expensive. The guest list is between 100 to 150 with one to four attendants in the bridal party. The semiformal wedding ceremony might be conducted in the late morning or early afternoon with a reception following. The invitations are still printed but might be on parchment with a more stylish design. The decorations are less elaborate at both the ceremony and the reception, with flowers and candles still appropriately used. The food at the reception is much less elaborate as well, consisting of finger sandwiches and cake with punch and coffee.

For the semiformal wedding, the bride might still wear a floor-length gown but might also wear a tea length dress with or without a veil. Her bridesmaids' dresses match hers in length and style. The men may either wear tuxedos or suits.

Informal or Casual—Guests for an informal wedding may be invited with a telephone call or handwritten personal invitation and usually number under a hundred. The ceremony can take place in a home or garden, a small chapel, or just about anywhere. The bride and groom each have one attendant and dress for the entire wedding party should suit the location and time of day. The reception for an informal or casual wedding is simple with cake and punch. Expenses for an informal wedding are obviously much lower than for a formal or informal wedding.

> **That's the Spirit**
>
> Fix your thoughts on what is true and honorable and right. Think about things that are pure and lovely and admirable. Think about things that are excellent and worthy of praise … and the God of peace will be with you. (Philippians 4:8–9)
>
> When your mind starts to spin with all the rules, rules, rules of wedding etiquette, calm yourself by practicing the truths in these verses and you will find God's peace.

Invitations and Announcements

Your invitation is usually the first indication to your guests as to the type of wedding that you are planning and sets the tone for everything that follows. It often becomes a family keepsake as well. There are tons of sources for invitations these days, and with the Internet you can check out all kinds of styles, wording, and get a pretty good idea of what's a good price to pay for the number of invitations you are ordering. With so much competition, hold out for some kind of a discount or free "add-on."

Invitations should be mailed four to six weeks prior to the wedding. When figuring the number of invitations you will need, don't forget to include everyone in the wedding party (and their spouses or dates) and your immediate family members (bride and groom). And don't forget to save a copy for yourselves!

> **"I Do" Do's and Don'ts**
>
> Do order a few more invitations than your guest list indicates because your guest list might change unexpectedly. Also, accidents do happen and invitations can be soiled or ruined. Plan on ordering some additional envelopes as well, in case you make goofs in addressing. Ordering 25 additional invitations after your order is delivered can cost 4 times as much as getting those same 25 extra invitations when you first place your order.

Deciding on your guest list is one of the first and toughest choices a bride and groom and their families have to make, because inevitably someone has to be left out. To help avoid hurt feelings, the only fair way to handle the guest list is to take the total number of guests your budget can accommodate and divide it in fourths:

one-fourth for you, one-fourth for your partner, one-fourth for your family, and one-fourth for your partner's family. If you and your partner are footing the bill for the entire wedding (ceremony and reception) then the two of you get to make all the choices on who to invite, but try to remain sensitive to your family's wishes.

Family Ties

Deciding on the guest list can be a very difficult time for you and both your families, especially if budget constraints require you to make deep cuts in the list. The family of the bride, especially if they are paying for the wedding, might feel they should be able to invite whomever they wish. The family of the groom might feel hurt and excluded, as if they are not even part of the very special occasion. You might not be able to give everyone what they want, but try to at least understand their points of view.

A great tip for assembling your guest list is to use three-by-five inch index cards. Consider giving each family a different color of card (blue = bride's family, green = groom's family, and so on) so you can easily keep track of your lists when they are merged. On each card write the full name and address of a couple or family you wish to invite. For families, don't forget to list the names of all the children under the age of eighteen if they are being included in the invitation.

Bet You Didn't Know

With a touch of your finger, you can tell the difference between an engraved invitation and one printed using thermography. Engraving uses a mold that stamps the lettering into the paper and then fills the indentations with ink. With thermography, the words are written out in glue and the ink color is sprinkled on top, then heated. If you run your finger over the invitation, you can feel the lettering. Engraving takes longer (allow six to eight weeks for your order to arrive). Thermography is much less expensive.

Say It with Style

The style of your wedding should be reflected in the invitation you choose. For a formal or semiformal wedding, the traditional style and third-person wording for the invitation is appropriate. There are also some beautiful invitations available—with color, designs, and even photographs—that do not conform to the traditional rules. The most important point is to choose an invitation you and your partner are proud to display. For a small, informal wedding, it is perfectly appropriate to send handwritten invitation in a style that matches your wedding as long as it includes all the necessary information.

Formal/Semiformal Invitations

The following are some guidelines for traditional invitations:

- All names are spelled out in full, without nicknames or initials.
- "Doctor" is written in full, unless the name that follows is long.
- "Mr." and "Jr." are preferred, although Junior may be used.
- No punctuation is used except commas after days of the week and periods after abbreviations such as "Mr." or "St. Peter's."
- The bride's surname is not listed unless it is different from that of her parents.
- The date of the wedding is spelled out: "Saturday, the sixth of June."
- The year can be eliminated on invitations, but if it is used, it is spelled out also: "Two thousand and three."
- When writing out the time of the ceremony, half-hours are "half after" as in "half after ten" for 10:30 A.M. You may also add "in the morning," "in the afternoon," or "in the evening" after the hour for clarification.
- An invitation to the ceremony only does not require an R.S.V.P.

Traditional wording for invitation issued by bride's parents:

> *Mr. and Mrs. John Evan Smith*
> *request the honour of your presence*
> *at the marriage of their daughter*
> *Emily Jean*
> *to*
> *Mr. Joshua Michael White*
> *Saturday, the sixth of June*
> *Two thousand and three*
> *at two o'clock*
> *First Avenue Baptist Church*
> *321 First Avenue*
> *Ashton, Indiana*

Traditional wording for invitation issued by bride and groom:

> *Miss Emily Jean Smith*
> *and*
> *Mr. Joshua Michael White*
> *request the honour of your presence*
> *at their marriage*
> *Saturday, the sixth of June*
> *Two thousand and three*
> *at two o'clock*
> *First Avenue Baptist Church*
> *321 First Avenue*
> *Ashton, Indiana*

Wording for invitation issued by bride's divorced parents (neither parent remarried):

> *Mrs. Margaret Ann Smith*
> *and*
> *Mr. John Evan Smith*
> *request the honour of your presence*
> *at the marriage of their daughter*
> *Emily Jean*
> *to*
> *Mr. Joshua Michael White*
> *Saturday, the sixth of June*
> *Two thousand and three*
> *at two o'clock*
> *First Avenue Baptist Church*
> *321 First Avenue*
> *Ashton, Indiana*

Family Ties

With so many brides and grooms coming from divorced homes these days, choosing the wording for your invitation can be difficult, if not painful, and open up old wounds or new issues regarding your family. Don't be afraid or embarrassed to talk about your feelings with your partner, your parents, or a trusted friend. Other couples have faced these same difficulties and have gone on to have beautiful weddings and successful marriages. For questions on wedding day etiquette for complicated families, Appendix A lists some suggested titles as additional resources.

Semiformal/Informal Invitations

When choosing nontraditional invitations consider the following:

- Follow the same conventions for writing and addressing as with traditional invitations.
- Discuss your top three choices of design with your partner and your parents.
- Choose a design and wording that you and your partner will be proud to display in your home and show to your children.
- Remember that your invitation sets the tone for your wedding.

Here are three examples with suggested wording for a nontraditional wedding invitation:

Example 1

Our joy will be more complete
if you can share in the marriage
of our daughter, BRIDE
to GROOM
on DAY
YEAR
at TIME
LOCATION
ADDRESS
CITY, STATE
We invite you
to worship with us and witness their vows
If you are unable to attend
we ask your presence in thought and in prayer

Example 2

> BRIDE'S PARENTS
> *request the honor of your presence*
> *at the ceremony in which their daughter*
> BRIDE
> *and*
> GROOM
> *will vow their lives to one another*
> *and become united as one in Christ*
> *on DAY*
> YEAR
> *at TIME*
> LOCATION
> ADDRESS
> CITY, STATE

Example 3

> *Our joy will be more complete*
> *if you can share in the marriage*
> *of our daughter*
> BRIDE
> *to*
> GROOM
> *on DATE*
> *at TIME*
> LOCATION
> CITY, STATE
> *We invite you to worship with us*
> *and witness their vows.*
> *If you are unable to attend, we ask*
> *your presence in thought and prayer*
> BRIDE'S PARENTS

The nice thing about a more informal invitation is that you can personalize it in many ways. We've given just a few suggestions to guide you but feel free to express yourselves and your unique relationship.

May I Take Your Order?

Ever wonder what a deckled edge looks like? (It's an uneven, feathery edge commonly found on parchment paper). Do you know the difference between embossing and stamping? What is "pearlized"? There is a wide range of paper and ink options for wedding invitations. Make sure you see an actual sample of your invitation before you order. There are three main ways you can order your wedding invitations:

1. From a mail order catalog
2. At a stationary store
3. Off the Internet

Mail order and Internet prices run about 40 percent less than the retail price most stores charge. Whichever source you choose, make sure you see an actual sample of the invitation you want before you place your order.

Most invitation orders can be delivered in one to two weeks. Plan on ordering your invitations at least three months before the wedding to allow time for delivery and another three to four weeks to address them so they can be in the mail the required four to six weeks before the wedding. If you're planning a holiday wedding, allow an additional two to three weeks to make sure your guests get their invitations on time.

Costs can vary greatly depending on the number of invitations you order (the per invitation price goes down when you order more), the type of paper, ink, and printing you choose, and the style of invitation and envelope, and so on. You can figure on an average price range of $125 to $175 for your standard invitation (invitation, inner and outer envelope, and tissue) based on an order of 100, but prices can vary from $25 to $900 so know your budget limits.

The Envelopes, Please!

Traditional wedding invitations come with two envelopes. The printed invitation is placed in the inner envelope along with any insertions and left unsealed. How you write your guests' names on the inner envelope is different from how it is written on the outer envelope:

To a married couple

        Outer: Mr. and Mrs. Robert James Brown

        Inner: Mr. and Mrs. Brown

To a married couples with children

        Outer: Mr. and Mrs. Robert James Brown

        Inner: Mr. and Mrs. Brown

                     Sally and Michael

To a single woman

        Outer: Miss (or Ms.) Elizabeth Parks

        Inner: Miss (or Ms.) Parks

To a single man

    Outer: Mr. Thomas Fox

    Inner: Mr. Fox

To a widow, or a separated woman

    Outer: Mrs. Robert James Brown

    Inner: Mrs. Brown

To a single man or woman and guest

    Outer: Mr. Thomas Fox

    Inner: Mr. Fox and Guest

> **Bet You Didn't Know**
>
> There's an easy 'touch test' (or even 'taste test') for distinguishing between the inner and the outer envelopes for your invitations. While they may appear to be identical, only the outer envelope has glue on the flap for sealing.

The inner envelope is then placed in the outer envelope so that the guests' names are seen first when the envelope is opened. The outer envelope is for mailing and should be hand-addressed, preferably in black ink, in neat legible handwriting. Some tips for addressing your invitations for mailing:

- Avoid abbreviations (except Mr., Mrs., Dr., or Jr.)
- Don't use symbols like an ampersand (&) instead of the word "and."
- Write out:

    North, South, East, and West

Street, Road, Avenue, Boulevard, Lane

States (Colorado, not CO)

Do yourself a favor and include a response card for your reception. A response card is a small card printed in the same style as the invitation, and should include a self-addressed, stamped envelope. The response card is a convenient way for your guests to respond to your invitation, and it will also help you get your final count in a timely manner.

If you have very many guests coming from out-of-town, it's also a nice courtesy to include a small map indicating the easiest route to the church and the reception, along with a simple set of directions.

Instructions for Proper Assembly Included

There are some basic rules for assembling and stuffing the wedding invitation envelopes:

1. Place invitation down, text side up.

2. Cover with tissue (optional).

3. Place reception card on top of tissue, text side up.

4. Affix standard first class postage to response card envelope and tuck response card under the flap.

5. Stack response card and any other enclosures (rain card, map, and so on) on top of reception card by size, placing the smallest enclosure on top of the stack.

6. Insert the invitation and all enclosures, folded edge first, into the inner (without glue) envelope.

7. Place the inner envelope into the outer envelope with the guest's name facing the flap.

> **"I Do" Do's and Don'ts**
>
> Do get help with addressing and assembling your invitations. In most cases, it's too much for the bride and her family to handle alone. Why not invite a couple of friends over (ones whose penmanship you admire) for an evening of fellowship while you work on your invitations? Most girlfriends will welcome any excuse to get together, giggle, and talk wedding talk!

After you have assembled a sample invitation, complete with all enclosures, take it to the post office and weigh it to determine the proper amount of first class postage for each invitation. Try to purchase stamps with an appropriate design.

Actually, It's an Announcement!

If you choose to have a very small wedding, you might still want to tell all your family and friends that you have gotten married. An announcement tells about your marriage *after* the wedding has taken place and is sent out as soon after the wedding ceremony as possible. To clarify: An invitation invites someone to attend your wedding ceremony and/or reception; an announcement tells someone that the wedding has already taken place.

The following is traditional wording for announcement issued by the bride's parents:

Mr. and Mrs. John Evan Smith
are pleased to announce
the marriage of their daughter
Emily Jean
to
Mr. Joshua Michael White
Saturday, the sixth of June
Two thousand and three
at two o'clock
First Avenue Baptist Church
321 First Avenue
Ashton, Indiana

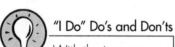

"I Do" Do's and Don'ts

With the increasingly good quality of printers and design programs, you might consider purchasing special paper and having a friend design a nice program for you on a home computer.

How to Get with the Program

Many couples choose to give guests a printed program of their ceremony to aid in corporate worship. A program is especially helpful if you wish to have guests sing a hymn or chorus or participate in a choral reading. You can probably order a wedding program from the same place you get your invitations, but it is likely to cost more. Check with your local Christian bookstore and see if you can purchase blank wedding bulletins and have them printed locally.

Your wedding program might include …

- The order of events in the ceremony.
- The names and roles of everyone in the wedding party.
- The title and composer of musical selections.
- Scripture readings.
- Poems and quotes and meaning of any symbolic elements.
- A personal greeting from the bride and groom .

What About a Wedding Website?

Emily Post doesn't cover this one. Tradition and etiquette aside, this is a fun and fabulous idea, especially if your family and friends are scattered across the country and around the world. According to Michael Winningham, creator of Wedding Websites at sfmediaworks.com, a couple can have their very own wedding website for one year for only $200. The web hosting is free, and each website is tailored to the personal needs of each couple.

Pages can contain important information for friends and family regarding the upcoming wedding (directions to the wedding, announcements, guest book, and so on) or provide help for out of town guest like links to hotel and air fair booking sites. A popular feature is "Our Story," a page with photos, old and new, that chronicle how the couple met, the proposal, and introduces the families. After the wedding, photos from the wedding day and the honeymoon can also be posted for everyone to enjoy.

To see an example website, check out: www.sfmediaworks.com/carrieandjames.

At the end of one year, the bride and groom receive the website on disk. All the information and photos can be sent via e-mail or regular postal mail. If physical copies of information or photos are sent, they will be scanned and returned. Contracts are provided outlining details for each wedding website.

> **That's the Spirit**
>
> Continue to love each other with true Christian love. Don't forget to show hospitality to strangers, for some who have done this have entertained angels without realizing it! (Hebrews 13:1–2)
>
> As distant relatives and friends from both families begin to arrive to help celebrate your special day, you might sometimes feel the strain of loving strangers (and some relatives are stranger than others)! Remind each other that God has called you to continue to love even those who are hard to love and to make hospitality an attribute of your life together.

Rehearsal Dinner

Don't let the word "dinner" throw you. There's more to this gathering than just feeding the wedding rehearsal participants. The rehearsal dinner is an occasion for gathering your attendants, family members, and out-of-town guests so they can get better acquainted, reminisce, and wish you wedding blessings. Because the rehearsal is usually held an evening or two before the wedding, it might work better to have the rehearsal dinner before the rehearsal itself. But don't skip the rehearsal! Everyone involved in the wedding will feel more at ease after a quick run through of the program.

> **"I Do" Do's and Don'ts**
>
> Don't worry if the rehearsal doesn't go off without a hitch. Even though some in your wedding party might act up during the practice run, they usually straighten up on wedding day because they know how important it is to you that things go according to plan. Relax! Laugh and let go of some of your own nervous energy. Your wedding day will be everything you want it to be, and more!

The Host with the Most

Traditionally, the groom's parents host the rehearsal dinner. That means that they are responsible for planning, coordinating, inviting, and paying for it. However, almost anyone can host the rehearsal dinner, including the bride's parents, grandparents, or a close relative or friend from either family. The rehearsal dinner can be as formal or informal as you and the host choose to make it. Just keep in mind the main purpose is to bring your two families and friends together so you all can get to know each other a bit better before the big event.

Y'all Come

The guest list usually includes everyone involved in the wedding party and their spouses, immediate family members from both families, parents of children in the wedding and their parents (or just the parents if the children are too young), and the officiant and his or her spouse. It's also nice to include any out-of-town guests arriving early for the wedding so they can immediately feel a part of the celebration.

Celebrate!

Whether you choose to have a fancy brunch, a sit-down lunch, a restaurant buffet, or a poolside barbecue, celebration is what needs to happen. Guests should be introduced to each other so they can get acquainted by name. One fun way to make introductions is to have the guests introduce themselves in turn, tell what their connection is to the bride and groom, and share how they first met the couple. Sometimes the attendants get a little dramatic! The groomsmen or bridesmaids (or both) might put on a little skit to get everyone laughing.

Another creative idea is to ask everyone invited to the rehearsal dinner to bring photos (old and new) of the couple to post on a board. If someone is willing to take on the project, you might collect the photos ahead of time, scan them, and create a PowerPoint presentation (complete with captions and sound affects) that can be projected for all to enjoy. Or a relative could collect short video vignettes of the bride and groom as children and compile a 5–10 minute movie.

Usually, the person hosting the event will offer a few comments and either offer a prayer before eating or ask someone else to do that honor. Toasting is traditionally a part of the rehearsal dinner. Christian couples who do not drink alcohol but still wish to participate in this tradition can offer good wishes and blessings. The best man often leads, followed by a word of thanks and appreciation from the groom to his parents and his bride. The bridesmaids and the brides might also have something to say. Before the end of the evening, many couples give out the gifts for the wedding party members and confirm any last minute details for the ceremony such as transportation arrangements, arrival time at the church, any special seating arrangements for the ushers, receiving line instructions, and so on. The host should be ready with a closing prayer to wrap up the evening and send guests on their way so everyone can get a good night's sleep.

> **Bet You Didn't Know**
>
> In Scotland, the mother of the bride will hold an open house before the wedding inviting some of the women who have given a wedding gift to the couple for the traditional "show of present." The wedding gifts are displayed unwrapped with the card indicating the gift giver. The occasion is meant to be an opportunity for the bride to get acquainted with the wedding party members and guests before the wedding.

Chapter 11

Perfectly Stunning in Bows and Bowties

Nearly every little girl grows up dreaming about her wedding dress, picturing in detail a beautiful gown of satin and lace with a long train and a shimmering veil. Choosing the right wedding dress might be the single most important choice you make for your special day, except for the groom, of course. It's also likely to be the most expensive single item in your wedding budget. In this chapter, we hope to help you pick the perfect wedding dress for your special day. We know you'll look gorgeous!

As the bride, you will be the center of attention on wedding day and your dress sets the style for what everyone else in the wedding party will be wearing. From the groom and grooms-men to the bridesmaids and flower girl, a lot of thought goes into planning the perfect attire for everyone involved in the wedding, and that includes Mom and Dad, too! Check your wedding budget before you start shopping! Then, go out and enjoy the experience of bringing together every button and bow that will be worn at your wedding.

Picking the Perfect Wedding Dress

If you've been dreaming of your wedding day since you were a little girl, then you already have a vision in your mind of how you want to look as you glide down the aisle toward the altar and your adoring groom. It should still be fun to look at pictures of dresses and try on some different styles. You might even discover that your tastes have changed since you were in kindergarten!

Two important things to keep in mind when looking for your wedding gown (besides budget, of course!) are the style and the season. If you have already decided on the style for your wedding—formal, semiformal, or informal—you will want to purchase a dress to match. You will need to know the season for your wedding because that will affect the material, length of sleeve, and other decisions about your dress.

A Vision of Loveliness

If you are struggling with what look you want or if you have a dream gown in mind but are finding it difficult to translate that vision for those helping you shop, try this little exercise. Put together your picture-perfect dress by making a list of words or phrases to describe the look you hope to achieve. Use photos from bridal magazines to help you visualize your perfect dress.

For example:

- *Think about your personal style*—Do you want formal and elegant or soft and romantic? Perhaps you are more the casual or thematic type of bride. If you find your dream dress, allow the dress to set the style of the wedding rather than the other way around.

- *Think about elements*—Looking at dress after dress might get overwhelming. Try focusing on parts of dresses you like—sleeves, necklines, bodice, train, skirt—instead of trying to find everything you want in one dress. If you decide that a beaded bodice is a "must have" that will help you narrow your search.

- *Think about you*—You might find a dress that is absolutely perfect on the model, but if it doesn't look good on you, you will not be happy with it. Be realistic about your body shape, height and weight, skin coloring, and hairstyle.

"I Do" Do's and Don'ts

Don't buy a dress that is too small for you with the intention of losing enough weight before the wedding to fit into it. Your partner loves you just as you are. Eat healthy and exercise regularly to keep in shape; excessive dieting at a time when you are already stressed is unhealthy. If you do lose a few pounds, it is easier to alter a dress down than it is to try to make a too-tight dress fit.

Learn the Lingo

As you start researching and shopping for your perfect dress, it will help to know some common terms used in describing the style, fabric choices, and other elements of wedding gowns and dresses. Here's a list of common terms magazines, websites, and bridal shop personnel might use.

Shape of gown or silhouette:

A-line, empire—Small bodice and scooped neckline bodice, waist-line is high, skirt is narrow, and length can vary.

A-line, princess—No waist-line seam, slim-fitting, looks good on most figures.

Sheath: Nontraditional, hugs the body from top to bottom.

Traditional ball gown—Full skirt that reaches ankles to floor, fitted waist and bodice, necklines can vary, and might be strapless.

Necklines:

High—Hugs neck with high band collar, might have cut-out, very Victorian.

Jewel—Round neckline at base of throat.

Portrait—Off the shoulder.

Sabrina—Rounded line that curves from the collarbone to the tip of the shoulders.

Dress lengths:

Ballet-length—Hem reaches to center of calf, between ankle and knee.

Floor-length—Formal, hem fully skims the floor.

High-low—Hem falls from slightly below the knee to ankle in the front, tapered to ankle, to train-length in back.

Knee-length—Hem comes to and covers the knees.

Short—Anything above the knee length.

Trains:

Sweep train—Shortest train, extends back 8 to 12 inches after touching floor.

Chapel train—Trails from waist for 3 to 4 feet.

Cathedral—Usually 6 to 7 feet, but can extend to 12 feet (Monarch), flows from waist.

Veil lengths:

Cathedral length—Head to train and measures about 12 feet.

Chapel length—Head to floor and measures about 9 feet.

Elbow length—Falls from head to brush the elbows.

Finger-tip length—Frames face and brushes the shoulders.

Types of fabric:

Brocade—Rich cloth with raised design woven in.

Chiffon—Thin, sheer cloth of silk or rayon.

Crepe—Thin, crinkled cloth of silk or rayon.

Eyelet—Cloth with open holes edged with embroidery.

Linen—Made from flax thread (from fibers of the flax plant).

Organdy—Very sheer, stiff fabric of cotton, silk, or rayon.

Organza—Sheer, chiffon-like fabric but crisper and stiffer than chiffon.

Satin—Silk, nylon, or rayon cloth with smooth, glossy finish on one side.

Silk—Smooth, soft fabric from silkworm threads.

> **Bet You Didn't Know**
>
> Most American bride's today pay hundreds of dollars for a white wedding dress they will wear only once. In the Victorian Age (1837–1901), most brides could not afford to purchase or wear a white wedding dress. What color dress did the Victorian bride choose? Pale blue, lavender, and light gray were favorites, along with perhaps navy.

Silk-faced satin—Smooth, lustrous silk-weave with a glossy face and dull back.

Taffeta—Fine, stiff cloth of silk or rayon with a sheen.

Tulle—Fine silk, nylon, or rayon netting used for skirts, veils.

Voile—Soft and sheer fabric, usually made of cotton, silk, or rayon.

Shop 'Til You Drop!

Or at least, that's the way you might start to feel after making the rounds of shops and stores. But the only way to really know if a dress is perfect for you is to try it on. Because so much depends on your gown, it's best to start shopping for your wedding dress at least six months before your wedding date. Tackle only one or two places a day—shopping for your wedding dress shouldn't become a chore! Go out armed with your list of attributes and any photos you have collected, a lot of patience, and comfortable shoes. If you encounter a large selection of gowns in a store, tackle them in groups of three. Save your favorite from each trio to try on a second time. Each time you try on a dress, you will have a clearer idea of what you're looking for.

Occasionally, all that homework pays off and a bride is able to pluck the perfect dress right from the rack in the first round. If you try on a dress that makes you shout "It's perfect!" and it fits your budget, go for it. But that's rare, so be patient. It's usually less expensive if you can purchase a dress off the rack, but you might need to place an order to get your perfect gown. It takes about three months for your order to be placed and your wedding gown to be made by the manufacturer.

Family Ties

There's hardly a more special time between mother and daughter than when you go shopping for your wedding dress. Make it a magical time—buy Mom lunch or dinner, take along a camera (just in case you're allowed to take photos), and truly enjoy each other's company. There will be many tense moments and tough decisions in the months to come, so make this a happy time.

A Fit Fitting

Whether you purchase your dress off the rack or special order it, you will need to plan for several fittings. Be sure to take your mother, your maid of honor, or another trusted friend along for your fittings. It's important to have the opinion of someone you trust at this special time, and it's more fun to share the moment with someone with whom you have a significant relationship. Don't forget to take in the shoes you are going to wear for the wedding when trying on dresses. Having the dress hemmed might cost you more than other alterations. It might be worth it to buy it for the perfect length even if it needs other alterations.

Your final fitting should take place a few weeks before your wedding. The last thing you should worry about on your wedding day is whether or not your gown fits. So make sure your wedding gown is ready early. Some places will hold your gown until the week before your wedding and they are probably better equipped to store it properly so that it doesn't wrinkle.

Here are some other helpful tips:

- Make sure the gown you choose makes you feel more beautiful than you ever imagined. You'll feel good if you know you look good.

- Wedding gowns tend to run small. So don't panic if you need a wedding gown that is a size or two larger than your normal size.

- Unless a dress shouts "this is it!" at you, take a day or two to decide on the wedding gown that you would like to purchase. Most bridal shops have a no refund, no return policy. Don't rush such an important investment.

- Use a credit card to pay for your wedding gown. Most cards offer some kind of buyer protection services. So if something does go wrong, you might be able to recover some of your losses from the credit card company.

- Expect to give an initial deposit of up to 50 percent of the cost of the gown.

- Be sure to get a written contract with specific and so on.

- Watch out for scam artists—the wedding business is full of them. Check out the wedding books and websites listed in the resources. Many will list typical scams and how to avoid them.

- Have fun! Whatever gown you choose, you will be the center of attention on your wedding day and you will be beautiful!

There can be many hidden costs in purchasing a wedding gown. Some are legitimate and need to be figured into your budget. Others you might be able to do without. Consider purchasing only your gown at a bridal store. It is usually cheaper to purchase items like shoes, bra, jewelry, and other accessories somewhere else.

"I Do" Do's and Don'ts

Can't find the dress of your dreams in the fabric and fit you want? Consider having a dress made for you. McCall, Butterick, and Vogue all offer designer patterns for wedding gowns and attire for everyone in your wedding party. If you are a gifted seamstress (or you have a close relative who is), you can save up to 75 percent of the cost of ready-made dresses by doing it yourself. Even if you hire a seamstress, you are more likely to get a custom fit and the price will be comparable to purchasing and gown and adding on alterations.

Icing on the Bride

As if your gown isn't spectacular enough, you get to dress up with all kinds of other finery: veil or headpiece, jewelry, shoes, and lingerie. Veils are very traditional and quite trendy these days with the sleeker look of a one-tier veil being preferred to the poofy look of a multitiered veil. Before you choose a headpiece or veil, you'll have to decide how you will wear your hair (more tips for hair care are coming up). Other factors that influence your choice of headpiece are the wedding gown, the level of formality of the wedding, the shape of your face, and the season.

Headpieces can be worn with or without a veil and have become quite stunning in their own right, so even if you choose not to wear a veil you can dress up your hair with a beautifully designed halo, headband, tiara, or crown. A simple wreath of flowers, silk or real, is another popular option for a hair accessory. The headpiece is a perfect place to bring in a touch of color so popular with today's brides.

One final piece of advice for choosing your veil and headpiece: Keep in mind that for most of the ceremony, your guests will be looking at the back of your head and gown, so make sure everything works together. Take a look from their perspective before you make your final choice.

The jewelry you choose will either add or detract from your overall look. Too much jewelry or not enough can both change the effect of the gown you have chosen for your perfect look. Try out some different styles at one of your dress fittings. In general, with a high neckline you should focus on earrings. Otherwise, go for a necklace that accentuates the neckline of your gown. Most of all, make sure your jewelry is comfortable.

And speaking of comfort, think shoes! You will be on your feet all day, so make sure that the shoes you choose are not only beautiful but also comfortable to wear. Shoes made of fabric and tinted to match your dress can also be embellished with beading or pearls for a stunning look. Choose flats or one- to two-inch heels and strapping that supports your foot well. And by all means, break them in by wearing them around the house for a few days before the ceremony. If all else fails, do what many brides end up doing—kick them off and go barefoot at the reception.

You'll want your gorgeous look to go from your head to your toes and to your skin, too! Choose special undergarments to give you that princess-like feeling from the inside out. You might need to buy a special undergarments (bra, panties, slip) that work with your gown, but also pick ones that are pretty to look at and comfortable to wear. Pay a little more for a nice pair of light-colored stockings (off-white or ivory) that fit properly for the style of gown and shoe you are wearing. Buy two pairs just in case you get a run in one on your wedding day.

That's the Spirit

Charm is deceptive, and beauty does not last; but a woman who fears the Lord will be greatly praised. Reward her for all she had done. Let her deeds publicly declare her praise. (Proverbs 31:31)

There's nothing wrong with wanting to be as beautiful and charming as possible on your wedding day. Just don't neglect investing in the things that will really last—your family, your friends, your relationship with your future husband, and your walk with God.

Decisions for Dressing Your Wedding Attendants

After you've chosen your gown, it's time to turn your attention to what the well-dressed bridesmaid will be wearing at your wedding. The style you have chosen for your own dress will be your guide, but you might also want to consult the Style Guide for Wedding Attire table at the end of the chapter. For many brides, choosing the attire for the wedding party is one of the most stressful decisions to make. We'll try to make it a little less stressful for you with some practical tips and words of wisdom.

Color Me Happy!

Because just about any color will compliment the bride's white gown, you have an incredible palette of colors and shades from which to choose for your wedding party. Keep in mind that the color you choose for the bridesmaids' dresses will also need to be coordinated with the flowers, the groomsmen's outfits, and dresses worn by the bride's and groom's mothers. While black is always classic and has become a popular choice for bridesmaids in recent years, most bride's still choose to add a splash of color to their wedding party. Whatever color palette you choose, there are various ways to incorporate it throughout your wedding. You can go with complimentary colors (opposites on the color wheel) such as yellow and violet or red and green. You can choose two or three colors that blend such as green, blue-green, and deep blue. Or you can choose a one-color (monochromatic) palette with a wide range of shades within that one color, as with lilac, violet, and deep purple. Have fun trying out color combinations with fabric swatches and flowers until you find the look that feels perfect to you.

Bridesmaids, Be a Blessing!

This note is just for bridesmaids (brides, you might want to find an excuse to leave this page open and lying about). All jokes aside, being asked to be a bridesmaid is an honor. The bride has chosen you to participate in the most sacred moment of her life. Please remember that this is *her* moment, not yours. Be patient and kind. It is very hard to put together a perfect wedding. Your bride wants you to look good as much as you do, but trying to find a dress that suits everyone in the bridal party might be nearly impossible.

Here's the best gift you can give the bride and groom: If you hate the dress, just try to make the best of it. Don't tell the bride how you feel unless she asks your opinion before the dresses are ordered. Focus on her happiness above your own and you will not only be the perfect bridesmaid but you'll be a real blessing to your friends, too.

Brides, Be Kind!

Yes, it's your wedding and you have the right to choose whatever you want for your bridesmaids to wear. But doesn't it also make sense to try to choose a color and style that will make everyone look their best? Some of your bridesmaids might be making a financial sacrifice to be in your wedding because it is their responsibility to pay for their entire outfit (we're talking and average of $100 to $300). Be kind and take into consideration a few things while shopping for the perfect look for your attendants:

- **Consider body types**—Not all body types are equal! Think about your attendants and try to picture each individual body type: petite or tall, slim or full-bodied. What dress style would look best on the majority of them? Is there a style that could be more easily adapted to suit their differences?

- **Consider the color**—Don't choose a color that will make anyone look washed out. What looks good on a fair-skinned redhead might not work on a bronzed blonde or a brunette.

- **Consider the cost**—Try to pick a dress in a reasonable price range for your particular group (something bridal magazines don't consider). Look for ways to help make this experience affordable for everyone by giving jewelry or some other accessory for the wedding as the bridesmaids' thank you gift. One mother of the bride graciously paid for all the attendants' shoes and had them dyed to match their gowns.

- **Consider their opinions**—Gather some ideas on styles and colors and then have a little get-together to ask everyone for their opinions. Take a few of them shopping with you from time to time (just be sure no one feels excluded). Don't be thin-skinned and take offense if your ideas are shot down. Remember you still have the final word, but the spirit of unity can be sweet!

- **Consider being different**—Traditionally, all the attendants wear identical dresses, but there's no good reason to keep this "rule" any longer. Dressing your bridesmaids in dresses that are similar in style but accommodates their individual body types, complexions, and even personalities can make for a beautiful wedding and a joyous celebration for everyone.

Where to Shop

You can get bridesmaids' dresses from a variety of sources, so consider the pros and cons of each before you go shopping. Most bridal stores have sample bridesmaids dresses that you can try on for style and color. If you decide to purchase from a bridal shop, each attendant will have to be measured and the dresses ordered. When the dresses arrive, they will need to be fitted and perhaps altered before the wedding. If you choose this route, get a really early start.

If you're going to order dresses anyway, check out some catalogs first. The prices and the return policies are usually better than at the stores. The major disadvantage is that you are depending on the accuracy of a picture to pick a style and color of dress. The same can be true about buying from the Internet. If you choose this route, make sure you can return the dresses for a full refund if for any reason you are not satisfied.

Many brides have been lucky enough to find beautiful dresses in a department store. Buying off the rack means better prices and the opportunity for individuals to actually try on the dress before you buy, and you can be sure of what you are getting. One drawback is if any of your attendants require an irregular size because most department stores carry a limited range of sizes. Sometimes it's possible to buy a larger size and have it altered, but that does not always yield a satisfactory result.

Two final options: You might rent (especially if you have your heart set on an expensive, formal gown that no one in your entourage will ever wear again) or you can have dresses made or make them yourselves.

Don't Forget to Accessorize!

Unless the bride requests that all the bridesmaids wear the same accessories, each bridesmaid will need to show good taste in her choices of shoes and jewelry. Let comfort and style guide you in both. Low-heeled shoes will be kind to feet that will be standing for most of the day. In most cases, jewelry should be simple and elegant. A necklace, earrings, and a bracelet are all appropriate (skip the watch, if you can).

Grooming the Groom

It's natural to focus attention on the bride and her attire, but the groom deserves some attention. After all, it's his wedding day, too! Almost every groom is willing to let his bride lead in setting the style for the wedding party. But it's important to include him in the decisions about what he and the groomsmen will be wearing. Chances are we're talking a tuxedo or a dress suit; here are some guidelines for what the well-dressed groom is wearing.

To Rent or Not to Rent

Is that even a question? We don't know too many grooms who own their own tuxedo. Considering that the average price of a new tuxedo is between $300 and $500, most men will choose to rent when a tux is called for (see the Style Guide for Wedding Attire table). Renting will cost about 10 to 30 percent of the price of a new tux, and you have the added perk that you can all match!

If your wedding style allows for you to wear a suit, you might seriously consider buying a new one. A good suit can be worn over and over again for many years to come, making it a better investment. Whether you rent a tuxedo or buy a dress suit, do consider buying a good pair of black dress shoes. Wearing your own shoes on your wedding day makes sense because your feet will get a workout! Yes, you can rent black shoes with your tuxedo, but they won't feel the same as your own (which you can break in ahead of time).

Renters Assurance

Most men enjoy shopping for a rental tux about as much as they enjoy a root canal. Just remember you are doing it for a good cause (what's her name?). Here are some tidbits about renting that might make the experience a little less painful for you and your men:

- Get recommendations from family and friends for a good formalwear store you can trust. You're going to need sound advice on what works and what doesn't.
- Put your best man in charge. Make him responsible for keeping track of all the rental arrangements, dealing with the store, and making sure the groomsmen tow the line.
- When you first meet the staff at the store, go with your gut. You want to deal with someone who will listen to you. If that's doesn't happen from the start, go somewhere else.
- Think one-stop shopping. Choose a store that can supply you with everything you need: from tux and trousers to tie and cufflinks.
- Get your groomsmen into the store at least three months before the wedding so they can be set up with matching duds.
- Finally, get the guys to go to the store themselves to pick up their stuff and insist that they try it on before they leave the store. That way if there are any problems, the store has time to make it right.

> **That's the Spirit**
>
> Who can find a virtuous and capable wife? She is worth more than precious rubies. Her husband can trust her, and she will greatly enrich his life. (Proverbs 31:10)
>
> ... and when a graceful figure is the habitation of a virtuous soul—when the beauty of the face speaks out the modesty and humility of the mind, it raises our thoughts up to the great Creator.
> —Sterne

Making Up for Matrimony

Have you ever seen a bride that wasn't just radiant? Love has a lot to do with it, but we suspect that most of those brides have also taken the time and effort to get their bodies in the best shape possible—if not for the wedding, than for the wedding night! To look your best when you walk down the aisle, you need to start your health and beauty routine about six months before your big day. But even with a few weeks to work on it, you can make a difference in how you look and feel.

Take Good Care of Yourself

Beauty starts with a well-balanced diet and regular exercise. That's probably not what you wanted to hear, but you can't afford to neglect either in the midst of your wedding preparations. Thirty minutes of exercise each day will help keep your body fit by flushing out toxins and giving your circulation a boost. The result will be clearer skin and more energy for all those prewedding errands.

Make fresh fruits and vegetables a regular part of your diet and don't forget to drink a lot of water (six to eight glasses a day to start). Finally, try not to spend too many sleepless nights worrying over wedding-day details. Instead, aim for eight good hours each night dreaming of your future spouse.

Beauty from Head to Toe

Start by deep-cleansing your face regularly with a gentle cleaner and moisturizing masque. If you're thinking of splurging on a facial just before the wedding, you should know that it could leave your skin red and blotchy if you haven't been taking care of it all along. You'll want to get your hair in good shape, too. Keep the ends trimmed, deep condition it about once a month, and don't overdue any chemical processes like coloring and perms. If you're thinking about a new style for the wedding, try it out well in advance to make sure it will work and that you are comfortable with it.

With all the emphasis on looking good, you might be wondering about make-up for your big day. Brides are naturally beautiful, so don't feel like you have to make any major make-up changes just because you're getting married. Keep in mind, however, that your face will be surrounded by white, making you look a little washed out, especially in your photographs. Experiment at home with small variations of your normal make-up routine. Try a more intense color on your lips and experiment with neutral eye colors. Slip on a white shirt to see what the effect might be when you're wearing your wedding dress.

Don't forget to pamper your feet and hands because they will be on display come wedding day. If you can afford the time and money, schedule a professional manicure and pedicure as soon as possible. Ask the attendant about ways to pamper your hands and feet at home. Then, a day or two before the wedding, have another professional manicure and pedicure if you can. Bottom line, be good to yourself!

Dressing It Up

Which style you choose for your wedding attire is not nearly as important as having it all coordinate. In other words, you don't want to mix a super-formal wedding dress with very casual attire on the groom or bridesmaids. This style guide might help you think through all the elements of wedding attire according to the style you have chosen for your wedding.

Style Guide for Wedding Attire

Formal Wedding

Individual	Attire
Bride	Traditional white or ivory floor-length gown with train; veil or hat; medium-sized bouquet; gloves, optional.
Groom	Tuxedo with black or gray jacket and striped trousers; white shirt with studs or cufflinks; bow tie or ascot; vest or cummerbund; black shoes and dark socks.
Bridal attendants	Long or tea-length dresses; gloves, optional; medium-sized bouquet; shoes/accessories to compliment dress.

Formal Wedding

Individual	Attire
Groomsmen/Ushers	Same as groom.
Mothers	Street-length dresses in elaborate fabric; hats, optional; shoes/accessories to match dresses.
Fathers	Same as groom.

Semiformal Wedding

Individual	Attire
Bride	White or pastel floor-length or ballerina dress with chapel-length veil; or white or pastel tea-length gown with fingertip veil or hat; modest/small bouquet.
Groom	Tuxedo or dark formal suit with matching trousers (appropriate to season); white dress shirt and dark bow tie; cummerbund or vest; black shoes and dark socks.
Bridal attendants	Long or tea-length dresses in elaborate fabric and complimentary color; shoes, stockings, and accessories; flowers for hair, optional.
Groomsmen/Ushers	Same as groom.
Mothers	Street-length or ankle-length dresses in elaborate fabric and dressy accessories.
Fathers	Tuxedos or dark dress suits.

Informal Wedding

Individual	Attire
Bride	Formal suit or street-length gown in white or color; small bouquet or single long-stemmed flower; contemporary shoes; no veil or train.
Groom	Business suit or matching trousers and jacket; dress shirt and tie; dark shoes and dark socks.
Bridal attendants	Dress length equal to or shorter than the bride's; small bouquet or single long-stemmed flower.
Groomsmen/Ushers	Same as groom.
Mothers	Suit or street-length dresses with coordinating accessories.
Fathers	Same as groom.

Planning Your Perfect Ceremony

Your wedding ceremony should be a unique and personal reflection of the love you and your future spouse share. It's like opening a small portal into your hearts so your friends and families can celebrate with you the wonder of how God has brought you together and the love that you share. It should also be a public declaration of the lifetime commitment you are making to one another. By saying your vows and making your promises before your friends and family, you are giving them permission to hold you accountable for fulfilling those vows and keeping your promises.

A Christian wedding has yet another dimension. Marriage is a sacred covenant, ordained by God and used by God to demonstrate his great love for his bride, the church. Your ceremony, should also incorporate worship—acknowledging God's presence at your wedding and inviting his blessing on your holy union. These are all important aspects to the wedding ceremony that you and your future spouse should talk through as you plan your service. Other more mature Christians might give you greater insight into the spiritual dimensions of marriage as you plan.

Order of Ceremony

Wedding ceremonies can vary significantly depending on your church or denomination. In some cases, the order of ceremony is fixed by the officiating minister. Sometimes certain elements of the service are required, but other parts of the service can be planned by the couple. Talk with the person who will be officiating at your wedding and see if you have any input on the order of service. If so, take a look at the following sample ceremony and start a list of elements you want in your ceremony. After you decide what you want, take it back to the person or persons performing your wedding and work out the final details. Though they provide spiritual and procedural oversight, your wishes should be respected. Here's a sample ceremony to use as a guide while putting together the pieces of your own wedding ceremony:

Processional

Welcome and Invocation

[Names of bride and groom] welcome you this afternoon to share with them as they create their covenant and commitment of love during this time of worship.

Because of the deep love [bride and groom] have developed for each other they stand before us today declaring their decision to join their lives together as husband and wife. We have been invited to witness this most sacred event.

Comments to Groom and Bride

[Groom's name, bride's name] the Bible teaches that marriage is to be a bonded relationship of one man and one woman, freely and totally committed to each other as companions for life. Our Lord declared that a man shall leave his father and mother and shall cleave unto his wife, and the two shall become one flesh.

Nothing is easier than saying words, and nothing is harder than living them day after day. What you promise now must be renewed and confirmed tomorrow and each day of your lives together. At the end of this ceremony, legally you will be man and wife, but you still decide—each day that stretches out before you—that you want to be married, that you will love each other.

Question to Groom/Bride

[Groom's name] will you give your life to [bride's name] to love her, satisfy her, and protect her as your wife and friend for the rest of your life?

[Bride's name] will you take [groom's name] as your husband, and will you love, honor and respect him, will you encourage him and be faithful to him for the rest of your life?

Question to Bride's Parent (s)

Who gives [bride's name] to be married to [groom's name]?

MARRIAGE ADMONITION/Sermon "Life Commitment"

[Groom, bride] as you begin your life together now as husband and wife, remember that you are entering into a sacred relationship. The vows you are about to exchange before God and these witnesses are a verbal expression of your commitment to and love for each other.

Real love is something beyond the warmth and glow, the excitement and romance of being deeply in love. It is caring as much about the welfare and happiness of your marriage partner as you care about your own. Love makes burdens lighter—because you divide them. It makes joys more intense—because you share them. It makes you stronger—you can reach out and become involved with life in ways you dare not risk alone.

The Scriptures teach us that this love is slow to lose patience, it looks for ways to be constructive. It is not possessive, it is neither anxious to impress nor does it hold inflated ideas of its own importance. Love has good manners and does not pursue selfish advantage. It is not touchy. It does not compile statistics of evil ... rather it is glad when truth prevails.

Love knows no limit to its endurance, no end to its trust, no fading of its hope. It can outlast anything! It is, in fact, the one thing that still stands when all else has fallen. This is God's love and the love that bonds your lives together.

I charge you both as you stand in the presence of almighty God, having deliberately and prayerfully considered the holy covenant you are about to make, that you do now declare before your families and friends your pledge of faith and commitment to one another.

EXCHANGE OF VOWS

You may choose to use these traditional vows or substitute your own:

[Minister to groom]

[Groom's name], will you take (name of bride) to be your wife? Will you love her, comfort her, honor and protect her, and, forsaking all others, be faithful to her as long as you both shall live?

[Groom's response] *I will.*

[Minister to bride]

[Bride's name], will you take [name of groom] to be your husband? Will you love her, comfort her, honor and protect her, and, forsaking all others, be faithful to her as long as you both shall live?

[Bride's response] *I will.*

[Groom to bride]
I, (groom), take you, (bride)
to be my wife,
to have and to hold
from this day forward
for better, for worse
for richer, for poorer
in sickness and in healthy,
to love and to cherish,
till death us do part,
according to God's holy law;
and this is my solemn vow.

[Bride to groom]
I, (bride), take you, (groom)
to be my husband,
to have and to hold
from this day forward
for better, for worse
for richer, for poorer
in sickness and in healthy,
to love and to cherish,
till death us do part,
according to God's holy law;
and this is my solemn vow.

EXCHANGE OF RINGS

Introduction

The rings you exchange to seal your vows will constantly serve as the outward and visible sign of your marriage, signifying to all that you belong one to the other. They are formed of precious metal into an unending circle. So may your relationship be pure and enduring. Let me assure you that if these solemn vows are kept inviolate, as God's Word demands, and if steadfastly you endeavor to do the will of your Heavenly Father, God will richly bless your marriage and establish your home in peace.

Groom (while placing ring on bride's finger): *[Bride], I give you this ring as a visible sign of my love and commitment to you, making it known that I am yours and you are mine.*

Bride (while placing ring on groom's finger): *[Groom], I give you this ring as a visible sign of my love and commitment to you, making it known that I am yours and you are mine.*

Prayer of Dedication

DECLARATION

[Groom, bride] in as much as you have consented together to enter this holy rite of marriage; having made public declaration of your love and commitment to each other for the rest of your lives; and sealed your vows with the exchange of rings. By the authority committed unto me, as a Minister of the Gospel of Jesus Christ, I declare you husband and wife, according to the ordinance of God and the law of this state.

What God has joined together, let no man separate.

THE KISS!!

Presentation of New Couple

It gives me great pleasure to introduce to you for the very first time Mrs. and Mrs.

_____.

Recessional

Bet You Didn't Know

In Germany, the traditional wedding day can actually last up to three days. First, German couples attend a civil ceremony with only family and close friends attending. The next night the bride and groom invite all of their friends, neighbors, and acquaintances to a big wedding party. On the third day, the religious ceremony takes place. At some time during the vows, while the couple is kneeling, the groom might kneel on his bride's wedding dress to show symbolically who will be "wearing the pants" in the marriage. However, when they stand, the bride might step on her groom's foot to show otherwise!

Announcements

Is there something you need to say to the people attending your wedding that is not a part of the wedding ceremony itself? For example, has there been an unexpected change of plans for the reception due to weather? Do you want to call attention to a certain feature of the service (for example, a responsive reading in the program or an honored guest who will be singing)? Are you inviting attendees to take home a small token from the ceremony? All these "housekeeping" items can be taken care of during the announcements—either right before or right after the ceremony itself and can be handled by the person officiating or a close family member or friend.

Question to Parent(s)

It is traditional in Christian wedding services for the officiant to ask "Who give this woman to be married to this man?" The roots of this question go back to the time when women were viewed as the property of their family. Although there is no legal or religious reason for this part of the service, it is symbolic of the bride's leaving her family and cleaving to her husband. It is also a moment many fathers anticipate from the time they hear the words "It's a girl!" so don't discard it lightly. However, if you have a complicated family situation, there are alternative ways to handle it.

You might have your father and mother stand and answer the question with "We do." If your father is deceased or no longer a part of your life and not present at your wedding, you might have a male relative or family friend escort you down the aisle, and he might answer with "On behalf of her mother, I do." If you just aren't comfortable with this element of the ceremony, talk with the person performing the service to see if the question can be skipped.

Charge to Couple, or the Sermon

Because a Christian wedding is viewed as a worship service, it is customary to include a short talk about the sanctity of marriage and the nature of marital love. This is usually done by the person performing the ceremony. However, if you and your future spouse are from different churches, this can be an opportunity to include a minister from another church. Before you make such arrangements, check with the officiant to make sure this is an option for you.

Some couples are put off by the idea of having a "sermon" at their wedding, so don't think of it that way. Instead, view it as an opportunity not only for you and your spouse to focus your thoughts on the sacred nature of marriage but also as a chance to encourage and challenge the hearts of those in attendance. There are many individuals and couples who attend weddings that find God speaking to their hearts about their relationships and their marriages because of the words spoken at a wedding ceremony. You might also consider the unsaved guests at your service. For some, it might be one of the only times they hear God's perspective on love and marriage. What a testimony!

An Act of Worship

The intent of Holy Communion, or the Lord's Supper, is to remind believers of the sacrificial love of Jesus Christ for his bride, the church. It evokes not only repentance for sins but it reinforces the unity of the body to which God has called all Christians. Communion, as an act of worship, is a fitting symbol for the marriage ceremony. Here is an example of communion as an element of the wedding ceremony:

> *As their first act of worship as husband and wife, [groom and bride] have chosen to celebrate the Lord's Supper together. The elements of the Lord's Supper remind us of his infinite love for us when he freely gave his life in our place. The bread is a symbol of his body, broken for us in an act of sacrificial love. The cup represents his blood, shed for the forgiveness of our sins.*

> *As you prepare to receive the elements, examine your hearts, confess your sin, and receive his promise of forgiveness.*

> BREAD

> *The Lord Jesus, on the night of his arrest, took bread, and after giving thanks to God, he broke it, and gave it to his disciples, saying, "Take, eat. This is my body, given for you. Do this in remembrance of me."*

> CUP

> *In the same way, he took the cup, saying: "This cup is the new covenant sealed in my blood, shed for you for the forgiveness of sins. Whenever you drink it, do this in remembrance of me. Every time you eat this bread and drink this cup, you proclaim the saving death of the risen Lord, until he comes."*

Ring Ceremony

For centuries, the ring has been a symbol of the eternal nature of marital love and fidelity. To the ancient Romans, the exchange of circular bands of iron was proof of a marriage contract. Renaissance jewelers developed a new kind of wedding ring, the gimmel ring. It consisted of interlocking rings symbolizing the union of two lives. Martin Luther and Catherine Bora were wed with an inscribed gimmel ring in 1525.

In the early 1900s, wedding bands engraved with orange blossoms and wreaths were very popular. The design was reminiscent of the days of the Crusades when brides received a head wreath of orange blossoms as a blessing. Today, the ring remains an enduring symbol of the marriage covenant. Here is an example of the exchange of rings as an element of the wedding ceremony:

Question

What token do you bring as a symbol of your love for each other and to seal the vows you have just exchanged?

Blessing of Rings

May the circlet of gold, which has no end, symbolize the purity, the unending love and affection that you have for each other. May these rings also be an outward and visible sign of your commitment to each other as husband and wife, symbolizing the inward and spiritual bond that unites your two hearts in an enduring love.

[To Groom] *Repeat after me:*

[Bride's name], with this ring I commit myself to you in marriage, promising to share all I am and have. I pledge my love and life to you in the name of the Father, the Son, and the Holy Spirit.

[To Bride] *Repeat after me:*

[Groom's name], with this ring I commit myself to you in marriage, promising to share all I am and have. I pledge my love and life to you in the name of the Father, the Son, and the Holy Spirit.

Unity Candle

Matthew 5:14–16 reminds us of our calling to be light to the world, allowing the light of Christ to shine through us to those still in darkness. Although candles have been a part of worship for thousands of years, the tradition of the unity candle is relatively recent. It is a powerful visual image of how two can join into one. Here is an example of the unity candle as an element of the wedding ceremony:

[Groom, bride] in a moment each of you will take a candle to symbolize your individual lives. You will use those candles to light the central candle as a symbol of the new relationship you are beginning today. Let me remind you that marriage does not wipe out your separate identity as individuals, but it does enrich you by helping you to grow and develop as people who are made in the image of God. If each of you will contribute your best to your marriage, you will become as one in life's most intimate and fulfilling relationship. This is my prayer for both of you as you begin this exciting journey together.

The Declaration, Kiss, and Introduction

This is the moment you've been waiting for—being declared husband and wife! And, of course, there's the kiss! When you feel this moment coming in your ceremony, take a deep breath, slow down, and savor every second. This might be the moment you remember most from the entire service. Finally, the officiant will have you face your guests and introduce you as Mr. and Mrs. and you will be off into the greatest adventure of your life.

Writing Your Wedding Vows

Your wedding vows should reflective three significant areas of commitment—your commitment to God, your commitment to marriage itself, and your commitment to each other. As you create your vows, keep in mind that the promises you make in these three areas are part of the sacred covenant and that you make these promises before God, your family, and each other for good reason. The marriage ceremony, both as a sacred and legally binding agreement, requires witnesses who are willing to hold the couple accountable and assist them in fulfilling their promises.

As you and your future spouse discuss your wedding vows, focus on three areas:

1. Your vision for marriage (see Chapter 3)
2. Your relationship (how you met, how your love has grown, what you mean to each other)
3. The commitment (promises) you are making to each other

So where do you begin? What should be included in your vows?

Marriage Is …

In the sample ceremony given at the beginning of this chapter, the person performing the ceremony makes a statement to the couple about what marriage is according to God's Word. Hopefully, you and your future spouse have already thoroughly discussed your vision for marriage and have formulated a statement of what you believe about marriage that you both can agree to. If not, go back to Chapter 3 and work on this some more. It is important that you can articulate what you believe marriage is and what God says marriage is before you can enter into a ceremony pledging to uphold that vision.

> **That's the Spirit**
>
> … the Lord witnessed the vows you and your wife made to each other on your wedding day when you were young … Didn't the Lord make you one … ? So guard yourself; remain loyal to [each other]. "For I hate divorce!" says the Lord, the God of Israel. (Malachi 2:14–16)
>
> When writing your vows, it's important to avoid using weak phrases like "I will try …." Marriage is *not* an "I'll give it my best shot" kind of commitment. When the going gets tough in your marriage, you need to be able to look back to your wedding ceremony and realize that you made promises that *can be kept* with God's help, regardless of the circumstances. We firmly believe that no Christian marriage *has* to fail. If two Christians divorce, it's because one or both of the partners made the choice *not* to honor their wedding vows.

What Loving You Means to Me

Think about your relationship with your future spouse and write down what you are hoping for in your marriage. Write down what you will give as well as what you hope to receive. Stay away from phrases stated with a negative like "I will never be unfaithful" or "I'll never ignore you." Instead, make a positive declaration such as "I promise to be faithful" or "I promise to make giving you the attention you need a priority." The following questions might help you think about your relationship. To begin with, you and your future spouse should do this exercise separately. Don't read your partner's responses until you've completed your own. Later you can get together, review your answers, and use them to write your vows.

Reflect on your relationship:

- Where did you meet? Describe the setting, the time, the weather, and so on.
- Why did you decide to pursue a relationship with each other?
- How has your life been impacted or changed because of this relationship?
- What do you love most about your future spouse?
- What is the dream or vision you have for your life together?
- List four reasons why you want to marry your partner.
- What passage from the Word of God has meant the most to you during this courtship?
- How did you feel when he asked you to marry him or when she said "yes"?
- How is your personal relationship with Christ enhanced by your future mate?

After both of you have completed your questions, read each other's responses. Take time to discuss thoroughly the answers. Out of these questions and the examples provided in this book you will find different themes and words you would like expressed in your own wedding vows. Remember, these are to represent you and your relationship. They need to be personal.

Promises You Make (and Keep!)

Your vows should also reflect any promises you want to make to each other in the presence of God and with your family and friends as witnesses. The following are promises that have been included in wedding vows. Perhaps there are some here you would like to incorporate into your own.

I promise …

- To live with you and love you forever.
- To love you as God defines love.
- To be an encourager in your life.
- To respond to you emotionally, spiritually, and physically.
- To laugh with you but never at you.
- To help you be all God wants you to be and all you want to be.

- To share and delight in your successes and to share equally your disappointments.
- To comfort you without trying to fix you.
- To care for you through any kind of sickness and in health.
- To adventure with you into the unknown.
- To be a person you can always depend on.
- To respect and accept your family.
- To pray for you and with you every day.
- To forgive you quickly when I have been offended.
- To thank you for who you are as well as what you do.
- To adventure into your life, to see it through your eyes, to hear it through your ears, to touch it through your fingertips.
- To be faithful in seeking the Holy Spirit to direct my thoughts and words.

Take time to write out your thoughts about these suggestions. You will probably need to write several drafts of your vows before you feel they are just right.

Family Ties

Many Christian parents pray for years that God will give their son or daughter the right partner for marriage. It's nice to honor such commitment. Some couples include their parents in the exchange of vows. Each set of parents recite a promise to continue to support the bride and groom in their new life together. Or you could vow to continue to honor and support your families who have contributed so much to the person each of you have become. If you have been blessed with loving and faithful parents, consider how you might acknowledge them in your ceremony.

Sharing Your Vows

Now that you've written your vows down, how will you share them during the ceremony? Many couples have little experience speaking in public, let alone making such personal declarations! Relax … the how isn't nearly as important as getting your message across to your partner. If your vows are short and easy to remember, you can take turns saying your vows to each other. Or you can choose to have the person performing the ceremony say the vows phrase-by-phrase so you can repeat them. Another alternative is to have the officiate read each vow and you respond with "I will" or "I promise." It's also all right to read them aloud. You don't have to memorize your vows unless you want to, but even if you do, have them printed and available … just in case.

Everyone gets nervous and a wedding is a prime time for the jitters! Practice reciting your vows just as you would for any speech or presentation. Read them out loud every day during the week leading up to the ceremony. This can help you memorize the words as well as keep you focused on why you are marrying this person. When the time comes to say your vows, share them in a loud, confident, and positive way. When you recite them at the wedding rehearsal, have someone stand at the back of the room or area to make sure you can be heard, and consider using a microphone if you can't. The promises you vow to each other are the most important and personal part of your wedding ceremony, so you don't want anyone to miss a word.

"I Do" Do's and Don'ts

Do consider preserving your vows in some special way. Have someone who does calligraphy write them out on nice paper in a size suitable for framing. At the time you sign your marriage license, also sign your vows. Placed in a frame, your promises can be placed somewhere in your home as a constant reminder of the love and commitment that binds you together. You might also print your vows in your wedding bulletin or program, if you choose to have one. That way all your guests, even those who have difficulty hearing you say your vows during the ceremony, will be able to participate in this important exchange between you and your spouse.

Music and Other Ceremony Elements

Music plays an important part in any worship service or time of celebration. It can be very helpful in creating the desired tone for your ceremony—formal, informal, worshipful, joyful, and so on. You can also use music to contribute to the message of your ceremony. For example, some couples have special songs that express their feelings for one another that they have performed at the ceremony or even sing to each other. Music is also a meaningful way to include others in your celebration by having everyone sing together and by inviting talented family and friends to perform.

Choosing the music for your ceremony can seem like a very difficult task to some couples. If you're having trouble, check first with the wedding coordinator at the church for recommendations. You can also set up an appointment with the organist or director of music to ask for guidance. Also, start paying attention to the music at other weddings you attend. You might hear a piece that fits your ceremony perfectly.

There are traditionally three main ways music is used in a wedding service—the processional, the recessional, and special music.

"I Do" Do's and Don'ts

Do think about your entrance! Traditionally, the bride enters on the arm of her father and is escorted by him to the altar where her groom awaits. Many brides have everyone stand and turn to watch her entrance. This can be signaled to the guests by the mother of the bride standing on cue to the music. Some brides are escorted by both their father and mother—one on each side of the bride. Other brides decide to make a solo entrance. There's no right or wrong way, but it is something you should think about and discuss together. You want your entrance to be meaningful and make a lasting memory for everyone concerned.

Let's Proceed with the Processional

The bridal party enters the sanctuary or proceeds to the altar to the processional. The processional music should have an easy rhythm to walk to—not too fast and not too slow. Many couples choose to have one processional for the wedding party and a different musical piece (such as "Here Comes the Bride") for the bride's entrance. Listed here are just a few suggestions of music to consider for your processional:

Wedding March ("Here Comes the Bride") from *Lohengrin*—(Wagner)

Suite in D major: Prince of Denmark's March ("Trumpet Voluntary")—(Clark)

Jesu, Joy of Man's Desiring—(Bach)

"Air On The G String" from *Orchestral Suite No.3*—(Bach)

Trumpet Tune in D Major—(Purcell)

"Air" from *Water Music*—(Handel)

"Give Me Forever, I Do"—(John Tesh)

"Romance" from *Eine Kleine Nachtmusik*—(Mozart)

"Hornpipe" from *Water Music*—(Handel)

Rondeau—"Masterpiece Theater Theme"—(Mouret)

"Can't Live a Day" (*In a Different Light* album)—(Avalon)

The Four Seasons—(Vivaldi)

Let's Go to the Recessional

This marks the beginning of your new life together. It should be inspirational and upbeat. (Most couples want to get out of the church as quickly as possible!) Try to select a piece that allows enough time for the entire wedding party to exit. Additional music can be added as guests are escorted out. Some possible recessional pieces include the following:

"O God, Our Help in Ages Past" (St. Anne's)(Watts/Croft)

"Wedding March" from *A Midsummer Night's Dream (Opus 61)*—(Mendelssohn)

"Joyful, Joyful, We Adore Thee" (Ode To Joy) from the 9th Symphony —(Beethoven)

"Hornpipe" from *Water Music*—(Handel)

Trumpet Tune in D—(Purcell)

"Entrance Of The Queen Of Sheba" from *Solomon*—(Handel)

Toccata from *Organ Symphony # 5*—(Widor)

"La Rejouissance" from *Royal Fireworks Music*—(Handel)

"Allegro Maestoso" from *Water Music*—(Handel)

Brandenburg Concerto No.3—(Bach)

Crown Imperial March—(Walton)

Magnificat in D, BWV 243—Opening Chorus—(Bach)

Bet You Didn't Know

Based on Psalm 90, the popular wedding hymn "O God, Our Help in Ages Past" was written by Isaac Watts in 1714. A prolific writer of hymns, Isaac Watts was unlucky in love. At five feet tall, he had a big head, a long hooked nose, and a sickly complexion, the result of many illnesses including smallpox. One woman did fall in love with his poetry and wanted to marry him. But when Isaac proposed, she rejected him because of his physical appearance. He remained a lifelong bachelor, gifting us with many hymns of comfort and praise to God.

Meaningful Melodies

Music can be woven throughout your ceremony. What other songs are meaningful to you and your partner? These can be contemporary love songs, classical selections, or hymns. Some churches have restrictions on the type of music that can be performed or played for any service, so work together with the coordinator or music staff to be sure your choices are acceptable (you can save more contemporary songs for the reception).

Readings

Another way to add meaning to your ceremony is to use readings of poetry, Scripture verses, quotes, and song lyrics. Some couples have written letters or poems to each other or to their parents to be read during the wedding ceremony. Readings can be done by you, your partner, someone from the wedding party, or other family members and friends you wish to include in the ceremony. Here are a few traditional samples of readings:

> *Because you love me, I have found*
> *New joys that were not mine before;*
> *New stars have lightened up my sky*
> *With glories growing more and more.*
> *Because you love me I can rise*
> *To the heights of fame and realms of power;*
> *Because you love me I may learn*
> *The highest use of every hour.*
> *Because you love me I can choose*
> *To look through your dear eyes and see*
> *Beyond the beauty of the Now*
> *Far onward to Eternity.*
> *Because you love me I can wait*
> *With perfect patience well possessed;*
> *Because you love me all my life*
> *Is circled with unquestioned rest;*
> *Yes, even Life and even Death*
> *Is all unquestioned and all blest.*
> —from *Pall Mall Magazine*

I love you not only for what you are, but for what I am when I am with you. I love you not only for what you have made of yourself, but for what you are making of me. I love you for the part of me that you bring out.

I love you for putting your hand into my heaped-up heart, and passing over all the foolish and frivolous and weak things which you cannot help dimly seeing there, and for drawing out into the light all the beautiful, radiant belongings, that no one else had looked quite far enough to find.

I love you for ignoring the possibilities of the fool and weakling in me, and for laying firm hold on the possibilities of good in me. I love you for closing your eyes to the discords in me, and for adding to the music in me by worshipful listening.

I love you because you are helping me to make of the lumber of my life not a tavern but a Temple, and of the words of my every day not a reproach but a song.

I love you because you have done more than any creed could have done to make me good, and more than any fate could have done to make me happy. You have done it just by being yourself. Perhaps that is what being a friend means after all.

Tribute
—from *Leaves of Gold*

"Where you go I will go, and where you stay, I will stay. Your people will be my people and your God my God. Where you die I will die, and there I will be buried. May the Lord deal with me, be it ever so severely, if anything but death separates you and me."
Ruth 1:16–17 (NIV)

Love never gives up.
Love cares more for others than for self.
Love doesn't want what it doesn't have.
Love doesn't strut.
Doesn't have a swelled head,
Doesn't force itself on others,
Isn't always "me first,"
Doesn't fly off the handle,
Doesn't keep score of the sins of others,
Takes pleasure in the flowering of truth,
Puts up with anything,

Trusts God always,
Always looks for the best,
Never looks back,
But keeps going to the end.
1 Corinthians 13:4–7 (The Message)

But the Lord watches over those who fear him,
those who rely on his unfailing love.
He rescues them from death and keeps them alive in times of famine.
We depend on the Lord alone to save us.
Only he can help us, protecting us like a shield.
In him our hearts rejoice, for we are trusting in his holy name.
Let your unfailing love surround us, Lord,
for our hope is in you alone.
Psalm 33:18–22

When using Scripture passages, check out different versions to get the reading that is most meaningful to you. You might also consider using a passage as a responsive reading. Responsive readings are a great way to involve everyone attending your wedding in worship. For example, check out this responsive reading from Ephesians 5:

Leader: *Follow God's example in everything you do, because you are his dear children. Live a life filled with love for others, following the example of Christ, who loved you and gave himself as a sacrifice to take away your sins. And further, you will submit to one another out of reverence for Christ. You wives will submit to your husbands as you do to the Lord.*

Women: *For a husband is the head of his wife as Christ is the head of his body, the church; he gave his life to be her Savior. As the church submits to Christ, so you wives must submit to your husbands in everything.*

Leader: *And you husband must love your wives with the same love Christ showed the church.*

Men: *He gave up his life for her … In the same way, husbands ought to love their wives as they love their own bodies. For a man is actually loving himself when he loves his wife.*

All: *As the Scriptures say, "A man leaves his father and mother and is joined to his wife, and the two are united into one."*

Leader: *This is a great mystery, but it is an illustration of the way Christ and the church are one. So again I say, each man must love his wife as he loves himself, and the wife must respect her husband.*

Prayers and Blessings

Prayers and blessings, directly quoted from Scripture or written specifically for you, are an important part of your ceremony. Again, the person performing the ceremony is most likely to deliver a prayer or blessing, but this is another opportunity to include others in your special moment. Think of how meaningful it could be to include parents, spiritual mentors, even children in this part of your ceremony. Make this part of your ceremony as personal and meaningful as any other part. We've listed a few samples for you here to get your creative juices going:

May almighty God, with His word of blessing, unite your hearts in the never-ending bond of pure love.

May your children bring you happiness, and may your generous love for them be multiplied to you.

May the peace of Christ live always in your hearts and in your home. May you have true friends to stand by you, both in joy and in sorrow. May you be ready and willing to help and comfort all who come to you in need, and may the bond of your love be a witness to God's love in every life you touch.

The Lord bless you and keep you;
The Lord make His face to shine upon you,
and be gracious unto you;
The Lord lift up His countenance upon you,
and give you His peace.
In the name of the Father, Son, and Holy Spirit, Amen.

The Big Day

The day you have been planning for has finally arrived. Use the checklists, guidelines, and tips in the pages that follow to keep your special day on-track and as stress-free as possible. Take good care of yourself in the days before your wedding, let others help you with errands, and, most of all, stay focused on your future mate and the exciting adventure you are about to undertake.

Your ceremony will focus on the lifetime commitment God is calling you and your spouse to as you pledge yourselves to each other. It will be a day full of promises that mark the beginning of your life as husband and wife. It will also be a time of rich memories as you celebrate with family and friends. From beginning to end, your special day will be packed with the people and things you love most. It will be over before you know it so relax, slow down, and enjoy every minute.

Chapter 13

From This Day Forward

Your big day is here! You and your family and friends have put in a lot of hard work to get to this moment. Planning a wedding can be very stressful as you work to balance your wants and wishes against everyone else's expectations. And of course you want everything to be perfect! You've already been the center of attention for weeks and now you are going to walk down the aisle dressed like a princess with every eye focused on you. Wow!

As the next several hours rush past (and they will) make every effort to slow down and smell the flowers, taste the cake, and revel in the delights surrounding you. You are building memories that will stick with you the rest of your life, so keep them on the firm foundation that you are deeply loved. Remember also to acknowledge that God is an invited guest to your wedding celebration.

You're Getting Married in the Morning

The day you thought would never come has finally arrived. In the next 24 hours, you're going to wish over and over again that you could slow down time because you will want to enjoy every second of every minute. You, your partner, and all your family have invested a lot in the ceremony and reception that will be taking place in a few hours. You're going to have a wonderful day, but first there are just one or two more details to tend to.

The Bachelor Bash

The purpose behind most bachelor parties is to give the bride and groom one last chance to "sow some wild oats" before they are locked into the monotony of matrimonial fidelity for ever and ever. Because that whole idea is contrary to God's views and vision of marriage, this is one tradition you might want to skip. But if your friends still want to throw you a party, ask them to skip the bachelor bash and have a pool party or backyard barbecue instead.

Try to schedule it several days before the wedding instead of the night before so everyone can be well rested and ready for a full day of activity on wedding day. Consider having the bride's get-together with the girls and the groom's party on the same night or combine the two parties into one big co-ed bash.

Giving Good Gifts

It's customary to give everyone in your wedding party a special gift to say "thank you" for taking part in your special day. These gifts can be given any time before the wedding but are often distributed at the rehearsal dinner. The gifts don't have to be expensive but should be as creative and personal as possible.

The bride chooses the same type of gift for each of her attendants (though they may vary slightly in color or style). She should also choose age appropriate gifts for the flower girl and ring bearer. The groom is responsible for buying each of his attendants a gift. It is not necessary to give others gifts, but it is a nice gesture to give something to your parents and to each other.

The following is a list of great gift ideas for everyone:

- Gift certificates (from a specialty store, catalog, day spa, or restaurant)
- Tickets (to a play, concert, or sporting event)
- Books (something that's a keeper like a classic devotional or inspiration title)
- CDs
- Jewelry

- Magazine subscriptions
- Gift baskets (for the bath, kitchen, garden, and so on)
- Picture frames
- Engraved pens
- Collectibles

You've just spent a small fortune on your wedding so you might not feel you can afford to give each other a gift. That's a perfectly okay choice. If you do decide to exchange gifts with each other just before the wedding, try to find something that will forever remind both of you of the love and joy you shared on your special day.

The following is a list of gift ideas for each other:

- Jewelry—watch, bracelet, ring
- Decorative treasure box
- Book of romantic poetry
- New Bible with a meaningful inscription
- Beautiful artwork
- Framed photograph of the two of you
- Handwritten letter expressing your feelings
- Leather or fabric bound journal

To Sleep, Perchance to Dream!

One of the best things you can do the night before your wedding is to get a good night's sleep. It won't be easy—your head is probably spinning with last minute details. You're mentally checking off every item on every checklist you've ever had. You've just spent several hours at the rehearsal focusing on the details of your cere-mony, and you're not at all certain that anyone was paying attention.

Your parents have assured you *again* that it's not too late to change your mind and your wondering if the rich food at the rehearsal dinner is making you sick. You've chipped a nail, you're getting a zit and no one seems to care as much as you. To top it off, you've just had a tearful few moments with the man you are promising to spend the rest of your life with—perhaps you snapped at him or him at you as nerves got the better of you both. No wonder you can't sleep!

Here are a few simple pointers that might help you drift off to dreamland:

- Try to relax! Take a few deep breaths and exhale slowly.

- Talk to God about it! Whatever it is you are thinking and feeling, he knows and understands. Let him carry it for a while.

- Take a bath! Soak in a tub of warm water with your favorite bath salts or bubble bath.

- Try some warm milk! It's an old remedy but one that really works. There's something in warm milk that helps your body relax. Drink it without chocolate, if you can, because chocolate has the stimulant caffeine in it.

That's the Spirit

This is the day the Lord has made. We will rejoice and be glad in it. (Psalm 118:24) Those who live their lives in obedience to God's Word and seek to follow Christ in all they say and do can face every day with joy. May your joy be multiplied on this your wedding day because you know that it is God who has brought the two of you together.

Bride's Guide for Survival

It's going to be a long day and you want to enjoy every minute of it. Brides who have made thoughtful choices in the final days before the wedding and who start the day off right are better equipped to watch over the final details in the plan, to enter into worship during the ceremony, and to participate fully in the celebration that follows. Here are some guidelines to help you outlast everyone on your wedding day.

Start Your Day Out Right

Hopefully you've planned ahead for a relaxing start to your wedding day. Try not to have any errands to run. It's best if the only thing you have to worry about is getting to the church on time. If yours is a morning ceremony, you'll probably get up just in time for a quick breakfast and start getting ready. Begin with at least a brief prayer and if there's time, a short reading from Scripture. Don't skip breakfast even if it's a light one. You're going to need a lot of energy. If your ceremony is scheduled later in the day, start with a massage to work out the tension and relax.

Pack a small bag of essentials to take with you to the ceremony and reception (your maid of honor can keep it for you). You might want to include: comb, brush, extra stockings, nail polish to match your color, cosmetics, any medication you might need, makeup for touch-ups, hairspray, lotion, and your I.D.

If you are planning on taking your photographs before the ceremony, consider ordering a fruit and cheese tray and bottles of juice or water to take to the church. With getting dressed, the photo sessions, and the ceremony, it might be several hours before the wedding party gets to eat. Wedding party members have been know to faint during the ceremony because they have gone so long without eating.

Family Ties

Find a special way to thank Mom and Dad for all they have done for you, not only with the wedding but for raising you in a loving home. Fix a special breakfast to share with them or take them out. Consider spending the morning with Mom at a spa getting a facial, manicure, and make-up. You'll both feel great and look beautiful when you're done.

Let Others Be Responsible

Wise brides realize that they can't do it all. The following Wedding Day Planner table lets you orchestrate the important parts of your wedding without having to oversee every detail. If you want to enjoy your day, you have to let go of some control and let others shoulder some of the responsibility for executing your plan. Choose a few good friends or family members to manage the details.

Wedding Day Planner

Assignment:	Assigned to:
Two Days Before:	
Call vendors to confirm reservations	_____
Put together a schedule and make copies	_____
Verify guest transportation	_____

continues

Wedding Day Planner *(continued)*

Assignment:	Assigned to:

Two Days Before:

Double-check wedding night accommodations _____

Confirm honeymoon reservations _____

Remind wedding party of the schedule _____

Put together emergency wedding kit _____

Other: _____

The Day Before:

Ensure marriage license and rings get to ceremony _____

Gather something old, something new, something borrowed, and something blue _____

Pick up and drop off wedding dress _____

Pick up and deliver bridesmaids' dresses _____

Confirm that all men have picked up their attire _____

Confirm flower delivery _____

Confirm cake delivery _____

Confirm transportation for ceremony and reception _____

Distribute copies of the schedule to everyone _____

Give out diagrams of where to stand during ceremony _____

Receive, check in, and unpack rentals _____

Take candid photos at rehearsal _____

Other: _____

Wedding Day Set-up:

Bring emergency wedding day kit _____

Receive flowers _____

Take bridal bouquets to bridal party _____

Help pin boutonnieres on male attendants _____

Set cake table with cake knife and server _____

Assist with final touches when the cake arrives _____

Help place centerpieces _____

Check the reception room set-up _____

Assignment:	Assigned to:

Wedding Day Set-up:

Set up candles for reception and ceremony area _____

Set up entry table and guest book _____

Set ceremony table (Bible, unity candle, flowers) _____

Attach reserved seating cards where applicable _____

Give wedding programs to person who will
hand them out _____

Check on sound system set-up _____

Test the microphones _____

Watch over wedding gifts table _____

Run emergency errands _____

Other: _____

At the Ceremony:

Identify people on photo checklist for photographer _____

Make certain officiant has the marriage license _____

Give officiant his fee or honorarium _____

Oversee musicians as they set up _____

Review ushers' duties with them _____

Check that wedding party everything they need _____

Double-check that best man has the bride's ring _____

Double-check that maid of honor has the groom's
ring _____

Other: _____

At the Reception:

Help direct guests to receiving line _____

Hand out final payments and gratuities _____

Decorate the getaway car _____

Review play list with musicians or DJ _____

Ensure departing couple gets "goody box"
of food _____

Transfer luggage to getaway car _____

continues

Wedding Day Planner *(continued)*

Assignment:	Assigned to:
At the Reception:	
Confirm getaway car is ready	_____
Gather guest to bid couple good-bye	
Gather all belongings from bridal dressing area	_____
Pack up and transport bridal gifts	_____
Help bride change into going-away clothes	_____
Take charge of wedding dress and accessories	_____
Oversee breakdown and return of rentals	_____
Oversee clean up of reception site	_____
Other:	_____

Assignment:	Assigned to:
The Day After:	
Return rented tuxedos	_____
Take bride's gown to be cleaned	_____
Take extra floral arrangements to elderly	_____
Other:	_____

Wedding Day Emergencies

Even at a perfectly planned wedding, something is bound to go wrong. But you shouldn't have to worry about it! Designate someone outside of your immediate families and the wedding party as the official "go to" person for emergencies. Make sure that person has a cell phone, a list of essential telephone numbers, and access to the wedding emergency kit. Here are some items you might want in your kit:

Medical:

- Antacids
- Clear bandages
- Smelling salts
- Tweezers
- Tylenol or ibuprofen

Personal:

- Bobby pins (white veil)
- Clear nail polish (for quick stocking repair)
- Curling iron
- Deodorant
- Extra earring backs
- Extra stockings
- Facial tissue or handkerchief
- Hair dryer
- Hairspray
- Mouthwash
- Sanitary napkins/tampons
- Static cling spray
- Toothbrush and toothpaste

General:

- Bottled water
- Clear tape
- Clean white cloth
- Corsage pins
- Crackers
- Mints
- Money
- Safety pins
- Scissors
- Sewing kit
- Spot remover
- Super glue
- Ziploc bags
- Other: _____

A Picture Perfect Day

With all the time and energy you have spent on this day, one thing you want to ensure is that you have a lasting record of the love, laughter, and tears. A good wedding photographer and/or videographer is the best way to have and hold onto those memories for years to come. You will want to review every special moment together and share them with others over and over again. Here are some guidelines for choosing the right professionals and all the details that go into making your wedding day picture perfect.

Choosing a Photographer

Don't trust your wedding memories to a friend with a camera. Hire a professional wedding photographer even if it means cutting back on something else. Start by asking other couples who have recently been married how satisfied they are with the results of their photographer. Look at their photos to get an idea of what he or she can do. Interview several photographers until you find the right one for you. Here are a few basic questions to ask during the interview:

- What packages do you offer?

- How many photos are included in each package?

- Will I get to keep the "proofs"?

- Do I have to guarantee ordering a set number of reprints from you?

- What is the cost for additional time or photos?

- How much is the deposit, and when is it due?

- When is the balance due?

- Do you charge for travel?

- Can I purchase the negatives? If so, when can I purchase them?

> **"I Do" Do's and Don'ts**
>
> Do include your partner in as many wedding-day decisions as you can. Hopefully you have already discussed your wedding-day priorities. Talk about how you want to handle the photography: Should it be before or after the ceremony? Who does your partner want photographed? What wedding-day events does he or she want photographed?

Make sure you see samples of his or her work. Ask about any special photographs you would like to have taken or any special effects you would like used. Just as important, hire someone you feel comfortable with and who you feel will listen to you and respect your wishes. Good photographers will only do so many weddings in a week, and their schedules book up fast. Start your search early so you have plenty of time to make your decision and so you can get the person you want. This is your story he or she will be telling.

It's All About Timing

There will be so much happening so quickly on your special day that you will want to make sure your photographer is in the right place at the right time—he or she can't be in two places at the same time! Professionals who have been in the business for a long time will advise you to consider your photographer when arranging your wedding day schedule.

The first decision you will need to make is whether or not to take photos before the ceremony. Although it is very sentimental to have the groom's first view of his bride be when she walks down the aisle, many couples today choose to have a photo session before the ceremony. This is especially important if the reception is scheduled to start immediately after the ceremony. It is a real nightmare for everyone to have guests waiting at the reception while photos are being shot after the ceremony.

It also means the photographer has less time to take photos of the cake and reception site set up. Here's a typical schedule to give you an idea of timing for photographs taken before the ceremony. Use it to talk over timing with your photographer because every situation will be unique:

12:00 P.M.—Bridal party arrives at church

12:15 P.M.—Individual shots of wedding party

1:00 P.M.—Private meeting of bride and groom

1:30 P.M.—Photo session with wedding party

1:45 P.M.—Guests begin to arrive

2:00 P.M.—Ceremony begins

3:00 P.M.—Ceremony ends

3:15 P.M.—After-wedding shots at ceremony site

4:00 P.M.—Reception begins

7:30 P.M.—Bride and groom leave

8:00 P.M.—Reception ends

If you will be taking your photographs after the ceremony, then you will want to schedule at least two hours between the end of the ceremony and the beginning of the reception. For photographers who charge by the hour (4–6 hours total) or who schedule by the clock (2:00 to 8:00 P.M., for example) timing might make all the difference to your budget and to the shots you get. If possible, try to contract for unlimited coverage with your package. Then you can space the events out as much as you want without having to worry about paying your photographer anything extra.

Know What Shots You Want

Don't expect your photographer to read your mind or to recognize Aunt Polly. The only way to be sure you get the shots you want is to make a list and go over it with your photographer ahead of time. You can use the Checklist for the Photographer. Before the ceremony, give a copy of the checklist to the photographer and designate someone to assist him in finding the people and places on the list.

Checklist for Photographer

Here are the special people and moments we would like you to capture in our wedding photos. If you have any questions, _____ will be your contact if we are not available.

People

Bride's family

Groom's family

Maid/Matron of Honor

Best man

Bridesmaids

Groomsmen/Ushers

Others (Readers, musicians, officiant, etc.)

Moments

Before the ceremony: Bride/Groom

Arriving at the ceremony: Bride/Groom

Ceremony

Reception

Processional/Recessional

Cutting the cake

Exchanging wedding vows

Throwing the bouquet

You may kiss the bride

Leaving for honeymoon

Signing the license

Special guests

Others:

Things

Wedding flowers

Altar/Sanctuary

Invitation

Rings

Others:

Advice from a Professional

Here's a list of great tips for everything from make-up to mugging for the cameras from professional wedding photograper Jerry Schrader. Jerry has had years of experience photographing picture-perfect weddings and knows just what to tell the bride and groom. You can check out his website at www.jerryschrader.com or contact him at 508-485-1987.

The following are tips for perfect wedding photos from a professional photographer:

Flowers: Avoid choosing flowers with long spikes. They are hard to photograph and intrude into portraits. Also, pure white bouquets do not shoot well. With all that white, you need a little color in your bouquet. Practice holding your bouquet tipped forward so the handle and your hands are concealed. Ask bridesmaids to hold their flowers in a relaxed way, so their hands appear graceful, elegant, and uniform.

Makeup: A wedding gown reflects a lot of light into a bride's face, especially if it has a full bodice and the bride has a large chest. Also, overhead light reflects off the bodice and bleaches makeup. Wear a little more to offset the effect, usually more blush. Make sure the makeup base you use matches your natural shade or your head will appear pasted on. When you are inspecting your makeup, look at your neck and whatever body that is exposed to be sure it's the same color and brightness as your face. Blend well and be sure there are no lines or edges, especially near the jaw line where the makeup ends.

Use a little lip gloss to highlight the lip. That little reflection can make a portrait sparkle! If your lips are cracked and dry, condition them for a month before the wedding so they can be their most attractive for your pictures.

I ask my brides not to release their makeup person until I have had a good look. Your makeup should not be obvious. Sometimes it takes a lot of makeup to make it appear as if you are not wearing any.

Double-check your bridesmaids. Try to get their makeup to match so you don't have a heavily made-up bridesmaid next to a girl who hates makeup. See if you can get the noticeably made-up bridesmaid to tone it down a little, and can we get a little lipstick and blush on the other?

Stay away from makeup fads, because you want your look to stand the test of time.

Men in your wedding: Cummerbunds are worn with the pleats up. The story is that they were worn to catch the crumbs at mealtime. The best way to tuck in a shirt is to reach into the fly and grab the shirttails and pull down. In a more discreet fashion, put your hands into your pockets, and using the pocket as a mitten, grab your shirttails and pull down. Many tux pants have a slit that allows you access to your shirttails.

Men often stand in what I call the jock pose, with feet shoulder-width apart and hands clasped in front. When the groomsmen (or ushers) are standing at the altar, every guest in the wedding is watching them. As difficult as it is, they should stand feet slightly apart, hands at sides, and try not to slouch.

Walking Down the Aisle: Brides should walk down the aisle slowly, head up, bouquet tipped slightly forward. You can look around, acknowledge best friends in the audience, wave, or otherwise interact. It makes for natural, interesting pictures, and your friends will appreciate the attention. Don't stare at the floor and walk solemnly. This is a celebration!

Bridesmaids should walk with their heads up, backs straight, bouquets tipped slightly forward, and smile. They should try not to be as animated as the bride, but it's okay to look and see who is there.

Readers: Ask your readers to practice their selection as much as it takes to get completely comfortable with it before the big day. Allow them to take their copy to the podium, but they should know the speech and be able to recite it audibly and clearly, without stumbling. And please, ask them to look up once in a while so the photographer can get a shot. If the reader is hunched over, nervously unprepared, there will be no way to compensate for this in the photograph.

The Ceremony: Worst-case scenario places the clergy (officiant) in the aisle with his/her back to the audience, and the bride and groom in front of them. No one can see any of the ceremony, and it's very difficult to shoot.

The best layout places the officiant in back of the bride and groom, with the couple facing one another. If the couple faces the officiant, with their backs to the audience, it is again very hard to see what is going on, and there are few good pictures.

Mugging for the Camera: I've changed my mind about this over the years; it makes for some fun pictures. But for the most part, it's best to act naturally. Don't stare at the camera. I will direct someone in the shot if it is needed.

Attitude: Often brides are nervous about being the center of so much attention. They want to play down their role so they don't appear to be showing off. But you are the center of attention and well wishes—don't be afraid to shine and go with the moment. Your friends and relatives have come to celebrate and will want to share this joyous occasion with you to the fullest.

A Star Is Born

Photos are great, but they can't record the actions and sounds of your wedding day joy. With video you can have a lasting record that will "speak" to you and your children about the day you started your family. Videography is becoming more common and more affordable all the time, but it can still be expensive depending on the area you live in and the type of recording you contract for. However, even if you decide you can't afford a professional videographer, find the best "someone" you can to make a video movie of your special day. It's a special memory keepsake.

Why Videotape Your Wedding?

Besides providing you with a precious keepsake of your special day, today's smaller and more advanced cameras allow a videographer to inconspicuously capture on film moments that you might otherwise not get to see. Just like with your photographer, you will still want to create a checklist of special moments and people for him or her to record. An experienced videographer will also ask you enough questions and get to know you well enough so that he can look for those "secret treasures" that might otherwise be missed. For example, he or she might look for comical moments like your bridesmaids doing the can-can just before the ceremony or sentimental moments like your 80-year-old grandparents stealing a kiss at the reception.

Who to Hire?

As always, start with recommendations from people you trust. Always ask to see examples of actual weddings that show a variety of options. Look for clear images, good quality recording, good composition, and an eye for detail. You'll also need to judge the creativity of the shooting and editing. Audio quality is just as important as the visual images, so listen for clarity and smooth transitions. Interview as many professionals as you need to until you find one you are comfortable with hiring. And don't be afraid to ask for references you may contact. The following is a list of questions to ask a videographer:

- How long have you been in business?
- What packages do you offer?
- Do you use professional quality equipment and supplies?
- What type of lighting will you use?
- What type of tape do you record on?
- Do you offer DVDs?
- How will you be dressed at the wedding?
- Are you unobtrusive?
- How many cameras do you use?
- Do you have back-up equipment that is comparable in quality to the original?
- Do you use high-band wireless microphones?
- Do you offer Non-Linear Digital Editing?
- Do you copy-protect or scramble the videotape?
- What are your guarantees and liabilities?
- Do you have a written contract?
- How much do additional hours cost?
- Will you attend the rehearsal?
- Are you familiar with both the ceremony and reception sites?
- Do you work with the photographer to ensure mutual cooperation?
- Are you there throughout the entire reception?
- Do you charge an additional travel fee?
- How much are additional copies of the wedding tapes?

There are two types of video recordings for weddings. A long-form wedding video records every moment of the wedding service from beginning to end. Likewise, nearly every minute of the reception is recorded from the traditional events like cutting the cake and tossing the bouquet to all the chatter and action of the guests until the bride and groom leave. A long-form recording has a running time of about 90 minutes.

Other couples are going to the short-form recording which captures the highlights of the wedding day. It's more like a living photo album rather than a running commentary. The short form still captures every important moment of the ceremony and reception but edits out the nonessential footage. The finished running time for a short-form video is about 30 to 40 minutes. Long or short is a matter of personal taste and an option to discuss with your videographer.

How Much Will It Cost?

There are several factors that influence the cost of videography. Depending on the area of the country you live in, a standard package can run from $300 to $3,000. You are primarily paying for the videographer's time and equipment. You can cut costs by choosing a package that uses only one camera and arranging the schedule so that your videographer can capture the most important moments in the least amount of time. It is also cheaper to accept raw footage as your final product because editing takes time and costs more. Even with those concessions, you will still get a higher quality recording than you can get from Uncle Bill.

Family Ties

If you have grandparents attending your ceremony and reception, assign someone from the family to watch over them. Sometimes they miss out on special family moments because they don't hear the directions or they simply get overlooked. Grandparents represent your heritage from the Lord and deserve to be honored on your special day.

Videographers can offer you other services beyond recording your wedding day. Consider having a video created to play at the reception that chronicles your two lives up to the wedding. Using still photos from the childhoods of both bride and groom supplemented by photos of their courtship, add a little background music and you have a wonderful piece of entertainment for your reception.

Note: Many places of worship and clergy do not allow supplemental lighting during the ceremony. Check this out before you meet with your videographers so you can get their advice. Unlike photographers, videographers are taping live, so they can't just take a break whenever they need or want one. Be sensitive to the fact that your videographer might actually work 8 to 10 hours straight on your wedding day. Assign someone to check in with him or her from time to time to see if they need anything and to make sure they get to eat and drink something at the reception.

A Place for Everyone

Keeping track of everyone on wedding day can be a tough job. It can be very disturbing to have someone from the wedding party suddenly disappear just when you need them for a photo or for some other reason. However, you don't want to have to keep track of everyone yourself, either. This is one thing you can delegate to your maid of honor and/or best man. Request that anyone in the wedding party or in the immediate families let one of them know if it's necessary to leave even for a short time. You will also need to think through the proper seating arrangements for family and special guests, as well as the order for the processional and recessional. It will feel good to have a place for everyone and everyone in their place.

Ceremony Seating

Depending on your location, your wedding party members, and your family situation, there might be dozens of "right" ways to handle seating. We will give here some general guidelines that you might adapt to your specific situation. One good rule to follow is that after the mother of the bride is seated, no other guests may be seated until the processional has been completed with the bride at the altar. Late arriving guests may then quietly slip into any available seat in the back.

The first two to three rows of seating should be reserved for family and special guests. The parents of the bride sit in the first row on the left-hand side as you face the altar. The groom's parents sit in the first row on the right-hand side. Grandparents should you seated next to or directly behind the parents, left side for bride and right side for groom. Additional family members and special guests may be seated next to the grandparents in the second row or in the third row.

"I Do" Do's and Don'ts

If you or your partner come from a divorced family, do talk over how to handle the seating arrangements at the ceremony and reception. When couples have stepfathers and stepmothers participating in or attending their wedding, things can get a little complicated. The best way to keep from disappointing anyone is to talk openly about your choices and decisions.

How to Go In and Come Out

Tradition and wedding etiquette dictate the order in which the wedding party enters and exits the sanctuary or altar site and exits. The entrance is called the processional and occurs in all weddings—formal, semiformal, or casual—in various forms. The exit or recession is not necessary at a very casual wedding (such as a small, home ceremony where guests mingle directly after the service), but does occur in all other weddings. At most Christian weddings, the officiant, groom, and best man (in that order) enter from the right front side and wait at the altar for the rest of the processional. Here are some general guidelines for the before and after parade. The listings are beginning with the first to enter and exit.

Processional	Recessional
Special guests	Bride and groom
Parents of groom	Flower girl
Mother of bride	Ring bearer
Groomsmen/ushers in pairs	Maid of honor and best man
Bridesmaids	Bridesmaids/groomsmen in pairs
Maid/matron of honor	Bride's parents
Flower girl	Groom's parents
Ring bearer	Special guests
Bride with father	Other guests excused by row

There are many contemporary variations on this plan which are perfectly acceptable. The only rule of thumb to follow is that the bride should always be the last to enter and the first to leave. One final word of advice: When you enter or exit, slow down and try to notice the people around you.

Your Carriage Awaits

You arrived at the church separately, but you will leave it as one. After you're pronounced husband and wife, you'll be ready to get on to the celebration. This sounds like a good time to discuss transportation options. Some couples want some type of special transportation to go from the church to their reception. Although you will probably read a lot in bridal magazines about renting a limousine, that's not always the best choice. And it's certainly not the only choice.

At the least, have the best man or one of the groomsmen act as your chauffeur and drive you to the reception so the two of you can sit back and relax for a few moments together before you face your guests. Another affordable option is to rent a classic car or a luxury car for the day (sometimes it's nearly as cheap to rent for the weekend). In some towns you can rent a horse and carriage—a dream come true for many brides.

If you have your heart set on a limo, do your homework before you decide on any service. The average cost for limousine service is $100 an hour. Try to get a good referral because the quality of service for transportation companies can vary greatly. When renting any form of transportation make sure first of all that they are fully licensed and have liability insurance. Here are a few other questions to ask:

- What is your minimum number of hours for rental?
- What is the cost per hour?
- Will you provide a back-up vehicle if necessary?
- What types and sizes of vehicles do you have?
- May I see the vehicles?
- Can I request a specific vehicle?
- What can you tell me about your drivers?
- How many drivers are available?
- How do they dress?
- How much of a gratuity is expected?

It's fun to treat yourselves by traveling to your reception in style. But even if you end up with a pumpkin and four white mice, all you really need is a reliable and comfortable ride to your wedding celebration where you can party the hours away.

Chapter
14

Let the Celebration Begin!

Finally, you can exhale! It's time for you and your new spouse to relax and have fun. Your reception is all about celebrating your marriage and enjoying great food, fun, and fellowship with your family and friends. Whether you choose a casual family get-together or a strictly formal affair, the "rules" are not as important as designing a reception that's right for you. As much as your ceremony was a reflection of your faith and love, your reception should be a reflection of your unique style as a couple.

With that in mind, there are certain elements to a reception that will define the type of affair it will be. The number of guests you wish to invite and your budget will have the greatest impact on your reception plan. Your reception can cost from 35 to 50 percent of your total wedding budget. It's an important expense that requires careful consideration, but it can be money well spent if it gives you memories you will cherish for a lifetime. No matter how you choose to celebrate, you and your guests will have a delightful time sharing good food and fun as you share in the joy of your union.

Location, Location, Location

One of the most important elements to any reception is location. Where you hold your reception will define the boundaries of style and ambiance for this celebration. Your budget will probably determine your wedding reception site—that, and the availability of the location you desire because the best and favored spots tend to book up early. But there are many location options to choose from—hotels, clubs, restaurants, gardens, and church halls—and a creative couple will either find or create the perfect place for their postnuptial party.

Finding the Right Fit

There are two basic types of reception sites. The first type charges a per person fee which includes the facility, food, tables, silverware, china, and so forth. Hotels, restaurants, inns, and catering halls are typical examples. The second type charges a room rental fee and you are responsible for providing just about everything else: the food, beverages, linens, and possibly tables and chairs. Civic locations such as parks, gardens, concert halls, and museums fall into this category, as well as most "at home" and many church receptions.

The advantage of the first type is that most everything is done for you. The disadvantage, however, is that your choices are limited. These types of places usually have package deals that prescribe everything from the menu choices to the room arrangement and table décor. Any deviation from the "plan" can cost you extra money. The advantages of the second type of site are that you have much more control over the selection of everything—food, décor, set-up, and so on. You can hire your own caterer or handle many aspects of the set-up (such as decorations) yourself, which often saves you money. The obvious disadvantage is that you will have a lot more to be responsible for and that can be stressful.

When comparing different locations, consider the proximity to the ceremony site and transportation, ambiance, available service staff, quality of food, parking, gratuity, set-up charges, and the cost of rental equipment needed such as tables, chairs, canopies, and so forth. If you are planning an outdoor reception, be sure to have a backup site in case of rain.

Ways to Save on the Reception

If you're on a tight budget and need to save some money, the reception is one area where cost-savings can be significant. Besides handling the catering yourself and booking civil sites, consider these additional tips for saving:

- **Create your own centerpieces.** There are many simple but elegant centerpieces and decorations that you can create yourself for a fraction of the cost of professional floral arrangements. Pillar candles in a floral candle ring, floating candles in a classy glass bowl, and potted flowers or plants are just a few ideas.

- **Reuse ceremony decorations at your reception.** Altar arrangements and arches look great flanking doorways or as a backdrop for pictures. Pew decorations and bridesmaids bouquets can be used as table accents, and your unity candle would make a great centerpiece for the bridal table.

- **Book at an "off" time.** Saturday evenings in May and June are extremely popular times for social functions and most locations know that and charge accordingly. By holding your reception earlier in the day, on an alternate day (Sunday through Thursday), and during an off-season for your region you might be able to get the location of your dreams at a fraction of the cost.

- **Forget the bridal packages.** Many package deals might include things you could care less about for your own reception. So you end up paying for food items or services you don't even want. Try ordering individual services and food items instead. And check out package deals other than "bridal" packages. Sometimes the cost for the same items is marked up just because it's for a wedding.

- **Choose a less formal plan.** Food may be served as a sit-down meal, a seated buffet (first course is served, main course and dessert is buffet), or buffet. Sit-down dinners are always more expensive than buffets. Give more value to what you want to serve instead of how you want to serve it.

That's the Spirit

A marriage is like a long trip in a tiny rowboat: if one passenger starts to rock the boat, the other has to steady it; otherwise they will go to the bottom together.
—David Reuben

Always keep yourselves united in the Holy Spirit, and bind yourselves together with peace. (Ephesians 3:3)

Grade "A" Catering

Food will most likely be the number-one item in your reception planning. Unless you are going to make all the food yourself, you will need to find a caterer. Even if you are considering a location that has a caterer on staff, you will want to interview that person to ensure you are satisfied with the quality of food and service they offer before you book the site. Because this part of the reception is so important (and costly), review the following guidelines before you make your decision.

Guaranteed Good Taste

There are many things that contribute to a good catering experience—quality and freshness of the ingredients, how it is prepared and served, and the professionalism of the catering staff. Get recommendations from family and friends and then interview the caterers you are most interested in and feel you can afford.

The following is a list of questions to ask the caterer:

- What are our menu options for our budget?
- Can we have a taste test of the food on our menu?
- When is the menu "set in stone"?
- Where is the food prepared?
- When will our food be prepared?
- What is the average serving size?
- Can we see a wedding during set-up?
- Are you familiar with my reception site?
- Will you be catering any other events the same weekend?
- How do your servers dress?
- For buffet receptions, how often will the food be replenished?
- Given the style of my reception, how many waiters do we need?
- What services are extra (cutting the cake, coffee service)?
- How is the charge for labor figured?
- How much does a dessert table cost?
- Is the wedding cake included?
- Do you provide a written estimate and contract?

- Are you licensed?
- What are your cancellation/postponement policies?
- Will you guarantee these price estimates? (For how long?)
- Is there a cap on price escalations?
- What type of tipping is required?

"I Do" Do's and Don'ts

You'll be very busy socializing at your reception. It's quite possible for the bride and groom to barely get a bit of the food they have spent so much time and money arranging for their guests. Do have the caterer prepare you a going-away package with samples for two. Later when you reach your lodgings, you might be very grateful for a tasty treat to enjoy at your leisure.

Don't be confused by all the rules for tipping at an event like a wedding reception. You can avoid the stress and unexpected surprises by following these simple tips on tipping:

- Inquire ahead of time about what's customary.
- Ask that all gratuities be included in your contracts.
- Ignore pressure from any vendors.
- Tip only for service rendered.
- Tip according to how satisfied you are with the service.

Ways to Save on Food

While you want to make sure the quality of the food at your reception is top-notch, there are ways to save. Check out a few of these ideas:

- **Limit your menu.** Remember the goal is to have good food and plenty of it. That can be accomplished with a limited selection and menu items that are in-season and take little preparation time.
- **Serve only cake and beverages.** Time your reception so that guests would naturally eat before they come and word the invitation accordingly: "Please join us for cake immediately following the ceremony."

- **Do it yourself.** It might sound impossible, but many couples cater their own receptions with the help of family and friends. Dessert buffets, punch/coffee/tea, and hors d'oeuvres receptions are all easy to pull together.

- **Hire a caterer for less.** A caterer who is just getting started in your area or who works out of his or her home might be more affordable and just as good as the seasoned professional. Ask around for good referrals.

Let Them Eat Cake

The focal point of every wedding reception is the wedding cake. Wedding cakes may be ordered from a caterer or a bakery. Some hotels and restaurants might be able to provide a wedding cake. However, you will probably be better off ordering your cake from a bakery that specializes in wedding cakes. When ordering your cake, you will have to decide not only on a flavor, but also on a size, shape, and color. The size is determined by the number of guests you plan to serve. Today's wedding cakes come in many shapes and size. You can choose from one large tier to two, three, or more, smaller tiers. The cake can be round, square, or heart-shaped. The most common flavors are chocolate, carrot, lemon, rum, and white cake.

Finding the Right Cake Maker

There are many options for finding a baker for your wedding cake. There are bakeshops that specialize in weddings, pastry chefs and caterers, independent bakers, and grocery stores. Ask recently married friends and relatives for recommendations. The wedding coordinator at your church, if there is one, might have some good ideas. If you attend a reception where there is a cake you like, don't be afraid to inquire about who made it. After you know the number of guests for the reception, start researching your options several months in advance; make an appointment and ask the following questions:

- May I see photos of cakes you have designed?
- Can we have a taste test?
- Can you decorate the cake with flowers? Who obtains the flowers?
- How far in advance is the cake prepared?
- Who will actually decorate, deliver, and assemble our cake?
- Do you give written estimates?

- Are there any additional charges not included in the estimate?
- Will you provide a written contract listing all the details (flavors, cake-shape, filling, and icing) along with rentals, delivery, and set-up fees?

Designing Your Cake

You have a lot of decisions to make when choosing your wedding cake. Cakes now come in a variety of flavors for both the cake itself and the icing and fillings. You might also want to consider having tiers or different flavors. Here are some of the elements to consider in designing you dream cake:

- **Cake flavor and texture**—You can have the traditional vanilla-flavored white, chocolate, chocolate and vanilla swirl, lemon, carrot, or just about any other flavor you can dream up, depending on your baker.
- **Filling**—Besides the traditional frosting-filling, you might consider fruit jam, butter cream, fresh fruit, mousses, and custards in flavors like chocolate, lemon, or berry.
- **Frosting and decorations**—The traditional butter cream can now come in many colors besides white for both the base frosting and the accent frosting. Other frosting options are whipped cream and meringue, and rolled fondant or marzipan. Decorating can be done in white on white, color on white, white on color and off-white. Flowers, swags, and basket weaves are common.
- **Cake toppers**—Beside the traditional bride and groom in either plastic or glass, you might also choose fresh or silk flowers, edible decorations, or any type of figure that is symbolic or has special meaning to you as a couple—birds, butterflies, hearts, and so on.

Is the Price Right?

Wedding cakes are usually priced per serving with the average range being $1 to $4 per serving, or around $500 to serve 200 guests. What you are paying for is the quality of the work and the taste—both of which can vary greatly from baker to baker. In addition to flavor, size, and cost, some baker's charge for set-up and delivery. The cake should be beautifully displayed on its own table decorated with flowers or greenery. If the baker, caterer, or reception site manager doesn't provide you with a pretty cake-cutting knife, you will need to buy or borrow one. If you plan on saving the top tier for your first anniversary, make sure it is not figured in the total of servings.

You might be asked to make a deposit of up to 50 percent of the total cost of your cake at the time you place your order. Some bakeries also require a deposit on columns, fountains, and plates used in assembling tiered cakes. Other bakeries use disposable columns and plates, saving you the rental fee and the hassle of returning these items.

Ways to Save on the Wedding Cake

You don't want to sacrifice taste and quality on the wedding cake; you can get both and still save yourself some money with these saving tips:

- **Make your own wedding cake.** The only thing that sounds harder than catering your own wedding is the idea of making your own cake. However, you can get step-by-step directions on cake baking and decoration that make it easy for even the least experienced bride to create her own cake.

- **Don't save the top tier.** Just how good can a cake taste after a year in your freezer? You can save from 10 to 20 percent by serving the top tier instead and ordering a small, fresh cake on your anniversary.

- **Buy a smaller cake.** Pair it with a large sheet cake or place it atop several fake cakes—foam cakes that are decorated and iced—to create the look of a tiered cake. If you are also serving a groom's cake or including a dessert table, plan on serving smaller portions of the wedding cake.

- **Go nuts with the sides.** The smoothly iced sides of a cake that are so popular cost more because of the labor involved. Asking your baker to roll your cake sides in nuts or coconut can save the baker time and can save you money.

- **Hire a freelance baker.** Cake decorators who work from their homes have lower overhead costs than professional bakers and can pass that savings on to you. The savings can be significant—$1 to $2 per serving.

The Groom's Cake

The groom's cake is an old southern tradition whereby this cake is cut up and distributed to guests in little white boxes engraved with the bride's and groom's names.

Today the groom's cake, if offered, is usually cut and served along with the wedding cake. Usually the groom's cake is chocolate cake decorated with fruit. Because of its cost and labor involved in cutting and distributing the cake, very few people offer this delightful tradition anymore.

Cutting the Cake

You can ask special friends to cut the cake as a way to include them in your wedding. It does take a little know-how. Remove the layer you want to cut. Never cut a layer while it's on top of another layer. About two inches from the outside of the cake, make a circular cut all the way around the cake. Then from the outside into the cut, slice pieces off. Repeat this process moving in two inches at a time, all the way to the center of the cake. You can have a pretty little lace apron made with your wedding colors for the servers to wear. It's a nice keepsake, too.

That's the Spirit

> We were filled with laughter, and we sang for joy. And the other nations said, "What amazing things the Lord has done for them." Yes, the Lord has done amazing things for us! What joy! (Psalm 126:2–3)

Your wedding celebration should be an example to others of the way God has blessed you, not just in a material way, but in the richness of your relationships and your love for one another.

Planning An Affair to Remember

Now that you have the perfect location and the best food your money can buy, it's time to turn your attention to what you want to actually take place at your reception. A great reception is one where everyone, especially the bride a groom, has a good time. What a "good time" means to you and your family and friends might vary, but there are some elements that are familiar to most wedding receptions. You can mix and match these elements to create an affair that is a unique expression of you and that everyone will remember fondly.

Meet and Greet Your Guests

Guests come to your wedding to see you! So while you are the guest of honor at every event, you must also demonstrate hospitality. That means making time meet and greet each of your guests during the course of the day. How you do this varies.

In some areas of the country and with small, informal celebrations, the bride and groom mingle systematically throughout the reception, stopping at each table or group of guests to receive congratulations and thank people for attending.

The receiving line is still an important part of many couples' celebration. Some couples choose to have their receiving line at the ceremony site immediately after the ceremony. After the recessional, the wedding party organizes and guests are directed to the receiving line as they exit the sanctuary or chapel. Other couples wait until they arrive at the reception. If you choose to have your receiving line at the reception, you may use it to greet guests as they arrive or shortly after the reception activities begin. Be sensitive to the number of guests you will be greeting and how long it may take for the last guest in the line to reach you. It's unkind to keep hungry guests waiting indefinitely to greet you, but it is equally undesirable to postpone your receiving line so that it is so late in the festivities that many tired guests give up and go home without ever getting the opportunity to speak with you.

Besides the newlyweds, deciding who will be in the receiving line is your call. Both the bride's and groom's parents may be included, as well as the maid or matron of honor and the bridesmaids. Usually the line begins with the mother of the bride, followed in order by the father of the bride, the mother of the groom, the father of the groom, and finally, the bride and groom. Any bridal attendants included would stand at the end of the line. Of course, the more people you include in the line, the longer it will take for guests to make their way through it.

If the upside of a receiving line is that it ensures that every guest has the opportunity to meet and greet the newlyweds, then the downside is that these exchanges must naturally be kept short. It is each guest's responsibility to greet the first person in the line with his or her name and relationship to the bride or groom. Introductions are then passed along through the line, keeping guests moving at a comfortable pace.

Time-Honored Traditions

For some, a wedding reception is not complete without observing certain traditions like tossing the bouquet and garter. Others skip these activities in favor of others that have more meaning for them personally. Remember, this is your reception and it should reflect your values and wishes for your special day.

- **The bouquet toss**—Originally, the bouquet formed part of the wreaths and garlands worn by both the bride and groom. It was considered a symbol of happiness. Today the practice of tossing the bouquet is similar to the tradition of throwing the garter. The single woman who catches the bouquet is believed to be the next to marry.

- **Tossing the garter**—This is the male version of the bouquet toss. In the United States, the groom traditionally removes the garter from the bride's right leg and throws it to a group of assembled unmarried men. The man who catches it is thought to be the next to marry. Many garters today provide the traditional "something blue." Some bride's wear two garters—one to toss and one to keep.

- **Cutting the cake**—One of the best-known traditions associated with the wedding cake is the joint cutting of the cake by the bride and groom. Before cakes became so grand, it was the sole responsibility of the bride to cut the cake for guests. Now the bride and groom symbolically cut the first piece together. Besides being a perfect photo opportunity, this act represents the first task of their shared life. Feeding each other a piece of the cake did not originate as the food fight it sometimes becomes. Instead, this action symbolizes the bride and groom's commitment to provide for and nourish each other.

You want your wedding reception to be filled with moments you will want to remember for years to come. As you plan the events for your celebration, think about the things that will mean the most to you as you look back on the day. Concentrate your money and energy in creating the opportunity for those treasured moments. But most of all, when the celebration begins, relax and enjoy everything to the fullest.

Speeches, Toasts, and Blessings

Usually the best man begins these proceedings by standing and offering a few words about the bride and groom. His words might be brief and sentimental or recount an amusing story. A brief prayer of thanks might also be in order. A toast is a short speech and a wish for the couple followed by everyone taking a drink. The drink does not have to be alcoholic. Others in the wedding party may also offer a few words and the bride and groom may respond with thanks.

It is also customary for many couples to have someone say a blessing for the food before eating. This honor may go to the father of either the bride or the groom, others in the wedding party, or a special wedding guest.

"I Do" Do's and Don'ts

The details of your reception and the order in which they occur is up to you. But no matter how formal or informal an affair you design, it's important to plan out a schedule and put it in writing. A written schedule will help others anticipate your needs and ensure that everything goes according to plan. However, don't get so hung up on keeping to your schedule that you forget to enjoy everything that is happening around you.

Shall We Dance?

To dance or not to dance is really up to you. Your reception can be exciting and memorable either way. If dancing is an important part of your reception plan, you will need to make sure that your location has space for it. You will probably also want to follow some of the etiquette and traditions associated with dancing at a wedding:

The first dance goes to the bride and groom to their favorite song.

Next, the bride dances with her father. The groom may ask his new mother-in-law to dance.

Finally, the groom dances with his mother and the groom's father dances with the bride while the bride's parent's dance with each other.

The dance floor is then open to the wedding party and other guests.

If dancing doesn't fit your style, there are other ways to celebrate and entertain your guests.

You can play music anyway. The right music can create the perfect atmosphere for your celebration. Music also helps people relax and can cover awkward silences as your guests get acquainted. Whether you hire a band, a DJ, or some other form of music, request selections that create the mood you want.

Place a disposable camera at each table for guests to use. An instruction card might suggest that the guests take shots of everyone at their table as well as their favorite moments during the reception. Many guests take their cameras home as a memento of the celebration. But others may choose to leave their camera for the bride and groom, giving the couple a perspective on their reception that they might have missed.

Get your guests to help you create a time capsule. At each table, place current magazines, newspaper articles, photographs, or other time-sensitive items. Have your guests write out predictions on how things will be 10 years from now including …

- Local news
- National news
- International news
- What the guest thinks he or she will be doing
- What the guest thinks the bride and groom will be doing

Put the predictions in an airtight container that the bride and groom can then open on their 10th anniversary.

Premier a slide show or video featuring the bride and groom. This could be the "Story of Us" and chronicle their relationship from first date to wedding day. Or, it could be their individual stories, including pictures of them growing up. Have a mixture of funny shots and more sentimental moments. The show can either be set up on a table to one side with a TV and VCR/DVD player or shown to the entire group at some point during the reception. If you plan on showing it all at once, be sure its not too long—10 minutes is probably enough.

Go with a theme reception. Consider doing things that fit with your ethnic background. Research wedding traditions from your country of origin and incorporate those in your celebration. Or, if your theme is medieval, recruit wandering minstrels or a court jester.

Ways to Save on Entertainment

You don't have to spend a lot of money on professional entertainment. You might choose just to socialize and enjoy the food and fellowship of your friends and family or try one of these cost-saving tips:

- Hire a DJ instead of a band. DJ's are usually more affordable than a live band. You'll get a wider variety of music and the DJ can also serve as a master of ceremonies.

- No money for a DJ? You can still have mood music by compiling some of your favorite hits on CDs and playing them through the sound system at your wedding reception.

- Recruit volunteers. Ask your musical friends or relations to prepare a song or two for the reception, or recruit church musicians for the reception.

- Keep it simple. If you just can't figure out how to entertain you guests for hours and hours then plan for a shorter reception. Schedule just enough time to observe any traditions you want to maintain, eat, and visit briefly then you and your spouse can get on with your honeymoon.

The Great Escape

When it's finally time for you and your spouse to take leave of your family and friends, you'll want to do it in a memorable way. But keep these guidelines in mind as you go:

- Before you slip out to change clothes, notify both the best man and the maid of honor. The maid of honor will assist the bride in getting changed while the best man notifies your family to gather your guests to bid you good-bye while he checks on your transportation.

- If you want to observe the "shower of rice" tradition, confirm with your reception location what is permitted and where. Few locations allow rice anymore. Some still allow birdseed, but many couples are going to bubbles or flower petals just to be safe.

- Remember that this is the last official event of your wedding day celebration but your happiness together has just begun.

The Honeymooners

Long before your wedding day, the two of you hopefully talked about your dreams and expectations for your honeymoon and agreed on the perfect way to begin your married life together. Both of you will welcome some time alone together after being "in the spotlight" for so long. You'll need a little time to unwind from all the stress and pressure of planning your big day. But all the hype you might have heard about the honeymoon might have created unrealistic expectations for you.

When planning for your getaway, try to view your honeymoon as a special vacation. Plan for a balance between fun and relaxing activities that allow you both to pursue your interests. And don't go outside your budget. If the purpose is for you to start your married life out relaxed and connected, going into debt in order to accomplish that goal doesn't make much sense. Finally, remember that wherever you go and whatever happens on your trip, you have a lifetime of adventures together ahead of you.

Planning Your Getaway

Vacation or honeymoon, the better the planning the better your time will be. With the average eight-day trip for two costing around $3,500 to $4,000, it can also represent a significant financial investment. That includes airfare for two, hotel, meals, tours, taxes, souvenirs, and snacks. Of course, there are ways to spend less (or more) and still have a wonderful time together! The place to start in planning is to figure out what your priority is for your time together:

- Do you want to go as far away as possible?
- Are your accommodations what matter most?
- Do you want to feel pampered?
- How do you want to spend your time?

To get ideas for planning your perfect getaway, talk with other couples and ask what it was that made their honeymoon plans perfect for them.

"I Do" Do's and Don'ts

If your honeymoon destination is taking you far away, do consider spending your wedding night somewhere closer to home. Many couples have found that being under pressure to make a flight or drive a long distance to your honeymoon destination the same day as your wedding adds unnecessary stress to your celebration day. And by the time you arrive, you are exhausted and crabby, too! Some couples even postpone their trip by two to three days so they can start their dream trip relaxed and refreshed.

Traditionally the responsibility for planning the honeymoon falls to the groom. But the wise groom includes his bride in the same way as the smart bride includes her groom in the wedding plans. Like the wedding, the honeymoon is for both of you, so you will want to start talking about it early. Here's a timeline to help you organize your honeymoon planning.

Planning Your Honeymoon Getaway

Six months before:

- Talk about the honeymoon you each want—tropical beach nights, mountain skiing, hiking and biking, or touring historical sites.
- Get recommendations from friends and family members on potential locations, hotels, and resorts.

- Set a budget and stick to it. Make sure you include everything—airline tickets, lodging, meals, taxes, tips, special activities and tours, and spending money for souvenirs.

- Start researching your top destination choices and travel agents or package deals.

- If you're planning a foreign destination, begin the process of securing passports if you don't already have them.

Four months before:

- Make your final decision on your honeymoon destination. If you're making your own reservations, begin to research hotels, airlines, and car-rental companies. Be sure to ask about special packages and discounts created just for honeymooners.

- Need a passport? It's time to submit those passport applications if you haven't already done so.

Three months before:

- Book your reservations and make all necessary deposits. Keep a record of all your reservation and confirmation numbers.

- Purchase your airline tickets. Seat assignments and boarding passes can be confirmed within 30 days of your departure.

- Ask about what official travel documents you will need and obtain them.

- Put together a list of things you will want to pack including clothes, toiletries, and accessories.

Two months before:

- Buy luggage, camera, and sunglasses. If you already own a camera, make sure it's in working order and pack extra film and batteries.

- Do you have an up-to-date credit card? Rental car companies don't take cash for a deposit—you'll need a credit card. And in many foreign currencies, you will get a better exchange rate with a credit card. A credit card is for convenience, not an excuse to go into debt.

- Make a copy of your travel itinerary, along with phone numbers where you can be reached, to leave with someone at home in case of emergency.

One month before:

- Check your list and make sure you have everything you will need for your trip (see the section "It's in the Bag") and complete any last-minute shopping.
- Get traveler's checks.
- Reconfirm all reservations and pick up tickets.
- Pack as much as you can ahead of time. Items that you won't need in the days ahead and clothes that don't wrinkle can go into your luggage now.
- Make a list of all the valuables you are carrying, including the numbers of your credit cards and traveler's checks, and put copies in your luggage.
- If you will need foreign currency for your honeymoon, exchange at least enough money ahead of time to get you from the airport to your hotel.
- Prepare a carry-on bag with one change of clothes, toothbrush and toothpaste, medications, and any other essentials just in case your luggage takes a detour and arrives after you do.

Choosing Your Location

Your destination is key to the rest of your honeymoon plans. Couples today have a lot of options and you can find some kind of package or deal to almost any location. Here are a few favorite honeymoon destinations to consider:

- **Tropical**—Hawaii, the Caribbean Islands (the Bahamas, Virgin Islands, Jamaica, Bermuda)
- **U.S. beaches**—California coast, Florida Gulf, the Carolinas
- **Cruises**—Alaska, Caribbean, Greece
- **Famous cities**—Paris, Rio, New York, Quebec, San Francisco
- **Mountains**—Rocky Mountains of Colorado, the Poconos in Pennsylvania

Whatever your interests, you can find the perfect location. You can go for the adventure—skiing, rafting, kayaking, diving—or the fun and entertainment of Disney World. You can plan a tour of historic sites and museums or stay close to home in a romantic B&B. Wherever you decide to go, make sure it is somewhere both of you can relax and enjoy and take time getting to know each other.

It's in the Bag

Packing for any trip is an art, but there are a few extra things to consider for a honeymoon trip. Depending on how far you are going and how long you will be gone, packing might make a big difference in how much you enjoy your time away. There's nothing more frustrating than to get somewhere and realize you've packed all the wrong stuff! The answer isn't to take more but to pack wisely! So do your homework about your destination—climate at time of your visit, formal or casual attire, and so on—and then follow these guidelines for perfect packing:

- Pack clothing that matches the climate and style of your destination. Choose wrinkle-free fabrics when possible. Plan for a few classic pieces (solid pants, skirts) that you can mix and match with a variety of tops.

- Go for comfort when choosing your shoes and clothes. Try to break in new items, especially shoes, ahead of time.

- Take the travel size of everything possible. Check ahead at your lodging to see they supply hair dryers, irons, and so on so you can skip those items.

- Pack the smallest bags possible (wheeled-ones are best). If you're flying, check on the latest luggage requirements for your airlines. Many have changed their weight limits per bag and more than one customer has ended up paying for extra weight in one bag when the same weight packed in two bags would have been free.

- Roll your clothes for tighter packing. Put all toiletries in Ziploc bags to prevent any leaking onto your clothes.

- Keep your valuables, travel documents, and money in your carry-on baggage. Stick in a healthy snack and a bottle of water along with any medication (including your chosen method of birth control) you might need during the trip.

- Plan for romance with a few special items like sexy lingerie, fragrant candles, massage oils, bath wash, and so on (see the romance tips in this chapter and in Chapter 19).

> **"I Do" Do's and Don'ts**
>
> With tightened security these days, it is important that your personal identification (driver's license or passport) matches your travel documents (your airline tickets). This will probably mean that the bride will travel under her maiden name. Keep a copy of your marriage license handy to prove you're married, but as far as reservations, travel under your maiden name until *all* documents reflect your new married name.

Managing Expectations

All newlyweds have such high hopes for their honeymoon. After all, it is the time you will be together as husband and wife. It's only natural that, just like with your wedding, you want everything to be perfect. So do be diligent to think through your trip and make a solid plan. But all the planning in the world might not protect your honeymoon from every little problem. You can plan for the weather, but you can't control the weather!

Use common sense when putting together your plans—don't make your schedule so crammed that you don't have any time to relax and just enjoy being together. Remember that you will need time to adjust to being together 24/7 and to explore your physical relationship with each other. Your honeymoon doesn't have to be perfect—it only has to be perfect for the two of you! Here are a few more honeymoon tips for you:

- Ask about the sleeping arrangements. Request a king bed if available. Sleeping together for the first time might be a challenge, so allow for some extra space. For cruises and overseas accommodations, double might be the best you can get.

- Be as extravagant as you budget will allow. This is a very special time for you as a couple. If your budget is limited, consider getting the best accommodations available closer to home rather than spending a fortune on travel and then having to skimp on your lodging and meals when you get where you're going.

- Take time to relax and unwind from the stress and strain of getting married. Keep your schedule light for the first day or two. Don't feel like you have to be joined at the hip the entire time. If he wants to golf and she wants to shop, why not? Having a little time apart is healthy and practical.

- Consider using a travel agent. It might not save you a ton of money, but a good travel agent will take care of all the details that you might forget during the months and weeks prior to the wedding. Letting someone else make the honeymoon arrangements can be a lot less stressful if it is someone you can trust to listen to what you want and do what you need.

That's the Spirit

Be humble and gentle. Be patient with each other, making allowances for each other's faults because of your love. Always keep yourselves united in the Holy Spirit, and bind yourselves together with peace. (Ephesians 4:2–3)

There can be a sudden release of emotions after leaving the wedding. Many grooms find themselves with crying brides and many brides don't know why they are crying. Or you might find you are irritated and crabby with this partner you have just pledged to love "'til death separates us." You've both been under a lot of pressure. This is the time to be especially gentle with each other in Christian love.

The Honeymoon Registry

Here's an interesting idea that you might want to investigate. Honeymoon Registry Services allow friends and families to contribute to your honeymoon expenses as their wedding gift to you. It works much the same as a standard bridal registry, only guests buy "pieces" of your dream honeymoon for you. For example, if you plan on honeymooning in Hawaii (a popular destination), all the costs of your trip are broken up into shares that can be purchased for you by your wedding guests. Your sisters can pool their money and pay for your 7 nights of lodging, Uncle Bob can give money for an authentic luau, Cousin Sue can buy 1/16th of your airfare, and your college roommate can pay for those snorkeling lessons you've always wanted.

There are several honeymoon registry services available on the Internet. Check out www.thebigday.com or www.honeyluna.com. These services charge a set-up fee and/or charge a service fee that is figured as a percentage (9–15 percent) of the amount contributed. They can also make your travel plans for you. The Internet services add "perks" such as a free wedding web page and a written acknowledgment of the gift for your guests. Some travel agencies advertise a honeymoon registry service, although all their service might include is allowing your friends and family to mail in checks toward your trip.

The Honeymoon Registry Service can provide your wedding guests with a convenient way to get you something you really can use and enjoy without the shopping hassle. You do need to make sure to choose the right service that will provide you and your guests with the best possible service. The Honeymoon Registry Service is not for everyone, but for some couples the honeymoon registry is a welcome alternative to toasters and towels.

> **Bet You Didn't Know**
>
> In ancient times, couples came together under very different circumstances. When a man decided he was ready for a wife, he would capture the woman of his dreams—usually without her consent—and carry her off to a secret place. There they would hideout from the bride's relatives for about 30 days (the time it takes for the moon to go through all its phases) and drink a fermented brew made with honey. Hence, we get the word "honeymoon."

While You're Away

If you have your first home already set up, don't forget to arrange for someone to pick up mail, bring in the newspaper, tend the plants and lawn, and take care of pets. Leave a list of numbers where you can be reached in case of emergency. Arrange for a family member or friend to stock the refrigerator just before you get home. After a relaxing trip, it will be nice to return to a home that is ready and welcoming.

Ways to Save

Whatever your honeymoon plans, there are ways to save so that your perfect getaway doesn't end up as a budget buster. Here are just a few:

- **Do your homework.** Visit websites related to your top destination choices. Check with state and local tourist bureau's in the area to get information on everything from accommodation to weather to restaurants to activities.

- **Try for the off-season.** Whatever your location, consider going when other tourist trade will be slow. Rates are generally lower and you won't have to fight crowds. Also watch out for special events that drive prices up (like the Super Bowl or Mardi Gras).

- **Shop early for the best prices.** There are a lot of Internet sites that offer great deals on airfare and lodging. Check them out.

- **Look for packages that represent good savings.** Don't limit your search to honeymoon packages only. There are some great vacation packages out there that also make great honeymoon deals.

- **Stay closer to home.** If you can't afford the trip to Tahiti this year, that's okay! Save it for an anniversary trip. Airfare is usually the biggest chunk of change honeymooners spend. Find the best accommodations at a great place you can drive to in a day and save a bundle.

Creating Honeymoon Intimacy

The best way to the perfect honeymoon is to focus on creating intimacy between you. As we said in Chapter 5, there's so much more to intimacy than sex. Yet so much emphasis for the honeymoon is placed on the sexual relationship. Your sexuality is at the heart of your identity—it's how God created you and is nothing to be embarrassed about. There is certainly nothing shameful about the sexual intimacy between a husband and wife. But it might take time for you to feel comfortable with this new part of your relationship. And remember, sexual fulfillment has to do with the whole relationship, not just the sexual act.

The Wedding Night

Ignore all the hype about sex and the wedding night! There's no law (at least, not any more) that says your marriage has to be consummated on your first night together. Only you and your partner can decide what is best for you. The physical union of a man and his wife is as sacred as it is sexual, so choose the time and place that is best for you. Take your time to explore and get to know each other physically. Learn what is normal for you and be realistic in your expectations. Talk with each other about your fears and concerns as well as your desires. Most of all, be patient with yourself and each other.

Setting the Mood

A quick look at the following lists of mood builders and ice breakers demonstrates that there is a lot more to sex than the physical.

Mood builders:

- Openness, acceptance, self-disclosure
- Willingness to discover, compromise, change, and learn together
- Submission to the needs of the other, unconditional giving is important
- Person-orientation, not performance-orientation
- Respect for your bodies

Mood breakers:

- Unrealistic, uncommunicated, high expectations
- Constant comparison
- Sexual intimacy as a reward or manipulation
- Criticism in any form
- Poor body hygiene
- Mental and physical fatigue

Check out these romantic tips for newlyweds:

- Your honeymoon romance starts with your destination. Romance is an adventure! Choosing a place that offers new sights, sounds, and experiences can be very stimulating.
- Reserve the honeymoon suite, even if it is just for one night. It's great to be pampered on your first night together as husband and wife.
- Think sensual. Try to appeal to all your senses: eat something pleasurable, add a romantic scent to the room with candles, oils, or potpourri.
- Bring your own music. It sets the mood and creates a lasting memory you can recapture time and time again.
- Add candlelight. The glow of candlelight is comforting and sensual. Stick with a variety of votives in deep holders. But remember never to leave a candle unattended.
- Create a keepsake. Take turns writing in a journal. Share a few thoughts and feelings about each day together. Pick up mementos, such as seashells, local wildflowers, ticket stubs, or other trinkets for keeping memories alive. Take pictures and have others take pictures of the two of you together.

- Surprise him or her! Turn the bathroom into a luxurious spa with a scented bubble bath, music, candlelight, and a bottle of your favorite bubbly beverage.

- Stay in touch spiritually. Pray together each evening at bedtime or start each day reading from a devotional book together. While watching a sunset or admiring a mountain view, remind each other of the many good gifts the Creator has given you.

The Gift of Sex

God has created you to desire each other and to enjoy sexual intimacy. It is a gift not to be taken for granted or given away to anyone outside of your marriage relationship. It is a spiritual act as well as a physical act—the completion of your marriage covenant. Too often today even Christian couples approach sex as primarily a physical urge to be gratified as quickly and conveniently as possible. But that takes away the wonder and magic. Physical intimacy isn't an event, it is something you develop over a period of time. Good sex starts in the mind and heart of both individuals before you get between the sheets.

True sexual intimacy is so much more about relationship than satisfying physical urges, and relationships take time. You are entering a new dimension in your relationship, so don't expect everything to come together perfectly in one or even a few nights. If you are initially disappointed with your sexual encounters as husband and wife, don't despair. Part of the beauty of a lifetime relationship is having the time to develop every area of your oneness over time.

That's the Spirit

You have ravished my heart, my treasure, my bride. I am overcome by one glance of your eyes ... How sweet is your love, my treasure, my bride! How much better it is than wine! Your perfume is more fragrant than the richest of spices. Your lips, my bride, are as sweet as honey. Yes, honey and cream are under your tongue ... You are like a private garden, my treasure, my bride! You are like a spring that no one else can drink from, a fountain of my own. (Song of Songs 4:9–12)

Don't forget that your God understands both the emotional and physical pleasures of sexual intimacy. Whatever your fears and concerns, hopes and dreams, you can tell him all about them. He created you both and knows you better than you know yourselves. Trust him to give you wisdom and courage to act lovingly in the area of sexual intimacy and physical oneness.

Pain or Pleasure

The first time you have sexual intercourse you might experience a little of both. For the bride, the presence of an intact hymen is the major source of pain. During your premarital physical, discuss with your doctor or nurse exercises that you can do beforehand to stretch your hymen. Also, it is important to be relaxed and sufficiently stimulated. Without sufficient stimulation, the vagina might be too dry for comfortable penetration. You might want to have a water-based lubricant available just in case.

Although the groom might not experience any physical pain, the experience can be emotionally painful. As a virgin, he might not be experienced enough to pace his responses. Premature ejaculation or the inability to obtain an erection are both possible results if nervousness and unrealistic expectations get the upper hand. Check out one of the books on sexual intimacy listed in Appendix A. Knowing what to realistically expect, learning to relax, and exercising patience and compassion for each other will go a long way toward making your first sexual encounters pleasing for both of you.

Sexual intercourse will get easier over time, but in the beginning frequency might be more a matter of comfort than desire. You will be using muscles in your body that you have never used in the same way before and you will no doubt be uncomfortable and sore. Don't let this discourage you. You can still enjoy getting to know each other, exploring each other's bodies, and enjoying the love you share without having sex all the time.

Is There a Problem?

If you are having difficulties in your sexual encounters, don't panic. Often the problem will resolve itself with love, patience, and honest communication. You must be able to talk about your sexual experiences as husband and wife. Tell each other what feels good and what doesn't, be willing to experiment with different positions and techniques. Put the satisfaction and desires of each other first, and no one will be last.

Give yourself time after the honeymoon to continue to work things out to your mutual satisfaction. But if after six to eight weeks, you are still having difficulty, don't hesitate to consult your physician. There are occasionally physical conditions that might require medical intervention. But in most cases, time and practice are the best healers.

One final note for the bride: Many brides are unaware that they can get an infection as the result of intercourse. Cystitis (or "honeymoonitis") occurs when bacteria invades the urethra, a situation common after intercourse because of the proximity of the opening of the urethra to the vagina. It can cause painful urination and require antibiotics. There are a couple of things the new bride can do to prevent this: drink lots of water and cranberry juice and try to urinate soon after intercourse to flush out the urethra.

Family Ties

After your honeymoon, be sensitive about sharing any details even with your closest family and friends. There are some things that your partner might prefer to keep just between the two of you. And there are some things that your family and friends might be uncomfortable hearing. This is an important part of your developing oneness with each other—knowing what to share and what to keep private between you two only.

A Lifetime for Loving

There is a custom in the Jewish faith that can help to keep the honeymoon experience in its proper perspective. For the Jewish bride and groom, the week after the wedding is spent not off in a remote location with only each other. Instead, the wedding feast is part of a seven-day period of rejoicing and blessing. Each evening, the bride and groom are the guests of honor at a dinner hosted by a different family. At the dinner, friends and family members celebrate with good food and fellowship. At the end of each dinner, the *sheva brachot* (seven blessings recited during the wedding ceremony) are recited again.

The custom has developed that each evening there are new faces around the table so that the joy and witness of the newlyweds can be shared throughout the community.

The seven blessings (*sheva brachot*) translated from Hebrew read:

1. You are blessed, Lord our God, the sovereign of the world, who created everything for his glory.
2. You are blessed, Lord our God, the sovereign of the world, the creator of man.
3. You are blessed, Lord our God, the sovereign of the world, who created man in his image, in the pattern of his own likeness, and provided for the perpetuation of his kind. You are blessed, Lord, the creator of man.

4. Let the barren city be jubilantly happy and joyful at her joyous reunion with her children. You are blessed, Lord, who makes Zion rejoice with her children.

5. Let the loving couple be very happy, just as you made your creation happy in the garden of Eden, so long ago. You are blessed, Lord, who makes the bridegroom and the bride happy.

6. You are blessed, Lord our God, the sovereign of the world, who created joy and celebration, bridegroom and bride, rejoicing, jubilation, pleasure and delight, love and brotherhood, peace and friendship. May there soon be heard, Lord our God, in the cities of Judea and in the streets of Jerusalem, the sound of joy and the sound of celebration, the voice of the bridegroom and the voice of the bride, the happy shouting of bridegrooms from their weddings and of young men from their feasts of song. You are blessed, Lord, who makes the bridegroom and the bride rejoice together.

7. You are blessed, Lord our God, the sovereign of the world, creator of the fruit of the vine.

Sometimes so much emphasis on the honeymoon is so contrary to the worshipful nature of the marriage ceremony that there is a disconnect. Sometimes the honeymoon environment creates an unwelcome feeling of isolation for the newlyweds. Perhaps as a Christian couple you can create a new tradition that will affirm that the marriage union (which does not end with the marriage ceremony) is a holy one and that the continuing joy of being husband and wife is meant to be shared in community with others.

Presenting Mr. And Mrs. _____!

Your wedding day is only the beginning of a lifelong adventure in marriage. After the honeymoon many couples discover that marriage is hard work—it takes continued commitment and communication to work through the many adjustments that come with married life. Your relationship with each other's families, shared finances, and changing expectations about what makes for a 'good' wife or a 'good' husband are potential areas of conflict. They are also opportunities for growth as individuals and as a couple if you practice good communication and conflict resolution skills.

Marriage is romantic and fun, as well as challenging. You can thrive during your first year of marriage. And as you learn to love your spouse in new ways and through the ordinary aspects of every day, your relationship can be a testimony to others of the power of Christian love and commitment. Before you know it, you will be celebrating your first year anniversary. Make it a true celebration of God's gift of marriage in your life!

Chapter 16

When the Honeymoon's Over

Imagine learning to swim without ever getting into a pool. You can sit in a classroom and learn human anatomy and how to breathe properly. You can work out at the gym and strengthen the leg and arm muscles you will need. You can study the laws of physics that allow you to propel yourself through the water. All that is good preparatory information. But until you actually get into the deep end, you can't really say you know how to swim.

Your first year of marriage is like getting into the deep end of the pool. No matter how diligently you have worked on your premarital counseling exercises, no matter how much you have learned about yourself and your partner and your families, you still have a lot to learn. The things you have learned "in the classroom" will be put to good use, but you will find that you will need to practice, practice, practice all those skills while living together daily.

Many brides and grooms forget that simple fact in all the prewedding madness. So if when the honeymoon is over you feel like you've been thrown into the deep end of the pool, take heart! Many happily married couples before you have experienced the same things you are experiencing and have survived. You will, too!

Paradise Lost?

Weddings are so beautiful and romantic! For months your thoughts have been on flowers and music, satin and lace! On your wedding day, you were the focus of attention and everyone was ready and willing to attend to your needs. Then, of course, there was the honeymoon—days or weeks in an exotic location far away from everyday responsibilities. You didn't have to cook or clean or go to work. Your only duty was to love and be loved by your new spouse. After all that, it's no wonder reentry into the real world can take some adjustment.

Post-Wedding Blues

Many newly married brides suffer feelings of disappointment, emptiness, and sadness immediately following their wedding day or after the honeymoon. And although it is less common among grooms, they, too, can experience an emotional letdown.

What causes post-wedding depression? You've probably anticipated and planned for your wedding day your whole life—and suddenly it's over! All that investment of time, money, and emotional energy for a one-day event can leave you feeling empty. You have been impressed with the permanence of this new relationship—your life has been forever altered—and you might be struggling with unmet expectations.

What are the symptoms of post-wedding blues? If you are having feelings of emptiness and purposelessness now that all the wedding planning and preparations are over or if you are sometimes overwhelmed with and unreasonable fear and anxiety that you have made a mistake and married the wrong person, then you are most likely experiencing post-wedding depression. You might also lack energy and be having feelings of disappointment and sadness that make you want to stay in bed—all day and all alone!

What can you do for post-wedding blues? Fighting post-wedding blues starts before the wedding. In the midst of wedding day preparations, remind yourself often that the wedding day is only the beginning. Remember, also, that almost every bride experiences some level of

> **"I Do" Do's and Don'ts**
>
> Don't overemphasize the importance of your wedding celebration. By staying focused on the marriage relationship instead of the wedding day, you can minimize the after-the-wedding-day letdown. Your wedding is for a day, but you will have many days ahead to enjoy the joys and wonders of your marriage together.

post-wedding blues. The tips listed here can help you beat the post-wedding blues. But if your feelings of depression persist after four to six weeks, talk to your doctor, a counselor, your pastor, or a trusted family friend. There might be another reason for your depression.

Blues Busters

Focus on your new life and love. The adrenaline high of the wedding will be replaced with new feelings of contentment and companionship.

Take care of yourself. Make time to exercise, eat right, and get the rest you need. Allow yourself time to recover emotionally and physically.

Plan a future treat. Give yourself something to look forward to. Arrange a weekend or day trip to a favorite place. Take up a new hobby or sport. Organize a post-wedding party with family and friends.

Take one day at a time. Don't give into the "for the rest of my life" panic. Whether married or single, God knows that if we focus on each day, the future will take care of itself.

Embrace change. Life is full of change, and marriage is one of the biggest catalysts of change. Try to see the changes you are experiencing as opportunities and adventures. Trust that God is in control and has the very best in mind for you.

Confront your expectations. Now that you are actually living together as husband and wife, you might have to face your expectations in a whole new way. Continue to talk and pray together about the roles you each play in your new relationship.

Honey, Your Humanity Is Showing

"I don't remember my husband picking his nose in front of me *before* we were married." Not a lot of emphasis is placed on normal bodily functions when they show passionate, beautiful, and young married couples in the movies! Not too many leading men passing gas in front of their gorgeous girlfriends. But I'm pretty sure it happens in real life!

So how do you handle seeing your practically perfect spouse in all of his or her humanity? First, it's important to keep your sense of humor. The fact that your partner feels comfortable enough in your relationship to let down his or her guard is good. But if you are starting to see behavior that you find rude, tasteless, or disturbing, don't be afraid to let your partner know how you feel. Some habits are made to be broken!

Where Is the Love?

If we had a dollar for every time we've heard a wife lament "But he was so romantic *before* we were married!" we both would be very rich! Perhaps men come with a special switch that automatically flips on during the pursuit and off after the conquest! At least, that's the way it feels to many new brides.

Sometimes the sudden change in your partner can leave you disillusioned. Imagine that your husband is a new computer program called Husband 1.0. You might be feeling like you need tech support right about now. There are hundreds of versions of this humorous exchange (Husband 1.0) in cyberspace. Here's our version:

Husband 1.0

Dear Tech Support:

Recently I upgraded from Boyfriend 5.0 to Husband 1.0 and noticed that the new program began making unexpected changes to the accounting modules, limiting access to wardrobe, flower, and jewelry applications that had operated flawlessly under Boyfriend 5.0.

In addition, Husband 1.0 uninstalled many other valuable programs, such as TableManners 1.0 and Romance 9.9 while also installing undesirable programs such as ESPN 5.0 and ToiletSeatUp 3.0. Conversation 8.0 no longer runs and WashingDishes 2.6 simply crashes the system. I've tried running Nagging 5.3 to fix these problems, but with limited success. I need help in maximizing the potential of this program.

Signed,

Disillusioned Wife

Dear Disillusioned:

Keep in mind, Boyfriend 5.0 is an entertainment package, while Husband 1.0 is an operating system and was designed by its creator to run with as few applications as possible. Do not try to uninstall Husband 1.0 and return to Boyfriend 5.0. Any effort to do so will activate hidden operating files (see your user's manual under HeartBreak 4.0).

Any new program applications can only be installed once per year, as Husband 1.0 has severely limited memory. Error messages are common, and a normal part of Husband 1.0.

Some users have had limited success with modifying Husband 1.0 by entering the command C:\I THOUGHT YOU LOVED ME. This command functions best when installed with the application Tears 6.2. Husband 1.0 should then automatically run the applications Apologize 3.0 and Flowers/Chocolate 7.0. But remember, overuse of this command can cause Husband 1.0 to default to GrumpySilence 2.5 or Fishing 5.1. In severe cases, your program might become corrupted by Resentment 3.0.

Instead, the creator of application Husband 1.0 recommends you read the manual. It might be necessary to reboot with Submission 2.0 so that Husband 1.0 and Wife 1.0 can interface more efficiently. Other upgrades to Wife 1.0 can also improve the performance of Husband 1.0. We recommend Lingerie 4.2, HomeCookedMeal 2.3, and Patience 3.0.

Again, thank you for choosing to install Husband 1.0. Please refer to the manual if you encounter any additional difficulties. We are confident that over time and with proper maintenance, you will derive great satisfaction from this application.

Signed,

Tech Support

Keeping the romance in your marriage is important. But it won't be automatic. You'll have to be intentional about it. Chapter 19 is dedicated to giving you a lot of advice and ideas for keeping the romantic love alive in your new life together.

That's the Spirit

I have found the paradox that if I love until it hurts, then there is no hurt, but only more love. —Mother Theresa

The fact that you have to work at your relationship doesn't mean there is a problem. Building a strong marriage will take faith and courage and a daily commitment to love even when it hurts.

Be on guard. Stand true to what you believe. Be courageous. Be strong. And everything you do must be done with love. (1 Corinthians 16:13–14)

After the Honeymoon, Everything Changes

The first year of marriage is a continuous cycle of change. Even couples who lived together prior to marriage confess that everything changes after the ceremony. For most couples, there are the challenges of learning to live together, figuring out who they are individually and as a couple, and adjusting to how their relationships with others have changed.

Home, Sweet, What?

One of the first decisions newlyweds face is where they will live together as man and wife. We understand that in some areas of the country, finding any place to live can take a small miracle. In that case, it might make sense to hold on to one of your single habitations. But in most cases, it is best to find a new place to start your life together as a married couple. Pray for direction—it's a decision with a lot of ramifications in your life. To help you make the decision for practical reasons, discuss together the following:

Economics—What can you afford to pay according to your budget? Don't forget extras like utilities and renter's insurance. If your place doesn't have a washer and dryer, where will you go to do laundry and how much will that cost? Take into consideration not only your immediate financial plans, but future plans as well. If you want to buy a home in the future, will the current rent and utilities allow you to save? Or can you live in a less fancy place in order to find that extra savings?

Location—Is it in a safe area of town? How close is it to work, public transportation (if needed), stores, and church? Is it a quiet neighborhood? Is it clean? We thought our first apartment was perfect! It was a very nice complex in a great location. But what we didn't realize until we moved in was that our bedroom window faced a busy street. Sleeping with the window open was next to impossible with the nightly traffic sounds. Finding a place too far from your work location can severely cut into the time and energy you have to give to each other. However, that decision may be driven more by economics than desire.

Size—Will you have enough space and for how long? That might seem like a simple question, but until you get both of your belongings together you might not realize how tight a space you have. Both of you will need some personal space as well. It's pretty hard to "get away" from each other when you only have two rooms! The second part of the space question is how long your current space will accommodate your needs. Every move you make costs money, so try to find a place with space you can live with for a year or two, at least.

"I Do" Do's and Don'ts

If choosing *where* you will live isn't hard enough, that decision opens up dozens of other decisions. If you or your spouse lived on your own for any length of time, you have probably accumulated a truckload of furniture and personal belongings. Deciding what goes with you into your new home can be difficult and cause conflict. Although many men don't seem to care much about interior decorating, they can be very protective of their "stuff." Merging your belongings in your new home will take communication and compromise for both of you.

"Who Am I?"

We've talked with you already about the sanctity of marriage and God's intent that the two of you become one. You made oneness a part of your wedding vows, the unity candle burned brightly, and you became one flesh on your wedding night. The unity of marriage should make you feel more connected, more grounded and content with who you are, right? So why are you feeling so confused?

With marriage, you not only accept a new role but you also step into a new identity. You are no longer a single adult, you are part of a married couple that God has brought together. You leave your family of origin and start a new family. You will leave your home and move to a new home—one you and your spouse are responsible to create. And as a bride, you are also changing your name. It's only natural that while you are adjusting to this "new" you, you might sometimes feel a little confused and alone. Remember that your identity is not in your name, what you do, or who you're with—it is in Christ alone you will find out who you are.

Bet You Didn't Know

A recent study reported in the May 2003 issue of the *Journal of Marriage and Family* found that companionship and compatibility have a different level of importance in the happiness quotient for married couples. Researchers tracked 73 couples for 13 years to see how doing things together affected their level of satisfaction with their relationship. One surprising discovery was that doing things together that both partners liked wasn't as important as the researchers had assumed. Instead, they found that compatibility—liking the other person and sharing similar ideas and values—was more important to marital happiness than companionship—doing things together.

"I Think We're Alone Now."

"In fact, I think everyone has forgotten all about us!" That is often how newlyweds feel in the first few weeks and months after they return from their honeymoon. Family members don't want to be seen as interfering with the couple's new life. Friends don't call or stop by for fear of interrupting a "private" moment. While everyone is assuming that the happy couple are more than content to spend every possible moment alone together, the young couple is feeling lonely and isolated. What can you do to break through the "privacy barrier" that everyone has erected around you?

Invite people over. Many couples feel they can't entertain because they don't have the space or the means. Don't let that be your excuse! Even in small quarters and on a tight budget, you can be hospitable. Keep it simple, but do reach out to others.

- **Stay in touch with old friends.** Your prewedding friends helped make you the interesting person your spouse fell in love with. There's no need to abandon them just because you're married now.

- **Go to social gatherings.** Get out and do things with other people. Attend social functions at your church or office. Happily married couples maintain a balance between their alone time and the time they spend with others.

- **Make new friends.** Both you and your spouse should keep your old friends. But you should also start making new friends together. Get to know other married couples in your church and begin to cultivate one or two friendships.

- **Visit family and friends.** Don't wait for family and friends to visit you. They might be waiting for some indication from you that you are ready to socialize. Let them know that you want to be included in gatherings.

Family Ties

One great way to connect with your family after the honeymoon is to host a post-wedding party. Invite both your families to watch you open your wedding gifts and eat leftovers from the reception. Sharing stories about the people behind the gifts—"Aunt Sally always gives silver" or "How sweet of Cousin George to send a gift! He taught me how to swim when I was 8."—can be a fun way to help your two families get to know each other better.

"I Haven't Had a Good Night's Sleep Since Before the Wedding!"

Sleep is one of the unexpected challenges of married life. Because of the differences in their metabolisms, men and women often disagree about room temperature and the appropriate amount of bed covers for a comfortable night's sleep. You might have also discovered that one of you snores or tosses and turns restlessly throughout the night. Sleep is a basic human need and essential to good health. Lack of sleep can cause you to have …

- Changes in mood—sadness, feeling overwhelmed, depression.
- Lower performance and concentration.
- Slower reaction times.
- Higher risk of accidents and injuries.
- Lapses of memory.
- Behavior problems such as angry outbursts.

If you think married life is leaving you sleep-deprived, you might need to make some adjustments to your sleeping arrangements. If one of you is a thrasher, consider a larger bed (a queen or king). If covers are an issue, use several layers so that each partner can put on or toss off covers to reach a comfort level. Try to find a room temperature that is in a midrange for both of you. There are even a variety of solutions for snoring—from nasal strips to medication to surgery. So don't despair—you can learn to sleep comfortably with your new spouse.

"Why Didn't Someone Tell Me?"

Married life is full of surprises, and every couples' relationship is unique, but you can't help but wonder why your married friends or family didn't let you in on at least some of the secrets of life together after the honeymoon! Hopefully, you have someone in your life who you can talk to honestly about the "after the honeymoon" realities of marriage. But just in case you don't, here are a few common "ah ha's" that other newlyweds have shared:

I thought sex would be more fun and exciting. There's so much hype these days about sex that many couples are disappointed when they finally pursue their passion. You might have been prepared for some pain and awkwardness during the honeymoon. But now that you've been married several weeks, you might be disappointed with your sexual experiences. Be patient! Don't expect great sex every time you try. Learn to enjoy the trying! Remember that there is more to intimacy than sex.

I didn't realize my partner had so many annoying habits! Chances are you are learning a lot of things about your partner that you didn't know before. Dating and courtship are designed to accentuate your strengths and similarities. But marriage and living together day after day has a way of focusing your attention on your differences. Different is just that—different! Don't assign a negative value to your partner's habits just because it's not the way you do it.

I didn't know my partner was such a slob! In almost every marriage, there is a conflict of expectations over cleanliness. What does "clean" mean to you? You and your partner might have been raised in homes with very different views about house-work. So try not to get upset if after you ask your partner to clean the bathroom, it appears to you to be almost as dirty as before. Be specific about what clean means to you and be willing to compromise if your partner doesn't see it the same way.

I just snapped at my partner for folding towels the wrong way—what's the matter with me! Laundry is another "skill" we usually learn from our family, so you and your partner might have very different views about it. One bride argued that the bath towels be folded in thirds. That was how her mother had always insisted it be done. When her new husband challenged the "why" of this absolute, the bride decided to ask her mother. It turned out that her mother always folded the towels in thirds because that was the only way they would fit on the narrow shelf of her linen closet! The moral? Be flexible—there might be more than one "right" way to do the laundry.

I can't believe we fight so much over food! Some couples fight more in the kitchen than in any other room in their home. Many newlyweds enter the kitchen convinced that there is a right way and a wrong way to fix almost any dish—and usually your partner's way is the wrong way! Food is often at the center of family traditions and cultural experiences. Is strawberry shortcake dessert or a meal? Do you stuff the Thanksgiving turkey with bread stuffing or cornbread stuffing?

> **Bet You Didn't Know**
>
> Many young couples feel like they are living in different time "zones" during their first year of marriage. Here's a time conversion table for the new husband who's trying to figure out what his bride's trying to tell him:
>
> "I'm coming." = "I need 5 more minutes."
>
> "Just a second." = "I need 10 more minutes."
>
> "It should take about 15 minutes." = "You might as well sit down."
>
> "Be there at 8:00 sharp." = "If you're late, don't bother."
>
> "Hold your horses!" = 5-minute penalty
>
> "I could get ready faster if you'd quit pestering me." = 10-minute penalty
>
> "Why don't you just go without me." = "If you do, I'll kill you!"

This Is Not What I Expected

Expectations are attitudes, dispositions, or states of mind that determine our behavior, or at least accompany it. Expectations are assumptions, often unspoken, that certain events will transpire and that relationships will develop in a certain way. Unfulfilled expectations, both of one's self and of others, produce frustration and increase stress which, if unresolved, will result in "burnout."

Expectation Check-Up

Now that you're married, your expectations about what makes for a good husband or a good wife might have changed. You might understand the complexities of the roles better and you probably have a growing understanding of what are realistic expectations for *you* and *your* partner in *your* relationship. To achieve satisfaction in your marriage you must know what you expect, know what is expected of you, and do what is expected better than others expected you could! Together discuss the following questions as part of your Expectation Check-up:

One area of married life that is better than I expected is _____ because …

_____

For me, the biggest surprise about living together has been …

_____

One area of married life that is harder than I expected is _____

because ... _____

In our marriage, my role is different than I expected because ...

_____

One area of our relationship that I hope we can change is ...

_____

One area of our relationship that I am totally satisfied with is ...

_____

You each entered marriage with *expectations* about the *other person* and about what is *supposed to happen* in the marital relationship. You had your own *expectations* of what makes for a *good (Christian) marriage*. Even with good communication about your expectations before the wedding, the reality might be different than you expected. And you can continue to expect your expectations to change as your learn more about yourself and each other and what works in your marriage relationship.

That's the Spirit

We can rejoice, too, when we run into problems and trials, for we know that they are good for us—they help us learn to endure. And endurance develops strength of character in us, and character strengthens our confident expectation of salvation. And this expectation will not disappoint us. For we know how dearly God loves us, because he has given us the Holy Spirit to fill our hearts with his love. (Romans 5:3–5)

You and your new spouse are bound to run into problems and trials in your marriage. It doesn't mean that you don't love each other or that God doesn't love you. Sometimes God allows us to struggle *because* he loves us and knows that the end result will be well worth the inconvenience or pain.

Dealing with Changing Expectations

As you continue to evaluate and communicate about your marital expectations, don't fall into the trap of thinking that things will get better on their own. Unfulfilled expectations can create frustration and anger.

Do admit that you have needs and tell them to your spouse.

Don't expect your spouse or any other person to meet all your needs.

Do recognize the affect of your past on your current relationship.

Don't let the past dictate the future. Today can be the first day of a new way of relating to each other.

Do talk with others about struggles you might be having.

Don't think your marriage has to look just like someone else's.

Do be flexible about your changing expectations.

Don't be unrealistic about your expectations or your ability to meet the expectations of your spouse.

Although expectations might change, God doesn't change. Let his Spirit and his Word provide the unmovable foundation on which you and your spouse continue to build your own unique and enduring marriage.

Family Ties

In adjusting to married life, you and your spouse will have to work through many differences—some big, some small. It will be tempting to want to seek the comfort of what's most familiar to you. If your family loves you, they will let you know that it is *not* okay for you to run to them every time you and your spouse have a disagreement. It might sound harsh, but your parent's home is not your home any longer; you must find a way to make a new home with your spouse.

The Best Is Yet To Come

There's no doubt about it—married life is an adventure! Your new life together will require discipline, practice, and patience. Never give up! Together you can build new traditions, positive experiences, and wonderful memories that will carry you through the many challenges you will face. If you discover everything about each other in the first year, what will you do for the next 60?

When it comes right down to it, being successfully and happily married is really very simple: Every day you must choose to love your spouse unconditionally. With God's help, you can! You see, it's all about attitude! Here are a few "Be" attitudes that have helped many couples find happiness in their first year of marriage:

- Be loyal.
- Be interesting.

- Be a team.
- Be content.
- Be romantic.
- Be a good fighter.
- Be disciplined.
- Be spiritual.
- Be positive.
- Be thankful.
- Be adventurous.

To be (or not to be) happy in your marriage relationship is more about choice than chance. Don't wait for your partner to change—look to your attitude first!

Setting Goals: Yours, Mine, and Ours

Part of every successful partnership is the ability to set common goals and then work together to accomplish those goals. Marriage is a partnership, and happy couples take the time to discuss and agree on goals. Couples who learn early in their marriage how to work together to fulfill their God-given purpose find that their marriage is stronger and that the rewards are worth the effort.

Good marriages don't happen by accident. You have a happy marriage on purpose. Most of the conflicts you and your spouse will encounter during your early years of marriage can be resolved with good communication and a strong commitment to each other. What kills marriages is when marriage partners start to move in separate directions—forsaking their common vision, common purpose, and common goals.

Setting Goals for Your Marriage

Your first year of marriage is going to be an adventure! You'll enjoy it more if you take the time to agree on where you are going and how you want to get there. Do you hope to start a family relatively soon? What romantic plans do you have in mind? Would you like to invest in a home? What are your other financial goals? Hopefully you have already discussed many of these questions as part of your premarital counseling. But in the many weeks or months that you have been preparing for your wedding, you probably set aside any thoughts of "after the wedding" goals.

In the following pages, we have provided you with five important areas for future planning along with guidelines for setting goals in each of these areas. We suggest you set aside a time each week for several weeks to build your vision for life as a married couple. Pick a time when fatigue and stress are least likely to be a factor— Saturday morning, Sunday afternoon or evening, or an evening early in the week. Read the Scripture passage provided in the sections of this chapter and pray together for God's wisdom and direction as you talk through your goals for the next year and beyond.

Initially, spend only a couple of hours discussing each goal. We've suggested a schedule, but you will probably find that all five areas are so interrelated that you can't talk about one without the others. The order isn't really important, except we do recommend starting with your spiritual growth goals. Setting your priorities with God first and focusing on what he wants for you will help guide you through your decision-making process on the other goals.

Here is a suggested schedule:

Week #1—Spiritual growth

Week #2—Marriage relationship

Week #3—Health and fitness

Week #4—Family planning

Week #5—Finances

Week #6—Reflect and commit

If you need more than one session to reach agreement on a goal in a particular area, take it. Remember, this is important stuff! Together you are charting the course of your married life. The time you spend now on goal setting will mean less time in conflict later. Trust us! This is more fun and much more beneficial to your long-term relationship.

Let's Talk About It

As you and your spouse set about discussing your goals, keep in mind the following four aspects of negotiating:

1. Respect each other's ideas and positions and listen with an open mind. Be accepting of any differences of opinion that might be expressed.

2. Be willing to compromise. Give and take is essential in any relationship. It's not as much about who's right and who's wrong as it is finding a point of agreement.

3. Only set goals you can both wholeheartedly commit to or keep negotiating.

4. Remember the purpose of setting goals is to draw you closer together. If during your discussion tempers flare or feelings get hurt, take a time out from the discussion and return to it later.

Dream a Little!

Goal setting should be fun! It's an opportunity to open your minds and hearts to an incredible array of possibilities. Although goals need to be realistic, don't be afraid to dream. You have a heavenly Father who has untold riches at his disposal and as his child, they belong to you as well. Too many Christians settle for too little too often. Socrates said "Wisdom begins with wonder." Take the time to wonder at all you can do with God's help.

That's the Spirit

Don't get caught up in what your family history, popular culture, or other people tell you is important. Your goals as a couple should be a reflection of your values and beliefs. "Test everything that is said. Hold on to what is good." (1 Thessalonians 5:21)

Does it agree with God's Word? Have you confirmed it in prayer? Is it in keeping with the leading of the Holy Spirit? Does it agree with your dreams and circumstances?

Directions for Goal Setting

Whether you're deciding on buying a house, having children, changing careers, or where to take your summer vacation, the following guidelines can help you set goals that you and your spouse can use to prioritize your life:

- Each of you should make your own list of what is important to you. Write down anything you would like to achieve in your first year, and the next three years in the following areas: family, health and fitness, financial, marriage relationship, and spiritual.

- Next, sit down and go over your lists together. If you have never done this, you might be in for some surprises. Do not ridicule or challenge a goal on your partner's list. You can be respectful even when you do not agree.

- Find those goals on your lists on which you can agree based on your life purpose as a couple and your shared values and beliefs.

Place each goal from your list into one of following categories:

- Short term (next twelve months)
- Midterm (next three years)
- Long term (three to five years)

This step might be more difficult than you might think at first. For example, you might both agree that you want to start a family, but you might strongly disagree about how soon you want to achieve that goal. This is an important step in the process. Take plenty of time to talk through the issues of timing because agreement will be necessary to help you prioritize your other goals.

After you have categorized the goals you agree on, go back to your lists and discuss the remaining goals. If you can reach agreement on any of the remaining goals through communication and compromise, add them to your Goal Planner.

Prayerfully consider each goal in your short-term list and discuss a realistic plan of action—how you and your spouse will work together to achieve that goal. It is important to be realistic and plan your actions based on what you know not what might or could happen. For example, if your goal is to buy a house, your action step might be to put a certain amount of money each month in an account for a down payment. Base the amount on your current incomes, not money you think might come your way.

Review all your goals and action steps to make sure (1) they are in keeping with God's purpose and plan for your individual lives and your marriage relationship; (2) they are realistic; and (3) they don't conflict with each other.

Be ready to celebrate when you achieve any of your goals! Plan a way of acknowledging God's faithfulness and your achievement as a couple whenever you complete a goal. Then, repeat the process and choose a new goal.

Setting Goals for Spiritual Growth

If you would have God bless your married life together, then you need to be intentional about including him from the start. Many couples invoke God's blessing during the wedding ceremony and then forget to consult him as the go about planning the rest of their married life. That just doesn't make sense! God's Word contains an incredible amount of wisdom and guidance that can help you and your spouse make the right choices throughout your married life. The first place to start, then, is to set goals that will draw you closer in relationship to him.

Questions to ask about your spiritual growth include: Are we individually and as a couple spending time studying God's Word? How can we grow in our prayer life? What should our involvement in ministry be and how can we serve the Lord together? What's one way I can help my spouse have a deeper relationship with God?

Scripture Reading: (Psalm 119:33–37) (see also Proverbs 3:5–6 and Ephesians 6:10–18)

Teach me, O Lord, to follow every one of your principles,
Give me understanding and I will obey your law;
I will put it into practice with all my heart.
Make me walk along the path of your commands,
For that is where my happiness is found.
Give me an eagerness for your decrees;
Do not inflict me with love for money!
Turn my eyes from worthless things,
And give me life through your word.

Prayer:

Without you, O God, we can do nothing. We invite you to be at the center of our lives. Open your Word to us, fill us with longing to be in intimate relationship with you, and teach us to pray. We want your will for our lives. In Jesus' name, amen.

Personal Goals:

His _____

Hers _____

Points to Discuss:

_____

Our Goals:

_____

Nurturing Your Relationship

After the wedding is when the real work of being happily married begins. How will you nurture the love that binds you together? Although spontaneity and surprise are critical ingredients to a simmering romance, planning can be beneficial as well. Now that you are both back to your busy schedules—trying to juggle work, church, recreation, family, and friends—you are probably beginning to see how easy it is for even loving couples to grow apart. In setting your goals, you must be intentional about how you will keep your marriage relationship a priority when other people and things begin to crowd in.

Think about …

- Planning time in your schedules to do things together that you both enjoy.
- Setting aside money in the budget for dates with your spouse and some weekend getaways.
- Talking about what each of you expects in the area of romance (see Chapter 19).
- Making a pact to let each other know when your needs in your marriage are not being met.

Scripture Reading: (Ephesians 5:23–25; 28, 33) (see also Song of Songs 7:1–13)

For a husband is the head of his wife as Christ is the head of his body, the church; he gave his life to be her Savior. As the church submits to Christ, so you wives must submit to your husbands in everything. And you husbands must love your wives with the same love Christ showed the church. He gave up his life for her …

In the same way, husbands ought to love their wives as they love their own bodies. For a man is actually loving himself when he loves his wife …

So again I say, each man must love his wife as he loves himself, and the wife must respect her husband.

Prayer:

We have found a treasure beyond price in each other. Help us not to take for granted the loving relationship to which you have called us. Renew in us the commitment to nurture our marriage and each other so that our home can bring honor to your name. In Jesus' name, amen.

Personal Goals:

His _____

Hers _____

Points to Discuss:

_____

Our Goals:

_____

Family Ties

Just because your mom and dad want grandchildren is not the right reason to start your own family. The decision to have and raise children is one you and your spouse need to prayerfully consider on your own regardless of any family pressures you might be experiencing. At the same time, don't let fear of responsibility or self-centeredness keep you from the joy of starting a family.

Planning Your Family

There is nothing more wonderful nor more terrifying than that moment when you and your spouse realize that together you have created a new eternal soul from your own bodies. Choosing if and when to start a family of your own is a decision that only you and your spouse can make together. Having a child will change your lives forever. If you and your spouse are considering starting your family soon, there is much you need to discuss.

Is this the right time? As newlyweds, you still have much to learn about each other. In the early years, you are forging a bond that will carry you through the many stages of your marriage—including parenthood. Enjoy this time together, just the two of you.

Are we ready? Every child deserves a mother and father confident and mature enough to handle the demands of parenting. The best gift you can give your child is a strong and healthy marriage—before and after he or she is born. Having a baby shouldn't be accidental—make sure that as individuals and as a couple you are ready for the challenge.

Be sure to think through the financial implications of having a child. Having a baby can add hundreds of dollars to your budget. Do you have adequate insurance coverage for the pregnancy, birth, and baby care? Consider the lost income during and after the pregnancy and whether or not you will have to upgrade your living space. At the same time, don't let money be the deciding factor because the finances will probably never be just right. If God blesses you with a child, you can trust him to provide for you and your child.

How will it affect our other goals? Whether you have one child or a dozen, children demand energy, time, and money. That's energy, time, and money that could be used to achieve some of your other goals. Having children needs to be important enough to you that you will not resent giving up or postponing other things that are important to you, too.

What do we believe about parenting? Hopefully you and your spouse have discussed the values and beliefs you hold about parenting and the roles of mother and father. Make sure you agree on the place a child should have in a home, how discipline should be handled, and the spiritual responsibility that parents have to raise their children to be children of faith.

Remember, decisions about whether or not to have children, how many children to have, and when to start having children are probably the most important decisions you will make during your married life.

Scripture Reading: (Psalm 127:3; 128:1–4;) (see also Mark 10:13–16)

Children are a gift from the Lord; they are a reward from him.

How happy are those who fear the Lord—all who follow his ways!

You will enjoy the fruit of your labor. How happy you will be! How rich your life!

Your wife will be like a fruitful vine, flourishing within your home. And look at all those children! There they sit around your table as vigorous and healthy as young olive trees. That is the Lord's reward for those who fear him.

Prayer:

We understand that bringing a child into this world is an awesome responsibility. We also know that every child is a sacred trust from you. Help us to make the choice about children wisely and in full agreement with each other. In Jesus' name, amen.

Personal Goals:

His _____

Hers _____

Points to Discuss:

_____

Our Goals:

_____

Keeping Fit and Healthy

There are many adjustments to married life together and many changes, as we've mentioned. One area that often takes newlyweds by surprise is how differently they eat and how that affects their health and fitness. In general, studies show that married people are healthier than single people. Yet many couples find that they pack on a few pounds after the honeymoon and time at the gym is often sacrificed for time with the new spouse. And, of course, there is the whole issue of sleep—or lack of it (see Chapter 16). It's not only okay to focus on yourself sometimes, but it is important that you take good care of yourself. And you can also encourage your spouse to do the same by setting goals together for fitness and health.

Consider these questions before setting your fitness goals:

- How have your eating habits changed since the wedding (for better or for worse)? For many couples, fast food becomes a trap in their effort to save time and money. Although it takes more effort to prepare food at home, it is usually much healthier fare and cheaper … don't forget the leftovers for lunch!

- What can you do to eat healthier? Some couples find it helpful to plan out some meals together, assigning duties to maximize the time spent on a healthy, home-cooked meal. For example, one person is responsible for shopping and another for the clean up. Preparation time is shared. You can have some great conversations about how your day went while chopping vegetables!

- What was your exercise plan before your wedding? For many singles, working out at the gym or sports and outdoor activities are as much about relationships and socialization as they are about fitness. So now that you're married, you might assume that your participation in these activities will have to stop. Not so! Remember, it's important for each of you to have some time away from each other. You might have to cut back on the number of such activities you engage in, but you probably shouldn't give them all up.

- What activities can we engage in together that will encourage our health and fitness? Try to find something that you both enjoy doing that will also be good for you. Tennis, golf, gourmet cooking classes, hiking, and so on. If you both tend to be couch potatoes, you might start by scheduling in an evening walk five nights a week. It's good for you, and it's also a great time to connect.

One word of caution in this area: The area of health and fitness can be a sensitive one. As a bride, you might feel your new husband doesn't find you attractive if he suggests you start working out. Likewise, a groom might feel threatened if his wife suggests he start lifting weights. Although you want to remain attractive for one another, setting goals for health and fitness is not about beauty or competition. It's about taking care of yourself and each other.

Scripture Reading: (Proverbs 3:7–8, 3 John 2) (see also Daniel 1:3–16)

Don't be impressed with your own wisdom. Instead, fear the Lord and turn your back on evil. Then you will gain renewed health and vitality.

Dear friend, I am praying that all is well with you and that your body is as healthy as I know your soul is.

Prayer:

Thank you for the incredible way you have created us. Help us understand how to care for our bodies. We ask for the discipline to make wise choices so that we can stay fit and healthy for each other, for others who love us, and for service to you. In Jesus' name, amen.

Personal Goals:

His _____

Hers _____

Points to Discuss:

_____

Our Goals:

_____

Establishing Financial Guidelines

Establishing financial stability is one of the most important goals of married life. It can also be an area of conflict for newly married couples. You and your spouse most likely have very different ideas about money and how it should be spent or saved. We will spend more time in Chapter 18 on resolving conflicts over finances. But for now, use the points listed here to talk with your partner about your current financial status and your plans for your financial future.

- Plan a budget (see Chapter 4)
- Tithing and giving to missions or the church
- Paying off debts
- Buying a home
- Insurance
- Savings and investments

Scripture Reading: (1 Timothy 5:8, Matthew 6:19–20, 24) (see also Matthew 25: 14–29)

But those who won't care for their own relatives, especially those living in the same household, have denied what we believe. Such people are worse than unbelievers.

Don't store up treasures here on earth, where they can be eaten by moths and get rusty, and where thieves break in and steal. Store your treasure in heaven, where they will never become moth-eaten or rusty and where they will be safe from thieves. Wherever your treasure is, there you heart and thoughts will also be …

No one can serve two masters. For you will hate one and love the other, or be devoted to one and despise the other. You cannot serve both God and money.

Prayer:

We first acknowledge that everything we have has come from your hand. Our material and financial blessings are a gift you have entrusted to us. Help us to hold them loosely, use them wisely and to honor you with all we have. In Jesus' name, amen.

Personal Goals:

His _____

Hers _____

Points to Discuss:

_____

Our Goals:

_____

Ready, Set, Goals

It has been the observation of many marriage counselors that married couples set patterns in the first year or two of their marriage that are then repeated over and over again throughout their marriage. Change is hard! And it gets harder the longer you have been engaged in an activity or behavior. That's why setting healthy and godly goals early in your marriage is so crucial to your marital happiness and success.

Write Your Goals Down

There's something solid about a goal that you write down. It's one thing to talk about things and another when you and your spouse take the time and effort to write your goals down; it brings an important added depth to your commitment. So write your goals down! Here are some quick tips for writing your goals:

- **Be specific.** The more specific you are the better chance you have of achieving your goal. Don't just say "We want to give more money to church." Instead, name an amount you will commit to give each month or a specific ministry you will support with an amount. Saying "We want to spend more time together" isn't nearly as effective or motivating as writing down the goal "We will spend three evenings a week together—two at home and one engaged in an activity or with others."

- **Keep it positive.** State your goal in a positive way rather than negative. For example, the goal "We will stop eating so much fast food" isn't very motivating and it doesn't really tell you what it is you need or want to do. A more positive way of stating the same goal might be "We will eat more foods that are healthy and make better choices when we eat out."

- **Review and adjust.** Yes, you are writing your goals down, but they're not in concrete! Be willing to review your goals on a regular basis and make adjustments to them so that you have a better chance of being successful in what it is that you really want—a healthy, happy, and God-honoring marriage.

That's the Spirit

One of the most awesome things about planning and writing down your goals is being able to look back and see all that God has done for you and thank him for his great faithfulness and love.

O Lord my God, you have done many miracles for us. Your plans for us are too numerous to list. If I tried to recite all your wonderful deeds, I would never come to the end of them. (Psalm 40:5)

Common Obstacles to Achieving Your Goals

If you talk to other young married couples that you know, chances are that you will be able to count on one hand those that have taken the time to make goals for their marriage. This is most likely because they have never really considered the importance of having goals for your relationships even if they are proficient at goal setting in their careers. Setting goals is a form of accountability as well as dream casting. If you are struggling to achieve your goals, check out these obstacles and see if any of them might be impeding your progress:

- **Lack of awareness**—Have you lost sight of your goal—the what, why, and how of what you are wanting to achieve?

- **Personal versus family**—Are you having difficulty surrendering your personal goals that conflict with the goals you and your spouse have agreed on?

- **Conflicting goals**—Have you set goals in one area that are keeping you from achieving a goal in another area? Which goal can you agree to change?

- **Negative thinking**—Do you find yourself saying "We'll never be able to do it!" That kind of thinking robs you of the will and energy to achieve your goal. If you really believe it is impossible, then you just made it impossible for you. Ask yourself, why did we choose this goal if we thought it was impossible?

- **Procrastination**—Waiting to get started on your goals postpones the joy you could be experiencing by achieving them. Why are you waiting?

Bet You Didn't Know

Corporate and business planners use a helpful concept: the 80/20 rule. The 80/20 rule asserts that a minority of causes, inputs, or efforts account for a majority of results, outputs, and rewards in ones life. Literally, that means that 80 percent of what you accomplish comes from 20 percent of the activities you engage in. Conversely, 80 percent of our activities account for only 20 percent of what truly matters most.

An example in society is the fact that over 80 percent of the crimes committed are done by less than 20 percent of the population. A more personal example would be that in your home 20 percent of your carpet is likely to get 80 percent of the everyday traffic and 80 percent of what you wear most often comes from 20 percent of the clothes in your closet.

Review and Reflect

After you've let some time pass, reflect on the goals you've made. Jot down notes on all you've accomplished and areas that still remain a challenge for you. Discuss openly what is going right and what still needs work. At this point, you might want to go back and adjust some of your goals and/or make new ones.

When you have achieved one or more of your goals, make sure you take time to celebrate! Even as you are planning your goals, talk about what you will do when one of your goals is met. Make it a true celebration. Think about whether or not you want to share the news with others or if you want to keep your celebration between the two of you. Regardless, celebrate! It is a sign of maturity and commitment that you set a goal, stuck to it, and made it happen, so pat yourselves on the back!

Chapter 18

Whatever Happened to Happily Ever After?

No matter how much you and your spouse love each other, you will encounter conflict in your marriage. It is part of the natural course of every intimate relationship. Just think how boring your life together would be if you were so much alike that you never disagreed on anything! In fact, learning to fight fair and resolve conflict in a healthy way can actually strengthen your relationship and build a better understanding of each other. However, couples who allow conflicts to go unresolved or who use unhealthy or unfair methods of fighting are planting seeds of anger, resentment, and discontent that inhibit the growth of true intimacy and might eventually splinter their relationship.

The first few years can be the most difficult as you and your spouse work through your differences but they are also the most important. How you deal with conflict in your relationship now can become the pattern that continues for the rest of your married life. Conflict is not a sign of failure in your marriage—it's an opportunity for growth. Your marriage will be happier and healthier as you learn the right ways to resolve conflict.

Happy Couples Are Couples Who ...

Happily married couples accept conflict as a natural result of a growing relationship and learn to deal with it in a healthy and godly way. Although every marriage relationship is unique, there seem to be some common areas that present challenges to most couples: adjusting to their changing roles, developing healthy relations with their in-laws, agreeing on how to handle finances, and establishing a balanced sex life. As you remain centered in Christ, you can accept conflict as an opportunity for growth and discovery and learn to deal with these and other areas of conflict.

"I Do" Do's and Don'ts

It's the little things that can drive you crazy! "Why can't he learn to put dirty dishes in the dishwasher?" "Why does she leave the cap off the toothpaste?" Do try to keep the little annoyances in perspective. But don't ignore problems that keep resurfacing in arguments. Chances are they are only symptomatic of unresolved issues that will eventually become major conflicts. Try to discover what the real issue is and use your best conflict resolution skills to find a solution.

Husband/Wife Hassles

Now that you are actually living together as husband and wife, there are some issues that might arise over the role each of you play in your new household. Even if you took our advice and discussed your expectations of marriage roles (see Chapter 3), conflicts are still likely to surface as those expectations play out day-to-day. Many couples discover that what they think in their heads about marital roles ends up being more difficult to live out than they anticipated.

Who does the housework? Who does the cooking? Who takes out the trash? Who takes care of the yard work? Many newlyweds find that they argue more in the kitchen than in any room of the house! There is, of course, no biblical reason why the wife can't mow the lawn while the husband makes the bed—if that is what works best for your marriage. But it will take a lot of honest communication to figure that out! Whether you take a traditional view or a less conventional view isn't as important as sharing the same view of what makes for a good husband or a good wife.

At the heart of many conflicts over marital roles is the unspoken issue of control. Almost anything can become a problem if the real issue is "Who's the boss?," but happy and healthy couples recognize when disagreements are escalating into a power struggle. That's when conflicts become destructive. It takes a mature man or woman to put the wants and needs of their mate ahead of their own desires. Make it your goal to promote each other's success and the health of your relationship above any preconceived notions of who should do what.

Happy marriages are those in which both the husband and wife are willing to make adjustments, establishing a balance in their roles so that they share in household responsibilities and the establishment of their home.

Living with In-Laws

Tensions over in-laws often grow after the honeymoon's over. You are, for better or for worse, a part of your partner's family now. Together you will need to find the best way to deal with conflicts that occur because of your relationship with in-laws. The place to start, as always, is with open and honest communication with each other. Here are some questions that might help you articulate your feelings and uncover the issues:

- What is your perspective of a typical visit to your in-laws home?
- Do you feel like one of the family?
- Is your spouse attentive or do you feel ignored?
- Are you uncomfortable with the role you are expected to assume while there?
- Are you comfortable with the frequency of your visits with your in-laws?
- What happens when they visit your home?
- Are visits to your home by in-laws unexpected?
- How does the communication style of your spouse's family make you feel?
- Are you okay with the level of affection that is displayed?
- Are telephone calls appropriate in length and frequency?
- Is advice given only when it is asked for?
- Do you feel comfortable asking your in-laws for their opinions?
- Do you know what your in-laws expect from you?
- Are you comfortable with those expectations?

Don't expect over-night intimacy with your in-laws. Just as your relationship with your spouse has grown over time—and must continue to change and grow over the years—the same is true of your relationship with your in-laws. Yes, there are horror stories about in-laws. We could tell you a few! But many couples have wonderful, loving relationships with their spouse's families. You can, too! Here are a few tips:

- Show your in-laws the same loyalty and respect you expect your mate to show your parents.

- Give them the benefit of the doubt. They are going to make some mistakes, but what most in-laws want is a healthy, loving relationship with their child and his or her spouse.

- Get to know them better by asking about their roots. Sometimes getting to know more about them as individuals and their own families not only explains the differences you might be experiencing but will help you appreciate them more.

- Set healthy boundaries and don't be afraid to say no. Discuss together the boundaries that are necessary for the success of your marriage: amount of time spent, how to handle disagreements with in-laws, gift-giving expectations, and so on.

- Have a plan for handling conflicts. Usually, the best thing to do is to let each spouse be the ambassador for his or her own family. In other words, if the wife has an issue with her mother-in-law, the husband should be her advocate and go to his mother on his wife's behalf. Likewise, if a husband is having difficulty fitting in with his wife's family, it is good for the wife to take some initiative to smooth the way.

- Always, always, always keep your marriage as the top priority. We hope that you never have to choose between your families and your spouse, but if you do there should be no question in your mind where your loyalty belongs.

If you are having significant battles with or about your in-laws already, we urge you to find a way to bury the hatchet (and not in somebody's back!) before you start having children. Things get a lot more complicated when children come into the picture. It is not only possible, but part of God's design for you and your spouse to have an independent relationship while maintaining a loving and supportive relationship with your families. You can work it out!

That's the Spirit

May God, who gives this patience and encouragement, help you live in complete harmony with each other—each with the attitude of Christ Jesus toward the other. (Romans 15:5) God does not ask us to do anything he will not enable us to do. Adopt the attitude of Christ who, even though he was God, did not demand his rights but humbled himself to the point of the cross, because he loved us. (Philippians 2:5–8)

Feuding over Finances

More married couples argue over money than any other subject! If you haven't discovered this truth yet, you will. It's not about how much money you make or how much you spend. It's all about managing your priorities and expectations. Unfortunately, the Christian perspective on wealth and possessions runs contrary to the world's view. You might not have been taught good money-management skills or how to live happily with less. You might already be heavily in debt and just can't see a way out. Whatever your individual financial situations were entering into marriage, you must now find your way together.

Overcoming a lifetime of habits and beliefs about money will not be easy. If you have not lived on your own, you might not have a realistic view of what it costs to live or the delicate balance between income and spending. The battle of the budget can be further complicated by the following conditions:

- One or both partners are accustomed to relying on credit to sustain their lifestyle. For many, this habit begins in college. Using debt to live on is borrowing against the future and as Christians your tomorrows should be in God's hands alone.

- You have a great difference of opinion on saving and spending. Money management is a reflection of deeper personal values. That's one reason why finances can create such conflict. If you can identify and agree on your values, it will make it easier for you to reach agreement on money matters.

- For some, money equals power and control. The spouse who earns all or most of the income might feel entitled to manage the couple's money as he or she sees fit. Although financial independence is good before marriage, after marriage there is no such thing as his money and her money.

- Planning for the future is an area many couples ignore—they figure there is plenty of time for that later. Every financial planner will tell you that the earlier you start, the better. Life insurance, retirement, and even a will, should all be considerations in your financial future.

If you find you are feuding over finances, take a deeper look at what the real issue might be. Does money represent power to you or your mate? Is your success and self-worth tied to your financial sate? Do you believe Christ's statements in Matthew 6 about who is really in control of your welfare? Talking honestly about your values and priorities might be more helpful in ending the feuding than money.

Try to locate a good Christian financial planner who can address the spiritual as well as practical issues of money and your future.

Sexual Tensions

We're not talking about unbridled passion, we're talking about differences in expectations about your sexual intimacy that might create conflict in your marriage. As newlyweds, remember that your sexual relationship will continue to grow and change. But the ability to express your sexual wants and needs with each other and to develop a mutually satisfying physical relationship is key to long-term marital success.

Difficulties in a married couple's sexual relationship are often rooted in a lack of understanding about a man's and woman's sexual differences and/or a lack of communication about your own sexual wants and needs. Your sexuality is so core to your personality that it is only natural that conflicts in this area can be hurtful. Again, you must be patient as you work out your sexual differences so that you can have a loving and fulfilling relationship that will last a lifetime.

It is important to realize that normal couples do have sexual difficulties. A 1978 study of 100 happily married couples noted that 50 percent of males and 77 percent of females reported sexual difficulties such as:

- Partner chooses inconvenient time
- Inability to relax
- Attraction to persons other than mate
- Disinterest
- Attraction to person of same sex

- Different sexual practices or habits
- "Turned off"
- Too little foreplay
- Too little "tenderness" after intercourse

If any of these difficulties are affecting your relationship, talk it out and seek help if you cannot resolve the problem together. A Christian counselor who understands the spiritual dimensions of sex might be just what you need to help you make the next step into a more satisfying level of sexual intimacy.

That's the Spirit

And so, dear Christian friends, I plead with you to give your bodies to God. Let them be a living and holy sacrifice—the kind he will accept. (Romans 12:1)

Our bodies ultimately belong to God, and sexual union is just another way to be "a living sacrifice" that will honor him as we honor each other with our bodies.

Fighting Fair

As you grow and mature in your relationship with each other, you will discover ways to control your arguments rather than allowing your arguments to control you. Without a healthy strategy, couples fall into destructive patterns—pouting, shouting, withdrawing, and fighting about the same issues over and over again without accomplishing anything! You need a plan—a set of rules that allows you to engage constructively on the issues and move ahead in your marriage relationship. In your battle plan, you will need to follow the "Rules of Engagement" and "Guidelines for Negotiating" if you're going to fight fair.

Family Ties

Keep your families out of your fights. If you are close to your parents and/or siblings, it will be so tempting to talk to them when you and your partner are having difficulties. But be careful that you are not turning to them only to gain support for your side of the disagreement. You should not put them in the awkward position of having to choose sides between you and your spouse. Neither should you demonstrate disloyalty to your spouse by sharing your personal conflicts outside of your marriage unless you have both agreed that it is appropriate.

Rules of Engagement

Too often when arguments erupt, couples are ill equipped at that time to deal with the real issues that are the point of conflict. If you understand that ahead of time and covenant together to observe the following rules of engagement, you stand a much better chance of resolving your conflict without hurting yourself or your mate.

Select an appropriate time. It is very important to select a time that will allow for the greatest understanding and cooperative effort. If you are hungry, physically exhausted, emotionally upset, or have a limited time before another engagement, real problem-solving should be postponed. If you do decide to postpone, set a definite time when you will revisit the issue.

Stay positive. When conflicts arise, you have the choice of accepting it as an opportunity to grow together or allowing it to become a wedge that separates you. It is your attitude toward the conflict and your commitment to finding a resolution that will make the difference.

Stick to the problem. You should each state the problem as you see it and discuss together what underlying issues might be contributing to the problem. But this is not the time to unload every issue, want, and need influencing your relationship. Nor is it the time to bring up past problems. One problem at a time is sufficient.

Listen carefully to each other. You need to really hear and understand each other. A good listener invites another to share what is on their heart. If you listen to each other, you soon will notice that you begin to take each other seriously. Listen to your spouse the way you want to be listened to.

Remain in control of your emotions. You cannot negotiate a solution to your problem if you let your emotions get control. That does not mean that you should hide your feelings. What it means is expressing your feelings without losing control and inflicting harm on your partner and your relationship. It also means not venting your emotions in a physical way—throwing and breaking things, or hitting or slapping your partner are not acceptable.

That's the Spirit

Keep the lines of communication between you and your spouse open so that anger will not have an opportunity to gain control.

And don't sin by letting anger gain control over you. Don't let the sun go down while you are still angry, for anger gives a mighty foothold to the Devil. (Ephesians 4:26–27)

Guidelines for Negotiating

How does the married couple arrive at a mutually acceptable solution? By learning to negotiate! As a couple, you can learn to work through your conflicts and achieve a win-win situation. Here are some guidelines to help you learn successful negotiating skills:

- **Take responsibility for your part in the problem.** In resolving marital conflict, you basically are saying to your mate that "we" have a problem. When you accept some responsibility for the problem, your partner perceives a willingness to cooperate and probably will be much more open to the discussion.

- **Believe that change is possible.** If you don't believe that change is possible, there seems little motivation to try to negotiate. Some things cannot be changed—those things you need to prayerfully let go of. But for everything else, you need to maintain the attitude and the desire that this conflict is an opportunity for positive change—in yourself, in your partner, and in your marriage. This is part of what makes the marriage relationship exciting.

- **Identify all your options.** After you own your part in the problem and agree that change would be beneficial, the next step is to find a solution you can both agree on. The solution is not always immediately obvious. You might need to brainstorm together and consider many options before you hit on the one that is best for you.

- **Agree to agree.** You must covenant together that you will pray and discuss until you can reach an agreement on the next best step for solving your difficulty. It's not fair to half-heartedly agree on a course of action. That makes it way too easy to say "I told you so" if the solution is less than successful. It also doesn't build the confidence and trust your marriage relationship needs.

- **Move forward with your changes.** Concentrate on your own behavior changes and allow your spouse to do the same. Show grace and patience, encouragement, and loving understanding. After a time, get together and reevaluate how your decisions are working.

Learn to Listen

Listening is a skill you can develop, and learning to be a good listener is essential to your marriage relationship. Here are some keys to good listening that many couples have found very helpful. A good listener …

- Keeps his/her mind focused on what the other person is saying.
- Asks questions to get more information and to clarify misunderstandings.
- Doesn't avoid listening because it is inconvenient or too time-consuming.
- Doesn't pretend to pay attention when he/she really isn't.
- Doesn't allow outside sights and sounds to easily distract him/her.
- Looks past what the person is saying to discover what he/she is feeling.

Many conflicts could be defused if couples would regularly practice the following listening exercise. It only takes 30 minutes and is well worth the effort.

Find a place where you and your partner can spend 30 full, uninterrupted minutes together. Sit face-to-face, knee-to-knee. The quieter partner begins. He or she will talk for 10 minutes about himself/herself. The other partner must give full attention and listen without interrupting, making comments, asking questions, arguing, correcting, agreeing, getting angry, or falling asleep. After the first 10 minutes, the other partner begins to talk about himself/herself for 10 minutes. The first speaker now listens, with full attention and saying nothing, as above.

Follow-up. For the final 10 minutes, discuss what you have been saying to each other. Also discuss what you have learned about your partner. Use the following questions to discuss what happened during your experiment in listening:

- Was it easier to listen or to talk for 10 minutes?
- What was it like not to be able to say anything while your spouse talked for 10 minutes?
- How did it feel to not be interrupted?
- What did you want to do, instead of listening, when you were required to remain silent?
- Did you ever wonder if your partner was listening during the 10 minutes while you were talking?

Overcoming Barriers to Fighting Fair

There's a big difference between the attitude that says "I want to be happy and I don't want to be hurt" and "I want *you* to be happy and I don't want *you* to be hurt." Self-centeredness is one of the primary barriers to fighting fair and a more common attitude than most couples want to admit. In your new relationship with your spouse, you might, for the first time in your life, be confronted with your own tendency to focus first on your own wants and needs.

When conflicts arise, many couples lapse into old unhealthy patterns of communication that they might have established in prior relationships or even earlier in their present relationship. Developing healthy communication patterns must be a conscious choice and will grow stronger with practice. Negativity and blaming are also common barriers to healthy conflict resolution, as we have discussed previously. Another common barrier to fighting fair is avoidance. You cannot deny conflict. Like negative emotions, the harder you try to push them down or cover them up, the bigger they grow. Avoidance can also take the form of emotional distance from the issues or even physical absence. As difficult as confrontation and conflict resolution can sometimes be, avoidance is never the answer.

One final barrier to resolving conflict in your marriage can be the misconception that every issue must have a winner and a loser. The "I win, you lose!" barrier is not for the happily married couple. You should always strive for the win-win solution—that's what good negotiation is all about.

If you can't seem to resolve your conflicts in a satisfactory way, don't be afraid to get counseling from a Christian professional or your pastor. It doesn't mean you're a failure. Take advantage of the wisdom of more mature believers who have gone through the same type of conflicts and have much information that is valuable to share.

Strategies for Reconciliation

Communicating honest feelings openly and resolving differences of opinion constructively might be two of the most difficult challenges of marriage, but they are well worth the time and effort when they lead to reconciliation between a husband and wife! Don't assume your mate should know what you are thinking or feeling. And don't assume your spouse will know what to do to help heal any wounds you might have. You must tell them what you want and need. Be specific. Say what you mean and mean what you say.

Affirming Loyalty to the Marriage

As newlyweds, you might still struggle with the idea that if you encounter conflict there must be something wrong with your marriage. You might fear that your marriage will not last. We hope we have helped you see that you can have a happy and healthy marriage even if it is not conflict-free. But it is important to reassure each other of your love and commitment to your relationship after a disagreement or fight. You will not always handle every conflict perfectly—you are, after all, imperfect human beings. Don't let your spouse wonder or have doubts about your continuing loyalty to him or her and your unswerving devotion to your marriage. Say it and show it—especially after a conflict.

Say the Magic Words

And they aren't "I told you so!" For many couples, saying "I love you" is easy. But there are more important words that you can say to express your love for your spouse. Learn to say "I'm sorry" and mean it. Don't use these magic words to dodge further discussion of a sensitive issue or to avoid responsibility. You must first own your part in any conflict and accept that your attitudes, actions, and words might have hurt your partner before you can sincerely say "I'm sorry" and mean it.

One final tip for using these healing words: always include specifically what you are sorry for. You'll be much further along the path to reconciliation when you say "I'm sorry for not giving you my full attention when you need to talk to me." rather than just saying "I'm sorry."

Practice Forgiveness

Never, ever take forgiveness for granted in your marriage relationship. It is fundamental to your continued intimacy—spiritually, relationally, and physically. The seed of unforgiveness will grow and fester and lead to negative feelings and behaviors—like bitterness and resentment—that will destroy your marriage. You must always ask forgiveness when it is necessary and accept forgiveness when it is offered. It is not the same as reconciliation, but it is essential to the process of being reconciled.

There is so much more in the area of forgiveness than we can deal with here. But we do urge you to develop a biblical understanding of forgiveness and practice it in your marriage. Consider the following statements:

- Forgiveness is a choice of your will; don't wait until you feel like forgiving.
- You don't have to forget in order to forgive. In fact, you need to acknowledge your anger and pain before true forgiveness can occur.
- You forgive for your benefit; not for the other person's benefit.
- Forgiveness means bearing the burden of the wrong done to you yourself.
- Forgiveness is costly, but freedom is what you gain from forgiveness.

Reestablish Trust

Part of the purpose of forgiveness is to heal any breech of trust that might have occurred between you. It takes a mature individual to extend trust and to be trustworthy. In *See Dick and Jane Grow Up* by Dr. David Hawkins, the author offers some practical steps related to the forgiveness process that can help you reestablish trust between you and your spouse:

- Acknowledging pain and earlier betrayal
- Talking about fear for the future
- Discussing options regarding ways to trust one another in the future
- Understanding and accepting that things will never be perfect
- Accepting that spouses might hurt one another again
- Acknowledging the hurt of not being trusted
- Sharing frustrations, working with one another to create deeper trust

How to Kiss and Make Up

You're in the final stages of a fight. You've reached an understanding even though emotions are still running a little hot. At this point, the following exchange takes place:

Husband: C'mon, honey, it'll all work out. Let's make love.

Wife: You want sex now?! Are you out of your mind? I'm not sure I even *like* you right now!

Making up after a fight can be sweet! But some couples rush too quickly to the bedroom, leaving issues and emotions unresolved. Although it's important to reconnect and share affection after a conflict has been resolved, rushing to the bedroom is not always the right thing to do. Often after (or even during) a fight, the man wants to make love while sex is usually the farthest thing from his wife's mind. Physical intimacy makes him feel safe while she needs to feel safe before she is ready for physical intimacy.

He wants to have sex to recapture the feeling that she loves him. But she needs to feel that he loves her *before* she's ready to have sex. She needs some emotional distance from the conflict. Sound familiar? It's another one of the differences between the genders that keep marriage interesting! Just remember that what you both want is love. As you are closing out an argument, start slow and follow these tips for making up:

- Sit together in a neutral area (not the bedroom).
- Hold hands and continue to talk with your spouse.
- Make sure that the conflict has been resolved.
- Have you agreed on a solution?
- Is forgiveness needed?
- Reconnect emotionally—restate your commitment to each other.
- Embrace and hold each other (be willing to stop here).
- Kiss and reassure your spouse of your love (be willing to stop here).
- Decide together whether or not you are ready for lovemaking.

In your first months and years of married life, you will no doubt encounter many conflicts. We pray that you will learn to view them as positive opportunities for growth in your marriage. Remain flexible, learn to compromise, stay committed, develop trust, and think "we" and you will have many happy years together as husband and wife.

Chapter 19

Remember the Romance

It's so easy and all too common for the every day stresses of life to push romance right out the window! After weeks, months, and years of waking up next to your spouse every morning, it becomes so easy to take him or her for granted. But if you want to have a happy marriage, you have to make romancing your spouse a priority. We've already talked about this in the chapter on setting goals (Chapter 17). But we want to emphasize it again here. No matter how strong your love for each other is on your wedding day, it can die—it can be starved to death through inattention, ignorance, and cruelty. You must choose to live a life of love daily.

Simply put, romance is intentionally demonstrating through words and deeds that you love and cherish your spouse. Cherish is a great word—it might even have been part of your wedding vows. To cherish means to hold dear and value highly (attitudes); to treat tenderly, to nurture and protect (actions); to cling to the idea of, to harbor in the mind (thoughts). Smart couples learn to cherish each other every day with their attitudes, their actions, and their thoughts. And smart couples cultivate those tender moments and "butterflies in the stomach" feelings that convinced you to spend the rest of your lives together in the first place.

The Art of Romance

What do you think of when you hear the word romance? Do you think of flowers and sonnets, candlelight and lace? Romance can mean different things to different people.

To be romantic doesn't mean you emphasize your emotions over your reason. The authentic romantic is able to integrate his or her emotions, thoughts, and attitudes into an honest exchange of honor and love. Romance is fun and personal and passionate and playful. Romance can lead to deeper intimacy—physically, emotionally, and relationally—in your marriage.

Family Ties

Your families of origin have influenced your idea of romance. You might have grown up in a household where signs of affection were often displayed or never displayed. Maybe in your family only women and wimps were romantic. Your family might have taught you that it is the size and cost of the gift that matters or you might have learned that even a single flower plucked from a garden can be very romantic. Examining what you've learned about romance from your family is a good starting point as you get in touch with your "romantic side."

Romance is R.E.S.P.E.C.T.

If there is anything as important to romance as love, it is respect. Love might have gotten you to the altar, but without respect it is impossible to build a lasting intimate relationship. Respect for your partner comes as love deepens, enabling you to demonstrate high regard for your mate. Love can be a fragile thing, but mutual respect brings strength to the connection between you. It's hard not to be attracted to someone who recognizes your worth as a person and treats you with courtesy and consideration. You can't help but love your mate when he or she gives you the gift of honor and esteem.

On the other hand, disrespect creates the opposite effect. When your spouse treats you as if you are less important than he or she is, you begin to feel undeserving of love and romantically unattractive. That makes connecting on an intimate level increasingly difficult. Disrespect sets in motion a vicious cycle—how we are treated affects how we view ourselves and how we view ourselves affects our ability to be intimate with our spouse. Often we show disrespect for our spouse without even being aware of it. A key to romancing your mate is to be courageous enough to confront each other when you are hurt by actions or words that are disrespectful and to be ready and willing to change hurtful behavior when confronted with it.

The Latin root for the word romance means "to write;" here's an appropriate little exercise to help you and your mate think about respect for yourselves and for each other. Create an acrostic with the word respect. Use each letter of the word respect to begin an attribute or adjective that describes you (because you need to start with self-respect). Then do one for your mate. Take a few days to put some prayerful effort into it. A dictionary or thesaurus can help you find the right words. Then schedule a time to share them with each other.

Example:

R = romantic

E = encouraging

S = secure

P = passionate about God

E = earnest

C = compassionate

T = trustworthy

Romance Is a Choice

Every day you can make the choice to romance your mate. You don't have to wait for Valentine's Day, your anniversary, or some other special occasion. In fact, if you do you will be missing out on a lot of lovin'! Romance is about paying attention to the details—how he takes his coffee, her favorite color, what turns him on, and what turns her off.

Romance starts with honesty from the heart, and that requires trust. You must choose to reveal your romantic desires and treasure the secrets your mate reveals. Romance is creative—looking for new and different ways to say, "I love you" with signs and symbols as well as words and actions. Together you and your spouse can create your own brand of romance—one that fits the two of you in a unique and satisfying way.

Bet You Didn't Know

You can use flowers to send your lover a secret message. Clover whispers "Be mine." A red chrysanthemum says, "I love you." Peach blossoms express "I am your captive." Roses have a secret code all their own:

Red roses	Love and respect
Yellow roses	Joy and friendship
White roses	Innocence, purity, and secrecy
Dark pink roses	Thankfulness
Pale pink roses	Grace and joy
Pale peach roses	Modesty
Coral roses	Desire
Orange roses	Fascination
Red and white roses	Unity
Sweetheart roses	Beauty and youth
Open rose over 2 buds	Secrecy

Romance Is Personal

Because romance is so deeply personal, if you want your spouse to know how to romance you, then you will have to tell him or her what your needs and expectations are. Here's a way to check out your R.Q. (romance quotient). Put your initials in front of the statement that is true for you and have your spouse do the same.

I fall in love with you all over again when …

[ ] [ ] You use your pet name for me.

[ ] [ ] You give up something you want so I can have something I want.

[ ] [ ] You take the time to make a card or write a personal note.

[ ] [ ] You buy me something expensive—just because.

[ ] [ ] You clean the snow off my windshield on your way to work.

[ ] [ ] You bring me a single rose.

[ ] [ ] You hold my hand in church during prayer.

[ ] [ ] You kiss my fingertips in a dark movie theater.

[ ] [ ] You take me to our "special place" for no special reason.

[ ] [ ] You wear perfume (or cologne) for me.

[ ] [ ] You "set the mood" for lovemaking with candles and music.

[ ] [ ] You make me laugh after a hard day.

[ ] [ ] You bring me chocolate.

[ ] [ ] You offer to make dinner when it's my turn.

[ ] [ ] You get up early to start your day in God's Word.

[ ] [ ] You write me a sexy message and tuck it in my underwear drawer.

[ ] [ ] You show up at work unexpectedly to take me to lunch.

[ ] [ ] You call just to say "I can't get you out of my mind."

[ ] [ ] You make up a silly song about us.

[ ] [ ] You fix me my favorite meal.

[ ] [ ] You brag about me to your family.

[ ] [ ] You get me tickets to hear my favorite band (or see my favorite team).

[ ] [ ] You roll over and hug me in the night.

[ ] [ ] You give me the "I'm so glad you're mine!" look in public.

[ ] [ ] You take time to prepare me for lovemaking.

[ ] [ ] You surprise me in the shower.

[ ] [ ] You take out the garbage without being reminded.

[ ] [ ] You tell all your friends how proud you are of me.

[ ] [ ] You tell me I'm beautiful.

[ ] [ ] You admire my strength.

[ ] [ ] You initiate prayer with me.

Did we miss any of your favorites? There are so many more ways in attitude, action, and thought that you can make your spouse feel cherished. Use the table to make up a list of his and her romantic wishes using the examples we've given and adding your own favorites. Write two separate lists and exchange them along with a commitment to romance the one you love.

His Romantic Wishes

_____
_____
_____
_____
_____
_____
_____

Her Romantic Wishes

_____
_____
_____
_____
_____
_____
_____

That's the Spirit

One of the most romantic stories ever written is in the Bible. Written by King Solomon, the wisest man ever to live, the Song of Songs details the loving relationship between the king and his bride. God understands your romantic longings and the desires of your heart. He wants to see your desires fulfilled in your marriage.

I am my lover's, the one he desires. Come, my love, let us go out into the fields and spend the night among the wildflowers … And there I will give you my love. (Song of Songs 7:10–12)

Romance Can Get Physical

In case you haven't noticed, men and women are different. Put a man in a room with soft music, candlelight, and his wife and he's thinking sex. Take away the soft music and the candlelight and he's probably still thinking sex. It's natural; it's normal so expect it. But if that man is assuming his wife's response will be the same, he might be in trouble. A woman needs romance to feel loved, and she needs to feel loved before she can be responsive sexually. Yes, these are generalizations and there are exceptions to every rule. The point is that the husband and the wife who learns and accommodates the physical and emotional differences of his or her partner is truly romantic!

Not all physical intimacy needs to culminate in sexual intercourse. Kissing is a very intimate and romantic way of expressing love. Although many couples take kissing for granted, with practice it can become one of the most romantic gifts you can give one another. And it's good for you: scientific studies have shown that kissing causes our brains to produce oxytocin, a hormone that promotes feelings of well-being and happiness. But beware! Kissing can be habit-forming: Kissing releases a chemical inside your mouth and at the edges of your lips that makes you want more. Want to become a better kisser? Here are a few tips to help you develop the art of kissing:

- **Slow down.** Too often kissing is rushed in order to get to the next step. Make kissing the goal and savor every sense it arouses in you and your spouse.
- **Pay attention to details.** Create a romantic mood with dimmed lights and music. Remember how many mints you consumed while dating? Think about the condition of your face and lips. All these details can contribute to a sensual kissing session.
- **Relax.** Don't allow for distractions—either mental or physical. Turn off the TV and the phone and set aside your "To Do" list until tomorrow.
- **Be patient and practice, practice, practice.** You'll get better and enjoy it more every time.

What you both want is to love and be loved. Be aware of your differences, put your spouses needs ahead of your own, and you will enjoy many romantic interludes together.

"I Do" Do's and Don'ts

Before your spouse walks out the door each day, do take the time to exchange a kiss. A study conducted by German physicians and psychologist concluded that workers who were kissed by their loved ones each day before leaving for work …

- Missed less work
- Had fewer accidents on the way to work
- Earned about 20–30 percent more money
- Lived about 5 years longer

So if you want to live longer and make more money, keep kissing!

Seriously, who would have thought that something so fun and romantic could actually be good for you! What a great way to start your day!

Why Woo When You've Already Won

Here are two common complaints that marriage counselors have been hearing for years. Wife: "He was so romantic while we were courting. But now that we're married, he's totally forgotten how to be romantic." Husband: "She's totally let herself go. She doesn't seem to care about being attractive anymore." Her knight in shining armor is rusty! His beautiful princess has gone back to her Cinderella ways!

When courting behavior stops after the wedding day, someone is making the huge assumption that the battle is over. But if the rising divorce rate, both inside and outside the church, has taught us anything, let it be to never assume you will not lose your mate! It takes two to begin a marriage, but it only takes one to end it. You will find plenty of forces working against your marriage in the months and years to come. Every day you should wake up and ask yourself "How can I win my partner's love today?"

Enemies of Love

It's not really accurate to say you are "in love." Love is not a state of being. Love is verb—it requires action. If you want to defeat the enemies of love, you will need to use your body, soul, and mind to continue to court your spouse. Be on guard for these dark knights, sworn enemies of love:

- *Count Complacency*—A spouse under the influence of this enemy is thinking, "*I'm* perfectly happy with things the way they are so there is no problem." Also defined as "annoyingly self-satisfied." Complacency perpetuates the illusion that everything is fine, nothing more is desired. It's not the same as contentment because it is one-sided, and in a marriage that can be deadly. You fight complacency by being attentive to the wants and needs of your partner.

- *Lord Laziness*—This enemy keeps a spouse unwilling to exert any energy for the sake of the romance. In other words, a lazy partner might care but not enough to get involved. This enemy encourages the "This will be good enough" mentality. Eagerness is the best weapon against laziness. An eager spouse keenly desires to romance his or her partner and can't wait to do so.

- *Baron of Busyness*—Busyness is the plague of our age. Newly married couples often find themselves lamenting "There just isn't enough time to do everything we need to do." The only way to fight busyness is with priorities. You must choose to make romancing your spouse a higher priority than work, church, friends, or family.

Dating Your Mate

Intimacy will grow as you spend time together. But as you've already noticed, life has a way of crowding love out of your schedule. Smart couples guarantee time to talk and connect with each other by scheduling regular dates with their mates. Establishing this habit early in your marriage will help you survive when the children come along and take up even more of your time and energy. You and your spouse can take turns planning your date night, remembering to plan for the other's satisfaction and not just your own.

Here are a few ideas for dating your mate:

- **The Classic Date**—Remember when dating meant dinner and a movie? It's still the classic way to woo. To save some money, go to the early showing of the movie and have dinner after.

- **The Afternoon-Delight Date**—Great for a Saturday! Concert and theatre tickets are usually cheaper if you go to a matinee.

- **The Lunch Date**—Surprise your mate by picking him/her up for lunch. Instead of going out, pick up some take-out and rush home for a quickie.

- **The Daring Date**—Try something neither of you has ever tried before. It doesn't have to be extreme!

- **The Quick Date**—Write an hour into both of your schedules just to sit and cuddle (or practice your kissing!).

- **The Road Trip Date**—Gas up the car and take to the road for the day. It doesn't really matter where you go. Road trips are a great way to get away from the demands and distractions of your life and it doesn't have to cost a fortune.

- **The Kidnapping Date**—No ransom required! Make arrangements at a local bed and breakfast (usually *very* romantic) or hotel. Pack a bag for you and your spouse. When your mate gets home from work, kidnap him/her.

- **The Stay-at-Home Date**—You don't have to go somewhere to have a date. There are a lot of things you can do right at home. Rent a video and pop some popcorn. Eat French bread and cheese in front of the fire. Read a book together, alternating reading aloud.

- **The Project Date**—Has your wife been longing for a flower garden? Does you husband wish he had time to refinish his desk? Why not do it together!

- **The Nature Date**—Take a hike! Get outdoors and enjoy the incredible world that God has made for our pleasure. Watch a sunset or sunrise together. Walk along the beach or through the woods.

"I Do" Do's and Don'ts

Don't think you can't be romantic because you don't have the money for a fancy meal, an expensive gift, or a weekend away. There are a lot of ways to keep the passion in your relationship burning without spending the down payment for your house! But it's important, also, to see romance as an investment in your future with your spouse. In fact, romances should have a line in your household budget! Find a balance—be willing to spend some money for the sake of romance, but don't feel like it has to cost a lot!

Extraordinary Romance for Ordinary Days

Every day there is a way you can romance your partner. Romance is about attitude, actions, and thoughts. Keep the passion alive by striving to find some way to woo your mate every day. Here are a few suggestions:

Fifteen ways to woo your lover:

1. Just hold hands.
2. Pamper your partner with a foot massage.
3. Tell your spouse how attractive he/she is to you.
4. Share a romantic dinner.
5. Light some candles.
6. Give your partner a back rub.
7. Share a bubble bath.
8. Leave love notes around the house.
9. Play and have fun.
10. Give your partner the day off from household chores.
11. Serve your partner breakfast in bed.
12. Share your dreams for the future.

13. Listen while your partner shares his/her dreams.

14. Pray together.

15. Cuddle and kiss.

Your First Anniversary

Congratulations! It was the best of times, and sometimes it was the worst of times, but you survived and hopefully thrived in your crucial first year as husband and wife. You have begun to set patterns for the rest of your years together and we pray they are healthy ones. Every year you are together marks a milestone in your life—milestones that should be applauded. Your first anniversary really does deserve a special celebration.

Whether it's your first or your thirtieth, there are traditional types of gifts for nearly every anniversary. Let the list guide you, but remember your gift still should be creative and personal:

Anniversary Date	Traditional Gift	Modern Gift
1st	Paper	Clocks
2nd	Cotton	China
3rd	Leather	Crystal, glass
4th	Linen, silk	Electrical appliances
5th	Wood	Silverware
6th	Iron	Wood
7th	Wool, copper	Desk sets/pen and pencil sets
8th	Bronze	Linen, laces
9th	Pottery, china	Leather
10th	Tin, aluminum	Diamond jewelry
11th	Steel	Fashion jewelry
12th	Silk	Pearls, colored gems
13th	Lace	Textiles, furs
14th	Ivory	Gold jewelry
15th	Crystal	Watches
20th	China	Platinum

continues

continued

Anniversary Date	Traditional Gift	Modern Gift
25th	Silver	Sterling silver
30th	Pearl	Diamond
35th	Coral	Jade
40th	Ruby	Ruby
45th	Sapphire	Sapphire
50th	Gold	Gold
55th	Emerald	Emerald
60th	Diamond	Diamond

Make Your Anniversary Sacred

Because more than half of all couples marry on a Saturday, chances are good you will celebrate your first wedding anniversary on a Sunday. Why not take the opportunity to reaffirm your commitment to the sacred vows you took on your wedding day? This can be done very privately, with a special time of prayer and recommitment with just the two of you. Or you might choose to include family, friends, or even plan something more public. Here are a couple ideas to consider:

- **Just for Two**—Get up before dawn on the morning of your first anniversary. Head out to a special spot where you can watch the sun rise together. Take along a basket with fresh fruit, cheese, and some yummy pastries. And don't forget a thermos of your favorite breakfast beverage—gourmet coffee, flavored tea, or exotic juices. As you watch the sun rise, tell each other why you would do it all over again (get married, that is!). Choose a Bible verse to guide you through your next year of marriage. Before you leave your special spot, pray together, thanking God for all you have learned and experienced in the past year and asking for his continued wisdom in the years to come.

- **Two and a Few**—After church, invite a few special friends or family members to join you for a simple lunch at your home. You might invite your best man and maid of honor, your parents, or another married couple that has inspired you during your first year. Spend some time looking over your wedding photos, sharing stories from your special day, and reliving the moments that brought you two together. Ask your guests to tell one area of growth they have seen in your marriage during the past year. Before everyone leaves, join hands and pray together that the next year will be one of continued growth and blessing.

- **With Witnesses**—If you attend the church where you were married, perhaps the pastor who officiated at your wedding would agree to have a prayer of rededication and celebration during the morning service. If this idea interests you, we suggest you contact your pastor several weeks in advance to make the arrangements. Because this isn't often done in churches today (although we don't know why!) you will need to be clear exactly what you want. Here's a suggestion of a prayer or blessing that could be used:

Heavenly Father,

We come before you today just as we did one year ago to celebrate again the union of this man and this woman in holy matrimony.

We praise you that you have walked beside them every day of the past year, guiding them and teaching them to live together as one.

We thank you for the witness their love has been to those around them.

We ask now that you would reaffirm in them the sacred vows they took and aid them in living them out each day in the years to come.

In Jesus' name, amen.

Make Your Anniversary Romantic

Contemporary author Amy Bloom describes marriage as "a long, intricate, intimate dance together and nothing matters more than your own sense of balance and your choice of partner." Isn't that romantic? Women seem to excel in traditional romance. But men, you can get in touch with your feminine side! Here are a few ideas to get you started:

- **Sensual**—Plan a romantic interlude that appeals to all five senses:
  - **Smell**—You can find sprays, oils, and candles in almost any scent these days often right in your grocery store. Rose and jasmine are appealing scents for women and men often prefer vanilla.

- **Sight**—The soft glow of candlelight can transform any room into a romantic retreat.

- **Taste**—Chocolate covered strawberries are not only delicious but can be fed to each other in a very sensual way.

- **Sound**—Music is the ultimate in setting the mood. Jazz, classical, pop—what's your mate's favorite mood music?

- **Touch**—Keep in touch: start with a back rub or foot massage with scented lotion or oil; stroke your mate's hair and face while you talk; hold those kisses just a little longer. You can probably see where all this will lead!

- **Soft**—Softness sets the mood for whispered desires and gentle caresses. You can create an incredibly romantic atmosphere with soft lighting from candles, soft music playing in the background, satin sheets on the bed or a thick downy comforter spread on the floor. Keep your touch and your voice soft, too.

- **Symbolic**—Use hearts, flowers, and chocolate in unique ways to show your love. Make heart-shaped cookies as a sweet treat or write special love notes on paper hearts and place them around the house. A single flower can be more romantic than a bunch and a potted blue violet can woo when you explain that it symbolizes faithfulness.

Bet You Didn't Know

There's a good reason why 80 percent of Valentine's Day gift-givers choose chocolate! For centuries, chocolate has been a symbol of romance. In the ancient civilizations of the Aztecs and Mayans, chocolate was believed to be a powerful aphrodisiac. In fact, the Aztec ruler, Montezuma, reportedly drank 50 cups of chocolate each day to provide romantic "staying power" to serve his harem of 600 women. The Mayans also shared a passion for chocolate. At their betrothal and wedding ceremonies, gold chalices containing a liquid form of chocolate were served. Even Casanova, the infamous eigthteenth century lover, believed chocolate made him a better lover. (By the way, according to the Chocolate Manufacturers Association, chocolate lovers prefer milk chocolate to dark chocolate by a margin of more than two to one.)

Make Your Anniversary an Adventure

Marriage is the ultimate adventure, so why not plan something adventurous to celebrate your first year! By breaking out the ordinariness of your life, you can bring some added spice to your relationship:

- **Mysterious**—The element of surprise can be hard to pull off when you share the same house, but it can be done. But keep in mind that surprises can backfire. If it does, keep it in perspective—you've got a great story to tell your kids someday. One way to take some of the risk out of the surprise while keeping the anticipation level high is to alert your spouse that something special is going to happen—giving the date and time—without revealing any details. That way you might avoid plans that conflict and disappoint.

- **Creative**—Think outside the "anniversary" box. Try recreating some aspect of your first date or when you proposed. What about your honeymoon? Can you go back for a night or a weekend? Or is there a way to bring your honeymoon destination home? If you honeymooned somewhere exotic, try to recreate that atmosphere with music and food. Maybe you didn't go there on your honeymoon, but you and your spouse have always wanted to go to Italy or France. Use those destinations as themes for your own anniversary adventure.

- **Fun**—Remember that this is a celebration, so have some fun! Love and laughter are kindred spirits. Be a little silly and allow your mate to be silly, too. Do something a little crazy with whipped cream. Stand outside your window and serenade your love. Dance, even if you don't know how!

Make Your Anniversary Memorable

It doesn't cost a lot of money to make a memory. Mark the milestone of your first anniversary in a way that both of you will always remember and record those memories in some way. The following sections give a few suggestions for making your first anniversary memorable.

Begin a New Tradition

While planning your wedding, you no doubt saw first-hand the power of tradition. Traditions can transcend time—bonding families together even across generations. Occasionally, a tradition starts by accident. One couple exchanges a handwritten letter each year detailing their favorite memories with their spouse during the previous 12 months. It just so happened that on their first anniversary, the husband was deployed overseas, but the letters they wrote that year became such treasures that they have continued the tradition every year since.

Why not start your own anniversary tradition? To become a tradition, it will need to be something that you repeat every year on your anniversary, so give it some serious thought. Also, it should be something not too expensive and not too complicated so that future circumstances won't necessarily affect your ability to keep it up. Here are a few ideas to consider:

- Exchange only handmade cards or gifts. It takes a little more thought and planning, but these can also become treasures.
- Order a smaller version of your wedding cake to share together.
- Go to the place where you first kissed and kiss again!
- Recite your wedding vows to each other.
- Stay up late dancing to your favorite song.
- Watch the video of your wedding and eat pizza.
- Write a letter to God expressing thanks for the specific ways your mate has blessed your life over the past year.

Do Something Unique

This is the opposite of traditional. Every year plan a new and different way to celebrate. Alternate taking turns planning your celebration—first year the wife, second year the husband, third year the wife, and so on. Reserve the date and time with each other, but keep the details a secret. The anticipation will be well worth it! And, if you are at all competitive, it will be fun to see how you can "outdo" each other each year to make your anniversary a time to remember.

> ### That's the Spirit
>
> Give honor to marriage, and remain faithful to one another in marriage … Jesus Christ is the same yesterday, today, and forever. (Hebrews 13:4,7)
>
> Take strength in the fact that the Christ that stood as a witness to your vows on your wedding day is the same Christ that has guided you through your first year as husband and wife. He will also be the same Christ who leads with you wherever the future takes you in your life together. As Winston Churchill said, "This is not the end. It is not even the beginning of the end. But it is, perhaps, the end of the beginning."

Start an Anniversary Diary

Do dream about where you want your marriage relationship to be in the future—10, 30, 50 years from now. Having a vision for where you want to go can help you get there. As part of your first year anniversary celebration, try writing a diary entry for each decade anniversary to come. Use a blank book or a notebook and leave a few blank pages between entries so you can write in your actual anniversary thoughts when you reach that milestone.

In *The Diary of Adam and Eve*, a humorous look at the first married couple, Mark Twain gives us a fictional glimpse into the final years of their marriage:

> Adam: After all these years, I see that I was mistaken about Eve in the beginning …. At first I thought she talked too much; but now I should be sorry to have that voice fall silent and pass out of my life.
>
> Eve: It is my prayer. It is my longing, that we might pass from this life together—a longing which shall never perish from the earth, but shall have a place in the heart of every wife that loves, until the end of time …
>
> Adam (at Eve's Grave): Wheresoever she was, *there* was Eden.

What will you be thinking and feeling about your mate at the end of your days together? Our prayer is that as every year of your marriage passes, you will find yourselves more in love, more committed, and more blessed by your oneness. With God's help, you can make sure it happens just that way!

Appendix
A

Wedding Resources

There are numerous resources available to couples who are contemplating getting married. In this appendix we have listed some of the best books and websites to help you build a stronger relationship before and after your wedding as well as to help you plan your perfect wedding day.

Books

Listed here are books that can help you with your pre-marital relationship and your marriage relationship. In addition, there are books listed that help with blended marriages, sexual intimacy, spiritual intimacy, and planning your wedding. Most of these books are available at your local Christian book store.

Premarital Relationships

Boehi, David, Brent Nelson, Jeff Schulte, and Lloyd Shadrach. Dennis Rainey, ed. *Preparing for Marriage*. Ventura, CA: Family Life and Gospel Light Publications, 1997.

Olson, David H., John DeFrain, and Amy K. Olson. *Building Relationships*. Life Innovations, Inc., 1999.

Wright, H. Norman. *Before You Say, I Do*. Eugene, OR: Harvest House, 1997.

Marriage Relationship

Cloud, Henry, and John Townsend. *Boundaries in Marriage.* Grand Rapids, MI: Zondervan, 1999.

Congo, Dr. David and Janet. *Lifemates: a lover's guide for a lifetime relationship.* Colorado Springs, CO: Cook Communications Ministries, 2001.

Wheat, Ed. *The First Years Of Forever.* Grand Rapids, MI: Zondervan, 1998.

Wright, H. Norman. *Communication: Key To Your Marriage.* Ventura, CA: Gospel Light, 2000.

Blended Marriages

Harvey, Alfred. *Marriage and the Blended Family.* Brentwood, TN: Faithworks Publications, 2001.

Romano, Dugan. *Intercultural Marriages*, 2nd Ed. Yarmouth, ME: Intercultural Press, 2001.

Webster, Joann. *Stepfamilies Done Right.* Lake Mary, FL: Strang Communications, 2001.

Wright, H. Norman. *Before You Remarry.* Eugene, OR: Harvest House, 1999.

Sexual Intimacy

Cutrer, William, and Sandra Glahn. *Sexual Intimacy In Marriage.* Grand Rapids, MI: Kregel Publications, 1999.

Gardner, Tim Alan. *Sacred Sex: A Spiritual Celebration of Oneness.* Colorado Springs, CO: Waterbrook Press, 2002.

Rosenau, Douglas E. *A Celebration of Sex for Newlyweds.* Nashville, TN: Thomas Nelson, 2002.

Spiritual Intimacy

Sell, Charles and Virginia. *Spiritual Intimacy for Couples.* Wheaton, IL: Crossway Books, 1996.

Stoop, David. *What Happens When Couples Pray?* Ann Arbor, MI: Servant Publications, 2000.

Wedding Planning

Engel, Marjorie. *Weddings for Complicated Families: The New Etiquette.* Boston, MA: Mt. Ivy Press, 1993.

Fields, Denise and Alan. *Bridal Bargains: Secrets to Throwing a Fantastic Wedding on a Realistic Budget* (6th Edition). Boulder, CO: Windsor Peak Press, 2003.

Flowers, Michael, and Donna Bankhead. *Catering Your Own Wedding.* Franklin Lakes, NJ: New Page Books, 2000.

Moore, Cindy, and Tricia Windom. *Planning a Wedding with Divorced Parents.* New York, NY Crown Publishers, Inc., 1992.

Websites

The Internet is another great resource for couples who are planning on getting married. Start with the sites we've given here. You will find lots of help from building a healthy relationship with your partner to planning your perfect day. The following sites will give you great tips and also refer you to additional resources to strengthen your future marriage.

www.couplecommunication.com
Interpersonal Communication Programs, Inc.
1-800-328-5099
Program teaches skills for talking, listening, resolving conflicts, and managing anger better.

www.covenantmarriage.com
Covenant Marriage Movement
1-800-268-1343
God intends for marriage to be a lifelong covenant relationship between a man and a woman, exemplifying selfless unconditional love, reconciliation, sexual purity, and growth.

www.divorcebusting.com
The Divorce Busting Center
1-800-664-2435
Helps couples overcome infidelity, stop excessive arguing, improve the odds when one spouse wants out, end the Blame Game, and find forgiveness.

www.ImagoRelationships.org
1-800-729-1121
The Imago process brings about transformation in relationships through mutual healing, which restores love, passion, and aliveness.

www.lifeinnovations.com
Life Innovations, Inc.
1-800-331-1661
Resources to help couples discover their strengths and growth areas and locate counselors for premarital counseling.

www.marriagealive.com
Marriage Alive Resources
1-888-690-6667
A unique approach to building thriving marriages through the integration of biblical truth, contemporary research, practical application, and fun.

www.pairs.com
PAIRS
1-888-724-7748
Practical skills for extraordinary relationships.

www.PREPinc.com
Fighting for Your Marriage
1-800-366-0133
The comprehensive PREP approach includes modules on fun, friendship, intimacy, expectations, commitment, and more. Over 20 years of rigorous marital research suggests that the program can make a real difference in couples' lives.

www.smartmarriages.com
The Coalition for Marriage, Family and Couples Education, L.L.C.
202-362-3332
CMFCE serves as an information exchange to help couples locate marriage and relationship courses.

www.successfulstepfamilies.com
Successful Stepfamilies
870-932-9254
Christian resources for premarital couples, stepfamilies, and the churches who serve them.

For good general and comprehensive information on how to plan your perfect wedding check out these sites:

- www.foreverwed.com
- www.theknot.com

For information and articles on destination weddings check out these sites:

- www.weddingchannel.com
- www.whollymatrimony.com

These sites will give you a lot of inspiration for floral arrangements, both silk and fresh, and help you plan a beautiful wedding from bouquets, to arches, to centerpieces.

- www.somewhereintimefloralboutique.com
- www.blissweddings.com/weddingfloral
- www.weddingbokay.com
- www.flowerfarmstogo.com
- www.wedding-favors-party-favors.com

Appendix
B

Wedding Budget Worksheet

Listed here are many items that go into the cost of a wedding. As you plan together, highlight those things that will be part of your dream day and pencil in the maximum dollar amount you are willing to spend for that item. Use pencil because you may need to go back and adjust or eliminate figures to get to a manageable bottom-line. Then as you begin to purchase items, add in your actual costs, continuing to adjust your budget as necessary to ensure that your perfect wedding is one you and your family can afford.

Category	Budget	Actual
Rings		
Engagement ring	_____	_____
Bride's wedding ring	_____	_____
Groom's wedding ring	_____	_____
Stationery/Printed Goods		
Invitations	_____	_____
Announcements	_____	_____
Reply cards	_____	_____
Postage	_____	_____
Stationary	_____	_____
Thank you notes	_____	_____
Printed programs for ceremony	_____	_____
Guest book(s)	_____	_____
Maps to reception (if necessary)	_____	_____
Other:_____	_____	_____
Ceremony		
Site rental fee	_____	_____
Pastor's fee	_____	_____
Music		
Decorations other than flowers (candles, canopies, aisle runner, arch, kneeler, candelabra, and so on)	_____	_____
Fee for custodian	_____	_____
Nursery attendant	_____	_____
Gratuity for traffic control officer	_____	_____
Other:	_____	_____
Bride's Outfit		
Wedding dress	_____	_____
Alterations	_____	_____
Headpiece	_____	_____
Shoes	_____	_____
Lingerie (slip, panties, bra, hosiery)	_____	_____

Category	Budget	Actual
Jewelry (earrings, necklace, and so on)	_____	_____
Other:	_____	_____
Groom's Outfit		
Tuxedo rental or suit	_____	_____
Shirt	_____	_____
Tie, vest, or cummerbund	_____	_____
Shoes and socks	_____	_____
Other:	_____	_____
Photography/Videography		
Engagement announcement photo	_____	_____
Wedding portrait	_____	_____
Wedding/reception photographs	_____	_____
Wedding albums	_____	_____
Informal/candids	_____	_____
Duplicates for friends and relatives	_____	_____
Video recording of ceremony	_____	_____
Video recording/interviews at reception	_____	_____
Editing charge	_____	_____
Duplicate tapes	_____	_____
Florist		
Floral decorations for ceremony site	_____	_____
Bride's bouquet	_____	_____
Bridesmaids' bouquets	_____	_____
Flower girl's basket	_____	_____
Ring bearer's pillow	_____	_____
Corsages for mothers and grandmothers	_____	_____
Corsages for friends (attending guest book/gift table)	_____	_____
Boutonnieres for groom, best man, ushers, fathers	_____	_____
Flowers for reception (cake top, cake table, centerpieces)	_____	_____
Bouquet to toss	_____	_____

continues

continued

Category	Budget	Actual
Transportation		
Limousine or Carriage	_____	_____
Parking	_____	_____
Gratuity for traffic controllers	_____	_____
Reception		
Site rental fee	_____	_____
Decorations	_____	_____
Food	_____	_____
Beverages	_____	_____
Servers fee or gratuity	_____	_____
Party rentals (tables, chairs, linens, china, flatware)	_____	_____
Music	_____	_____
Personalized napkins	_____	_____
Favors	_____	_____
Cake knife	_____	_____
Toasting goblets	_____	_____
Other:	_____	_____
Cake		
Wedding cake	_____	_____
Delivery and set up fee	_____	_____
Groom's cake	_____	_____
Top	_____	_____
Other:	_____	_____
Gifts		
Bride's attendants	_____	_____
Groom's attendants	_____	_____
Groom to bride	_____	_____
Bride to groom	_____	_____
Thank you gifts for parents	_____	_____
Thank you gifts for other wedding helpers	_____	_____
Other:	_____	_____

Category	Budget	Actual
Rehearsal dinner		
Food, beverage, and gratuity	_____	_____
Room rental (if applicable)	_____	_____
Flowers or decorations	_____	_____
Other:	_____	_____
Honeymoon		
Hotel accommodations	_____	_____
Transportation	_____	_____
Meals	_____	_____
Entertainment	_____	_____
Passports (if necessary)	_____	_____
Traveler's checks	_____	_____
Other:		
Additional expenses		
Luncheon for bride's attendants	_____	_____
Marriage license	_____	_____
Physical/blood test for bride	_____	_____
Physical/blood test for groom	_____	_____
Hair stylist	_____	_____
Makeup artist	_____	_____
Manicurist	_____	_____
Bubbles, birdseed, or petals for exit	_____	_____

Index

A clear, Christian family focus

christian family guide

Christian Family Guides are warm, conversational books jam-packed with expert content, Scripture quotes, meditations, family perspectives, and helpful resources.

Well-known Christian book author and former editorial director for Moody Press, Jim Bell Jr., serves as the *Christian Family Guide* series editor.

ISBN: 0-02-864436-0

ISBN: 0-02-864442-5

ISBN: 0-02-864443-3

ISBN: 0-02-864493-X

ISBN: 1-59257-078-X

ISBN: 1-59257-090-9

Christian Family Guide to Managing People
ISBN: 0-02-864454-9

Christian Family Guide to Starting Your Own Business
ISBN: 0-02-864476-X

Christian Family Guide to Family Activities
ISBN: 1-59257-077-1

Christian Family Guide to Family Devotions
ISBN: 1-59257-076-3

Christian Family Guide to Surviving Divorce
ISBN: 1-59257-096-8

Christian Family Guide to Parenting a Toddler
ISBN: 1-59257-049-6

Christian Family Guide to Getting Married
ISBN: 1-59257-174-3

Christian Family Guide to Losing Weight
ISBN: 1-59257-191-3

ALPHA